# QUIET
# PRESENCE

BY
D    E HENDRICKSON

Amoskeag Great Flag. This picture, taken by Harlan Marshall in 1914, illustrates two points about the French-Canadians and Franco-Americans: they were capable of astounding amounts of work, as the size of the flag indicates, and they were enthusiastic about their affiliation with the United States.

(Courtesy, Manchester, N.H., Historic Association)

# DYKE HENDRICKSON

# *Quiet Presence*

DRAMATIC, FIRST-PERSON ACCOUNTS —

THE TRUE STORIES OF FRANCO-AMERICANS

IN NEW ENGLAND.

*Guy Gannett Publishing Co.*

 PORTLAND / MAINE

*14,249*
*1/8/83*
*6.95*

*First edition printed in the United States of America by*
*K.J. Printing Co., Augusta, Maine, April, 1980.*
*Published by Guy Gannett Publishing Co., Portland, Maine 04104*

*Library of Congress Catalog Card 80-50218*
*ISBN #0-930096-06-1*

*Cover photo: 1898, in Fort Kent, Maine—a religious*
*procession comes up the street.*
*(Family collection of Rose Nadeau, Fort Kent)*

# Dedication

*To my grandmother,*
*Edith Carter,*
*whose devotion to*
*work and family*
*has been like that*
*of the Franco-Americans.*

# Table of Contents

# Foreword

The Franco-Americans are the invisible minority group of New England. Not to themselves, of course. Over the years they have clung together with remarkable cohesiveness, and are quite aware of their own culture. But for a group that ranks as the largest minority in northern New England, and a major tenant in industrial communities of every New England state, they have not achieved the visibility and power of other ethnics.

The Irish, for example, control much of Massachusetts. The Italians are dominant in the political and economic apparatus of Rhode Island. The Yankees retain control in all six states, and the blacks, too, are gaining a niche in the ethnic mosaic. But in a region where 2.5 million of the 12 million inhabitants possess some, if not all, French blood, the Franco-Americans do not have a high profile.

Because the Franco-Americans lack high visibility, not a great deal of interest has been shown in their past. Historians have not been active in studying the Francos. Few objective journalists have approached this subject. We know there are many Franco-Americans in the region, but we don't know much about them. Not many New Englanders are aware of the French-Canadian migration of the 19th century that helped populate virtually every industrial city in the region. They do not know the difficulties of moving to a new country, learning the language, and taking the best job one could find. But because those of French-Canadian ancestry do number close to 2.5 million, the presence, albeit quiet presence, of the Franco-Americans should be more than a footnote in New England history. This book is one look at Franco-Americans.

"Quiet Presence" is an outgrowth of the desire to know more about the Franco-Americans of New England. In 1977, shortly after the phenomena of "Roots," I wrote a series of articles on the Franco-Americans for the Maine Sunday Telegram. The response was gratifying, as Francos and non-Francos alike were touched by a look into this past. Of special interest to readers were the stories about the individuals whose families settled here. Those who told their own stories told them best. It was evident that a greater investigation of the Franco-Americans was merited. This is the result.

It is hoped that "Quiet Presence" will help to fill the void of information about this ethnic group. Greater knowledge of the Franco-Americans will undoubtedly provide a greater appreciation. To have spent 12 hours a day, six days a week in a textile mill was a formidable chore. Such a life deserves respect and recognition, not derision and lack of awareness.

The interviews presented here were conducted in English. In many cases, a friend, clergyman, or family member was present to ensure fluid and accurate communication. Some interviews, like that of 90-year-old Adelard Janelle, took a half-dozen hours broken into several sessions. Others lasted two or three hours, and were later checked by telephone. The choice of whom to interview was not scientific. Millworkers chosen were usually referred to me by community leaders or priests. Those who could be regarded as academic leaders or political figures were interviewed because through my research, I felt they had something to say.

Sections that deal with historical developments were gathered in the orthodox manner of consulting books, newspapers, census data, government documents, and the theses of graduate students. Research was undertaken at the New York and Boston Public Libraries. It also was carried out at the Merrimack Valley Textile Museum in North Andover, Mass., the library of the Association Canado-Americain in Manchester, N. H., and in many other libraries. And much of the information here was uncovered in the kitchens of Franco-Americans themselves. There is much to say for verbal history.

# Acknowledgments

This book was made possible through the help of many people. I would mention Bob Moorehead at the outset. Bob was managing editor of the Maine Sunday Telegram in 1977, and saw the validity of a detailed treatment of the Franco-Americans. A series was written for the Telegram and eventually was developed into a book.

As the idea grew into a text, I received expert help and guidance from Dr. Paul Chasse, a native of Somersworth, N. H., who teaches at Rhode Island College in Providence. Dr. Chasse is among the most knowledgeable in the country about the French presence in America. His warmth and generosity were truly valuable.

Providing a guiding hand for research in the St. John Valley was Father Clement Thibodeau. An important source in southern Maine was Professor Madeleine Giguere of the University of Southern Maine. She was invaluable by providing statistics of Franco-American population centers throughout New England, and is also an authority on French-Canadian and Franco-American home life.

The staff of the Merrimack Valley Textile Museum in North Andover, Mass., was highly professional. The resources they provided were excellent. Robert Perreault, librarian at the Association Canado-Americain in Manchester, N. H., was a good resource, as was Norman Rioux at the heritage center in Lewiston. The staff of McArthur Library, Biddeford, is to be acknowledged, as is that of the Lewiston Public Library.

An important, and talented, contributor to the book was Gordon Chibroski, who handled all of the photographic work.

Crucial to the book, of course, were the many, many Franco-Americans who permitted me into their homes, and their lives, as I pursued my research. Without exception, they were gracious and helpful.

Final recognition is extended to my wife, Vicki. Producing this book was a far greater task than I imagined. I could not have done it without her aid and encouragement.

For over three centuries French settlers and their descendants have played an important role in shaping the cultures of two of North America's great nations.

Mr. Hendrickson's valuable work documents for the English-speaking American reader the history of the Franco-Americans of New England -- a group whose diverse backgrounds yet unified spirit contribute significantly to the region's economic, commercial and agricultural success.

In an era of re-examination of our pasts -- when a search for roots speaks as much for our personal pride as it does for our individual sense of security, Mr. Hendrickson's book is a welcome addition. It tells a fascinating story, encourages the reader's understanding and admiration and underlines the debt we owe to our Franco-American neighbors. Not only does it satisfy our intellectual appetites, it also provides for our basic needs: a fine recipe for a delicious omelette.

Kenneth M. Curtis
Ambassador

A youthful Adelard Janelle, second from left (sitting), with members of his National Guard unit in about 1907. The bottle at center is believed to be part of a joke.

(From family collection of Adelard Janelle)

Adelard Janelle at age 90, with Lewiston's St. Peter and St. Paul's Church in the background.

(Photo by Gordon Chibroski)

# Chapter I

## Adelard Janelle

# A Franco-American Remembers

"I started working in the mills when I was 12," recalls Adelard Janelle. "I was an oil boy."

"The hours were from 6 in the morning to 6 at night, but if you were good, they sometimes let you go out to play before the day was over. Oh, we had to say we were 16 to get work there, but they never took it seriously. When the truant officer was about to come by, they'd send us home for the day."

"I started at 55 cents a day – $3.30 a week. I gave it all to my mother, of course, because that's the way we did it then. I was the oldest of the children, so it was expected that I would enter the mill. It was natural for all French-Canadians to work, really. In those days, we started in our teens or earlier – today they want to go to college."

Adelard Janelle will be 91 this year. It is not unusual that he should have been a participant in the mill work that the French-Canadians were engaged in years ago in New England. It is unique though, that he remembers so much of what he saw and lived. Born in 1889, he witnessed part of the great continental migration from Canada to the New England states (1860-1900). Janelle and others like him are some of the few direct links to one of the most significant, if unheralded, events of 19th century New England: the migration of the French-Canadians.

The immigrants arrived by the thousands to work in the textile mills, the shoe shops and the lumber yards; it was their labor that helped the industrial revolution of the 19th century achieve production heights that it did. And largely because of that migration, New England is heavily populated with the descendants of the French-Canadians, the Franco-Americans. It is said that more than 2.5 million New Englanders possess at least some French blood, making it one of the most populous minority groups in the 12 million-person region.

Adelard Janelle is a Franco-American. Though he spent his days in the mill city of Lewiston, Maine, thousands of Francos have congregated in communities such as Pawtucket, R. I., Fall River, Mass., Manchester, N. H., Mansfield, Conn., and Winooski, Vt.

Those of French descent have often been overlooked in this six-state region that is better known for its native Yankees, or its highly visible Irish. Elderly Francos are often ignored on the streets as simply whispers from a forgotten past; younger Francos no longer speak French or continue the customs of their forefathers.

But those who have been settled here for close to a century, who individually spent 40 or 50 years working in the mills or raising a houseful of children, should not be forgotten. They have stories to tell. They are not necessarily glamorous tales, they are simply memoirs and recollections of what a blue-collar life in another land was really like. But as early pioneers of industrial America, the French should be heard. They can be disregarded no more easily than can the massive red brick buildings that anchor the downtown sections of countless New England towns and cities.

Like other New Englanders who are descendants of French-Canadian immigrants, Adelard Janelle has a story. His and others like his are important because they portray the lives of this hard-working people who left farms in Quebec to seek "streets paved with gold."

They did not know the language of the country, nor were they familiar with the jobs, the customs, or the communities they chose. But as a result of hard work, close family relationships, an abiding faith in the Catholic Chuch, and the ability to create cohesive ethnic communities, they have evolved into an ethnic group whose presence is felt in all six states.

The story of the Franco-Americans has not been well-detailed in

English, which is why Adelard Janelle is an important character. He was present during the migration; his life is one thread in the fabric of a gallant ethnic group in this country.

And he remembers.

"My family came to North America in 1729," said Janelle, a student of genealogy as well as of Franco-American history. "That was Jean Francois Janelle, and he came from just south of Paris."

"The Janelles were farmers, but in the 19th century, life on the farms in Quebec was hard. The crops were poor – you could only make a few dollars a year. So in May/1878, my grandfather, Michel Janelle, left Canada for the United States. He brought his wife, 11 children, and a nephew, Afix Marcotte, who was 18 and very close to the family. That's the Marcotte who started the stores in Lewiston, and left his estate to the Marcotte Nursing Home."

"Well, my grandfather had been living in Wooton, in the eastern townships of the Sherbrooke area, on land the government gave so people would settle. But the family left. My grandfather intended to go back, after making some money, but he never did."

"The family went by horse and buggy first, then by train – a special track was built in 1874 to connect Lewiston-Auburn with the Grand Trunk that went six miles past. He got a job right away in the Lewiston Bleach and Dye works. I don't know exactly what he did, but he was in the washroom. He never complained."

"My grandmother? She had been a teacher of elementary children in Quebec. She made between $9 and $15 a year, plus room and board, before she got married in 1857. She didn't work after that."

"My father, William Janelle, was 18 when the family came down, first to Greene, then into Lewiston. He was a weaver with the Androscoggin Mill right away; there were jobs in those days as soon as you got there. Weaving was a low-paying job, paying maybe $7 or $8 a week, but the pace wasn't bad. It wasn't hard work, except for the hours, which were 12 hours a day, six days a week."

"He left the mill in 1884, though. There was a strike. The Knights of Columbus were trying to organize in Lewiston – it was 10 cents a week for dues, I remember hearing."

"The strike didn't succeed. The French would always go work somewhere else during a walkout – they'd be mason-tenders, wood-cutters, or foundrymen. The Irish were the organizers but the French would work. They were proud, and it wasn't until much later that the French would join unions. Another thing was that a lot of French thought they would be going back to Canada – it wasn't across the ocean like Ireland – so they didn't get as involved. That's why they were slow to naturalize, too."

"Well, my father left during the strike, and after 1884 worked on a tree farm, for David Cowan, who had a small mill; and then for W. E. Cloutier, who was in wood, coal and lumber. My father started the William Janelle wood and coke business after he learned the trade, just after the turn of the century."

"My father married in 1888, to the daughter of French-Canadians, Genevieve Rousseau. I was born in Greene, but we moved to Lewiston when I was seven. That's my city."

Janelle's family is an unusual example of first generation success. Fortified by some funds from sale of the farm in Quebec, the sons and daughters of Michel Janelle, (Adelard's aunts and uncles), had notable success in business ventures. Most started in the mills but were able to move on to other endeavors.

Everett Janelle worked in a grocery, and was able to own one in his lifetime; John B. Janelle moved from clerking in a clothing store, to ownership, then to real estate; Phillip Janelle started in the mills, then went into baking, having a delivery route on horse and buggy, before returning to mills. Oliver was foreman in a shank shop, while Adelard's father, William, was able to rise to ownership of the wood and coke business.

Lionel Janelle was the most adventurous, but with mixed results. He went to California searching for gold but was unable to strike it rich.

Three of the four Janelle daughters went into business for themselves; pioneering the A. Janelle and Co., hats, corsets and millinery goods. The fourth devoted her life to helping her mother.

Adelard went into the mills in 1901.

"It was natural for a Canadian to go to work. I guess they wanted to be a man before their time. I didn't mind the work, though."

"I was an oil boy in the spinning room, oiling frames. There would be 35-40 cylinders on each side of the frame, and I would be in charge of oiling and cleaning, and making sure it was running as it should. The older men were generally good to the boys; we all spoke French and got along well. The only English there was spoken by the foreman; in the early years the bosses were English but later, the French moved up, and they became foremen and supervisors."

"My friends on the block went to work in the mills, too. When the work was done we acted like kids, and when the boss let us out for being good, we'd play baseball or roller polo, or go swimming. I knew some boys who went back to Sherbrooke to the colleges (secondary schools) to learn English. Then they would come back, and find it easier. I dropped out but I never stopped studying. I went to night school, then to Bliss Business College. I always wanted to learn."

Janelle left the mill in 1904, and was soon selling bleach water for a living. He also worked with his father's wood and coke business, and by 1918 was selling furniture as a trade. Janelle did not participate in World War I. He was a member of the National Guard from 1907 to 1913 and was about to be activated in 1918 when the war ended.

Janelle, never one to be dulled by the same occupation, began selling insurance in 1924.

"I started selling to mostly French," he remembers. "It was hard, though. The people didn't have the money to spend on something like this, and they didn't really believe in it. They didn't know very much about it."

"One plan they would buy was funeral insurance. You'd be sure to get a coffin and a hack; two horses and cart. Insurance on children sold, too. It was 10 cents a week for a $100 policy. They'd say, 'I'll take five weeks', and I'd sell it. But they didn't have much money – it wasn't a good business."

The year 1930 arrived, and Janelle, a Republican in a city rapidly becoming Democrat in nature, found himself in politics. A Republican administration was elected, and he was appointed clerk in the municipal welfare office at $35 per week.

"It was an accident, really, but it was a job during the Depression," he said. "It was a difficult job, because the French people would have to come in for aid. The French are proud. They didn't like it. But they had to eat. They had to pay rent. When the Democrats got elected the following year, I was out. And I was glad to be out."

The bilingual Franco had a number of jobs through the 30's, barely hanging on as hard economic times slowed down the mills, damaging the economy of the city. In 1935, for instance, he was the all-night assistant to the city works department. Two years later he was a janitor at the library.

Janelle's later working years were spent in greater comfort, indirectly as a result of his Franco-American roots. He was an assistant manager at the Montjanard Club from 1943-1955. Following that, he took a similar position at the Franco-American Club. He retired in 1966.

His life, then, was spent in Lewiston, a cultural and social experience squarely within the Franco-American lifestyle of the times.

"I remember the days at the train station," he said. "Some weeks as many as 100 people would come into the city. They would usually have a friend or relative waiting, and after they got off the train, they would get into the horse-drawn cars, and head off to their new apartments or houses. There were big families then. Sometimes a husband would be followed by his wife and 12 or 15 children."

"A lot of families said they would go back to Canada, but they never did. But they visited. Starting in the 1880's, they would have excursions, train trips, that would go to Sherbrooke, Montreal, Quebec. Some families would go for a whole month. Others would just see their old homes and come back in a few days. Excursions cost $3 or $4 per person, and continued through the 1920's. That shows the French didn't forget their homes."

The elderly Franco-American commented that his family was close throughout the years. Married in his early 20's to Rose Michaud, the couple raised their children with church and culture in mind. One son went into funeral work in Lewiston before leaving for Hartford,

Conn., to pursue a warehousing job with the Xerox Corp. One daughter worked for years in the local department stores, at one time being the supervisor of the lunch counter. Two other children went into the Lewiston mills.

"I never told them what to do for work," Janelle recalled. "They went to schools here, then looked for a job. I didn't tell them to go into the mills, or not to go into the mills. But the jobs were there, and they didn't mind the work, so two of my children did enter the mills."

"Really, the mills didn't cause people to complain, especially in the early days. Before President Roosevelt, the work was slow, you didn't have to watch too many machines. But when he was President, there was a 40-hour work week, and the mills speeded things up. That was 1933. And there used to be just one shift, but with the 40-hour week, they started going all day and night, three shifts."

"But mostly, the mills weren't bad. Just the long hours."

Janelle lives a quiet life these days. Residing with wife and daughter in a three-story wooden tenement in the Franco-American section of town, his world is considerably smaller than it has been. Eye problems limit his mobility; the fact he's 90 years old has deprived him of some of his strength.

But the knowledgeable historian is not without means. In summer, 1978, he and several nephews drove toward Quebec in search of the Janelle family. It was an outgrowth of his studies of genealogy, and the trip seemed appropriate as a milestone of 100 years from the migration of the early family. The mission was accomplished.

"I saw the house that my father was born in," he said with no small degree of pride. "I saw the farm my family used to own. We met members of the Janelle family, and I was surprised that it was so easy to communicate. They showed us around. They asked about our homes and families."

"And do you know, even though we had been gone for so many years, they had heard of our side of the family. They knew the story of our Janelles."

A French-Canadian family, and the means of transportation used to get them to the nearest train station. Thousands of families in the late 19th and early 20th century left Quebec on carts such as this as the first leg of their journey to New England.

(Family collection of Marcel Mathieu, Lewiston)

This is Biddeford, Maine, in the 1870's, and represents the kind of community that immigrants saw when they arrived from the farmland of Quebec.

(McArthur Public Library, Biddeford)

# Chapter II

## Before the Migration

Adelard Janelle might not have found his way to Lewiston at all had history taken a different course. Descended from the French who came to North America in the 17th and 18th centuries, Janelle could very well be reading to his great-grandchildren in Trois-Rivieres today, or writing his memoirs in Levis. But one historical event dictated a major change for all French on this continent: France fell from power in the New World in 1759. Though they had been successful in claiming much of North America, they were not able to maintain control of their early holdings. When they gave up Canada to the English following the 1759 "Conquest," all French in North America were adversely affected.

The French have a lengthy history on this continent. An early visitor to America, Samuel de Champlain, organized a colony in 1604 and France quickly spread its influence from Quebec to New Orleans. Though sparsely populated, the land it claimed was astounding in size. While the English colonies were developing along a strip of the east coast no wider than 210 miles, the French laid claim to much of the territory between the colonies and the Mississippi. Trappers, traders, and explorers during the 17th and 18th centuries, the French were prominent in the new land.

Friction between France and England was as natural as it was immediate. In the conflict between the two that followed, the future of the continent was at issue. Had France been able to emerge the dominant force, the forefathers of the Janelles would likely have stayed and enjoyed the good life in New France.

But the English, who had the support of their crown which New

France did not, were the victors. After protracted skirmishing, the two factions met in the "French and Indian War." Victorious in the Battle of Quebec in 1759, the English obtained full concessions in the Treaty of Paris, 1763. France was toppled from power, stripped of economic means, and its colonists directed into roles of small farmers, or "habitants." Frustration, and later, hostility, grew following the conquest. When dire economic circumstances put pressure on habitants in the mid-1800's, many emigrated to New England.

The 19th century, in fact, was a period of great migration for the French in Quebec. Hundreds of thousands left the province. Some went to the Canadian west, others departed in the direction of the Midwest. A great many came to New England.

But numbers hardly tell the story. People do. Adelard Janelle provides one personal account of a family's arrival in New England, and the life that was encountered through several generations. There are many like Janelle who have stories to tell.

The French in North America . . . .

The French became interested in the "New World" in 1524 when King Francois I sought wealth for his European domain. Expeditions were underwritten by the crown, for it was eager to compete with other European powers in search for riches.

Included in the early voyages were trips by the Italian Giovanni di Verrazano and the Frenchman Jacques Cartier. Cartier, significantly, discovered the Gulf of St. Lawrence in 1534. He made further forays toward the heartland of the continent, resulting in vast land claims.

Samuel de Champlain founded a colony on the mouth of the St. Croix River in 1604, marking the initial French presence in New England. The following year, he discovered the Merrimack River, and later went down the St. Lawrence to Quebec and Montreal. Though the French were not immediately successful at colonization, their far-reaching explorations put their flag on many shores.

Other early wanderers were Brule, Nicolet, Jolliette and Marquette, LaSalle and Iberville. It is estimated that 5,000 American communities have French names as a result of their early explorations.[1] The English language also reflects this exploratory past, as evidenced by vocabulary words such as levee, portage, bayou, butte and prairie.

The purpose of exploration varied. France was not primarily interested in the new land for colonial purposes. Many voyages sponsored by the crown were in search of gold, silver, or other assorted riches.

Failing to produce such wealth, it later lowered its expectations by simply demanding revenues from the fur trade.

Another reason for the vast travels of the French in North America was adventure. The "coureauseurs des bois" or frontiersmen, were a hardy bunch who roamed the continent in search of new fur sources – and new adventure. Truly intrepid, they were this continent's most swashbuckling breed – and often in temperatures of 30 degrees below zero!

A major purpose of French exploration, however, was the desire to spread the Catholic faith. In 1642, French missionaries contributed to the founding of Montreal. In following years, clerics spread like tributaries through the new land with the goal of bringing the word to countrymen and "savages" alike.

From the beginnings of the colony, the church provided more support than either the crown or the court. Historian Mason Wade writes that "the destiny of New France was shaped by the fact that in the 17th century, the great age of Catholic Revival in France, the renewed energy of the Church found in America an outlet from the restraint imposed at home by the dominance of the state."[2] Such a foundation produced a church-oriented province of Quebec. It is not surprising, then, that one of the key characteristics of the French-Canadian immigrants in later years was their attachment to their Church.

Though the French were more interested in political events in Europe, King Louis XIV made Canada (an Indian word for "group of huts") a royal province in 1663. It was a largely unsettled region. Only the St. Lawrence River Valley with Quebec and Montreal possessed an urban dimension. Its loose string of settlements south to New Orleans was formidable.

Some effort was made to populate the nascent Canada. In the mid-17th century, a small stream of colonists trickled in from France.

Dr. Gerard Brault, an eminent authority on the French who teaches at Pennsylvania State University, says that those arriving in New France were Normans and Bretons. There were also settlers from Anjou, Poitou, Le Perche, L'Isle de France. Some were officers of the crown, or leaders of missionary projects. There were soldiers, too, notably from the regiment at Carignan.

Of the non-military settlers, it is said that many were apprentices and part-time tradesmen. Successful merchants and established professionals were in the minority, as they saw little reason to leave comfortable lives for a future of hardship.

The rural sectors of France provided many recruits. The countryside was in a stagnant state; peasants barely survived, as harvests were meager and the jobs hard to find. Some historians relate that the peasants would come to towns and cities to beg when times were bleak. Thus urban entrepreneurs often persuaded the downtrodden rural poor to travel to the new world. They could convince the poor into a life of uncertainty more easily than they could entice the prosperous. Some recruits evidently felt they had as much of a chance overseas as they did at home.

Marriageable women went to New France, too. They also sought an improvement of unsatisfactory status. Reports indicate that of the 1,100 women who went to Canada between 1665 and 1673, 900 were orphans who had not married.[3]

(It is said, too, that "ladies of the night" were often "persuaded" to relocate to New France. Few historians elaborate on this point, however.)

Wade adds that "they (immigrants) were not all the best citizens; some were young men of good family who had fallen into disgrace . . . . they amused themselves gallantly with the habitants' wives and daughters, and introduced scandalous songs . . another immigrant group consisted of poachers, smugglers and counterfeiters."

Thus New France got both the good and the bad.

Though the flow of immigrants continued through the early 18th century, the French did not populate their colonies like the English. State leaders in Paris encouraged development of New France for some years, but their energies were diverted in about 1672. Any major commitment was discouraged in favor of King Louis XIV's plan to dominate Europe. Voltaire's description a hundred years later of Canada as "a few acres of snow" might sum up the enthusiasm even then that the leaders of French society possessed for its faraway colony.

So while France was withdrawing from its colonial support, the English sent ship after ship across. This crown wanted to create a colony; this crown felt domination of the new land would result in commercial and strategic advantages. By 1750, New France had a population of 60,000 while England's colonists numbered 1.25 million.[4]

The French that did settle were forced to make the greatest of efforts in adapting to their new environment. It was necessary to survive. The growing season was short; the land, particularly north of the St. Lawrence River plain, was not especially fertile. If a family were interested in farming, it would spend months, in some cases years, clearing an adequate number of acres. Those who discuss the early days sometimes differentiate between the woodsman and the farmer, but at times a man was both.

The newcomers also were challenged by long, harsh winters, a rude change from the more temperate European climate. The wildness of the country, its lack of population, and the absence of urbanization made life difficult. And Indians sometimes were a threat to survival. Though the French were to become known for their ability to cultivate friendship with the Indians, they experienced hostility from time to time.

If the French did not mold an urban environment for themselves, they were able to build up a massive string of trading posts throughout their territory.

They created a chain of forts along the trade route between Montreal and New Orleans. The forts served as relay stations for travelers; another purpose was to act as bastions to keep the English out of certain territory. By the mid-18th century, 20 such forts were manned from Montreal, through New York, Pennsylvania and Illinois, and down through Tennessee, Alabama and Mississippi.[5]

Such holdings in the heartland of the continent did not go unnoticed by the English. On the contrary, it fostered friction that led to war. England saw the Spanish to the south, the French to the west and north. They viewed such encirclement as a certain threat to future plans.

The two countries had been battling in Europe for years. They were to fight again in North America. England was unwilling to accept France's promise of dominance in the New World, particularly since the Anglos held the balance in men and supplies. The vast expanse of French holdings was a plum worth reaching for.

The French and English colonists, then loyal to the crown in London, battled over the rich fur trade in the St. Lawrence Valley.

Feelings intensified in the early 1700's. In 1713, the Treaty of Utrecht that ended the War of Spanish Succession between Great Britain and France dealt the latter a humiliating blow. In the peace agreement, France ceded to England its claims to the Hudson Bay territories, to New Foundland and to Acadia (Nova Scotia).

Two events in the following years were characteristic of the increasing hostility between the two. In 1745, an army of New Englanders captured the French fort at Louisbourg on Cape Breton Island. Ten years later, English troops forcibly ejected thousands of neutral French Acadians from their homes in Nova Scotia. A full-scale armed conflict was not far behind.

What is known as the French and Indian War, and in Europe the Seven Years War, was an outgrowth of the many antagonisms between the two competing powers. Fully underway in 1756, it pitted the undermanned, but inspired, French against the cumbersome forces of England and its colonies. The French were in no position to have to defend a border thousands of miles long. In the end, they were unable to do so with limited number of soldiers.

Support from Paris was minimal; so little, in fact, that it is said that France didn't lose New France, it abandoned it.

Despite the fact that the French were defending a massive area, from Cape Breton Island to Fort Frontenac on Lake Ontario, and Fort Ticonderoga on Lake Champlain, and Fort Duquesne in Western Pennsylvania, they seemed to be winning in the early stages. For three years, Montcalm's campaign against the English in New France was successful. He registered victories at Oswego in 1756, at Fort

William Henry in 1757, and Ft. Ticonderoga in 1758, the latter when outnumbered 15,000 to 3,857.[6] But though the French and their Indian allies battled nobly, they were overcome by superior numbers with greater resources.

The day of destiny for North America was Sept. 13, 1759. The English won the battle of Quebec, and therein lay the outcome of the war.

It was on the towering cliffs of Quebec that the English general, James Wolfe, and his forces defeated the army of Gen. Marquis de Montcalm on the Plains of Abraham. Wolfe was repulsed several times as he attempted to climb from the banks of the St. Lawrence to the level terrain behind the cliffs. Folklore has it that bribery finally bought knowledge of a secret pass up the cliffs, and the English were able to ascend to the fields where they could effectively engage the enemy.

The Battle of Quebec has been immortalized by both artistic rendering and historical account. There are Wolfe and Montcalm, in graphic oils, dying on the field of conflict; there is the history of North America, turning decisively on one afternoon of fighting. Perhaps not enough drama can be attached to this confrontation, for history has indeed been affected by the outcome.

It is said that the French have never fully surrendered, though, not even today.

A visit to historic Quebec City has not been underway very long before one notices the tremendous amount of history featured in the picturesque city. The Plains of Abraham have been kept intact, with frequent signposts marking battle sites. Statues of French heroes rise from manicured flower beds; city maps present a wealth of information about the famous confrontation.

Although not all Franco-Americans today are aware of the history of their people in Canada, the segment of the French prominence in North America is one of the most remarkable reverses of fate on record. France was a major landholder in the New World at the outset of the 18th century. Just 100 years later, it had lost everything.

France gave up Nova Scotia, Newfoundland and the vast Hudson Bay Region in the Treaty of Utrecht in 1713. In 1763, France lost

Canada. And when Napoleon signed the Louisiana Purchase agreement in 1803 that gave up claim to the heartland of southern North America for a modest $15 million, France was without holdings on the continent.

If those of French descent have been accused of harboring a defensiveness about their presence on the continent, the dramatic losses of the 18th century might account for some of that feeling. The French had not ceded their spirit, however, and in years to come gathered together for cultural survival in the Anglo world. In the years immediately following the Conquest, the English and French fashioned a coexistence out of need. Quebec was in ruins; rural regions in the St. Lawrence River Valley lay in an unproductive state because of the chaos that the war had brought. Survival came first. But, as the early post-war years led to a rebuilding, friction between the two groups resurfaced.

The English were assertive in taking over government land and commerce, which left the French with the unrewarding jobs as farmers and small merchants. By British law, no Roman Catholic could vote, nor be elected or appointed to public office. Though the Quebec Act of 1774 allowed the French the right to religious and political activities, it was with apprehension that the French faced the future.

French-Canadians were split in their loyalty during the American Revolution, in part because of pressure from their English leaders. But France showed its traditional antagonism by being a strong ally of the colonists. At the Battle of Yorktown, for instance, when Cornwallis surrendered to Washington in 1781, French soldiers and sailors outnumbered the revolutionary forces by three to one.

It is said that 47,989 French officers, soldiers and sailors participated in land and sea operations. The numbers are impressive, particularly when noting that the strength of the American army never exceeded 38,000 regular soldiers.[7]

French Canada, then, was entering the 19th century under a cloud of defeat and frustration. Their nascent colony had been shattered; their government was dominated by the unsympathetic victors.

"No real understanding of French Canada is possible," writes

Wade, "without a realization of what its history, perhaps the most colorful for its span of years of any of human record, means to French-Canadians, whose most popular historian, Francis Parkman, has made familiar the phrase 'our master, the past' and established it as a principle for action in the present."[8]

\* \* \* \* \* \* \* \*

Friction among the victorious English and the defeated French was to be a theme of Canadian political relations for years. Even a cursory glance at Canada today, and the prominence of the Parti Quebecois, shows that it still is. Yet political considerations were not the only relevant aspects of life in the provinces in the years following the Conquest. The difficulty in making a living was of paramount significance. It was to be a key factor in families' decisions to leave Canada for New England.

Many an observer of later-day mill life has wondered why the immigrants would pursue this taxing way of life. Remarkably enough, many preferred it to the lives they had in Canada.

Rural Canada was poor. The years following the Conquest were barren and unproductive for most French families. The French had been trappers and traders. Now they were thrust into roles as small farmers, roles they were untrained for. The English would sow the seeds of industrialization in Quebec and Montreal, but the French were not to be a part of this new wave of economic activity and prosperity. Discrimination, if not outright exclusion, kept the habitants anchored to the earth.

It was on the spreading farm plains that feelings of discontent slowly evolved. Unenviable lives on the farm eventually caused many to consider leaving.

One difficulty for the habitants was the land itself. Fields, particularly north of the St. Lawrence, were not greatly productive. The climate was dry; the growing season short. Wheat was the key crop for decades, with peas and potatoes other staples of the earth. Yet they were not often raised, or marketed, in profitable quantities.

It was even difficult to earn a profit from a bumper crop. Consider the small farmer's problems: roads were poor, and thus they had trouble transporting their crops to a proper market. Communication was minimal, so growers had little knowledge of market prices until they actually reached the community market. When cash money began replacing the barter system in Quebec in the early 19th century, the depressed state of the province made cash a very scarce commodity.

It might be added that many historians have labeled the French ill-suited to farming.

The tools of the habitants were rudimentary, and their techniques outdated. Because they were rarely exposed to the outside world, they did not learn new farming methods. Habitants refused to rotate crops; they were wary of attempting new types of produce. Even the French have written that the rural peasants were stubborn to the point of hurting themselves when it came to agricultural technique.

And a harsh critic, Englishman Lord Durham, says worse. Commenting on the rural residents of Quebec in the early 19th century, he found it hard to understand that "the French-Canadians clung to their ancient prejudices . . . with an unreasoning tenacity of an uneducated and unprogressive people."[9]

Also reflective of doubts about agricultural quality in Quebec were the "Canadian cattle." Critics, mostly English, mocked livestock of Quebec for being lean and stringy.

The livestock raised by the habitants was attractive only to the undiscriminating; the crops harvested were of subsistence quantity. Historians agree the French-Canadians did not thrive on the farm. Yet poor results were not from a lack of trying. Farmers labored 12, 14 or even 16 hours a day. Children, too, worked in the fields. Their preoccupation with the crops was a major reason their formal educations were minimal.

Lack of financial success did not mean the habitants considered their lives meaningless. They stressed their Catholic faith, their belief in the family, and their occasional soirees with friends and neighbors. They were tenacious in retaining their language, religion and culture, despite England's increasing pressure to belittle these values.

As the 19th century progressed, however, the land could no longer sustain all its inhabitants, even at its minimal standards. Large families that divided the family farm again and again were running out of space.

For generations, fathers had subdivided original holdings among sons. A dozen acres down by the river would go to the oldest upon marriage. A few years later, the east meadow might be passed to the next boy. As the parents aged, they would sometimes pass the farm over to a designated son and his wife, in exchange for care in their old age. The process would then begin again.

The original farms from the days of seigneural grants were not large enough to be split indefinitely, especially when the Catholic families had so many sons. Few could find cash-paying jobs in the rural countryside, and thus the first soul-searching about migration must have been in the early 19th century.

The huge expanse of Canadian territory should have provided alternatives to staying on the family homestead. Indeed, beginning in 1820, the English did encourage relocation. But the opening of the eastern townships required some cash outlay. Few habitants possessed hard currency.

The situation became pressing after 1820. Farmers could barely support their families, yet were unable to accumulate enough money to move to an area that might be more productive. And compounding their difficulties was the appearance of the wheat midge.

The presence of the devastating insect cut into the region's leading crop in the early 19th century. In some cases it forced farmers into rotating crops, a most round-about stimulus to agricultural reform. Even so, it was another factor that threatened thousands of habitants who could hardly afford further deterioration in the size of their harvests.

Frustration, both with the English and the obstinate earth, was building in many hardworking French. Lord Durham, who arrived from England to study the situation in French Canada, wrote that

"I expected to find a conflict between a government and a people; I found two nations at war within the same state."[10]

The result was Papineau's Rebellion. Frustration from poverty and from the lack of representation in government as well as the lingering distaste for the English culminated in this brief uprising in 1837-38. Led by Louis-Joseph Papineau, it pitted 2,000 rebels against an organized state force of more than 8,000.

The end was predictable. The rebels were armed with shovels, sharpened sticks and other lamentable weaponry when they rioted in the villages of St. Denis, St. Charles and St. Eustache. The English swept down in short order, and put the upstarts to a rapid rout. But the fact that the French would go through with such a rebellious action seems proof of acute frustration.

The English were stern in their response. They were out to show that they would tolerate no more disturbances. At least a dozen leaders were hanged in 1838, martyrs to the quest for rural reform. One thousand were imprisoned; many more fled. Papineau himself got away, and returned following an amnesty in 1842 to be a provincial leader in later years.

The dissatisfaction that prompted a minority to rise up against the English was present in countless Quebec households. Habitants wanted a better life. They were prepared to reach out for it.

The opportunity to seek something better did present itself. Word reached the Quebec countryside that quaint New England villages were turning into booming mill towns. Mill agents were SEEKING workers; CASH money was being paid. Though some French families decided to head for the Canadian west, or America's Midwest, most opted to head straight south to New England.

Could it really be worse there than on the unproductive countryside of Quebec?

The great majority of today's Franco-Americans can trace their heritage to ancestors from Quebec Province. Hundreds of thousands of immigrants came south in the 19th and early 20th centuries. Yet a unique segment of the story of the Franco-Americans does not involve Quebec. Some Franco-Americans, especially in Maine and Connecticut, are those of Acadian ancestry. They have a story, too.

Acadia was a term for the north Atlantic maritime region that today is known as Nova Scotia, Prince Edward Island, Cape Breton Island, lower New Brunswick and a large segment of Maine stretching to the Kennebec River. As usual in historical matters relating to eastern North America, a confrontation between French and English is involved when outlining the significance of Acadia.

According to historian Father Thomas Albert, the first French families came to Acadia in 1632. His monumental work, *The History of Madawaska*, states that most Acadian families came from Brittany. Some, though, were originally from Poitou and Saintonge.

Dispute arose between England and France as to who controlled Acadia. The English claimed the entire territory following the Treaty of Utrecht (1713), for they were, in fact, deeded tracts in Nova Scotia and Cape Breton Island, where the strategic Ft. Louisbourg was located. But France continued to occupy New Brunswick, and half of Maine. And French still resided in Nova Scotia.

The situation in Acadia was to prove disastrous to the French. In spite of their French origin, the Acadians agreed to a qualified oath of allegiance to the British Crown. They were to have freedom of religion, and exemption from military service. They specifically did not want to have to bear arms against fellow Frenchmen if England and France went to war. After Charles Lawrence became English governor of Nova Scotia, though, he demanded in 1755 a new oath under which they would have to take up arms against Frenchmen. When they rejected this, Lawrence said they were guilty of treason. He ordered them banished, and their property confiscated.

Eight thousand Acadians, especially in the Minas Basin region in Nova Scotia, argued they had been British subjects for nearly 45 years. It did no good. They were rounded up in churches and meeting halls, and sent away in boats chartered by Lawrence and led by Col. John Winslow. Unsuspecting villagers did not have an opportunity to meet with their families before being loaded on ships. They were deprived of a hearing to determine wrongdoing. They were simply "dispersed," and hence this ignoble chapter in North American history is called the Acadian Dispersal. The abductions continued in other Acadian villages that year. Personal tragedy was a daily occurrence. Husbands were stolen from the arms of their wives; sons, as many as a half-dozen in a family, disappeared without a word regarding destination.

The initial English force sent to Acadia to accomplish the mission was 2,000 strong. They were acting in the military interest, but their action was tainted by cruel personal administration. No consideration was given to the families of the deported; conditions on the trip itself were harsh. It is hard to imagine the male population responding to the King's call in the morning, then disappearing in the afternoon. But such was the nature of the Acadian Dispersal. The English did little to humanize the maneuver. "Let's drink to the happy voyage of the Acadians," reads Winslow's log as he left with a full ship of neutral French.[11]

Father Albert writes that 8,000 were taken to exile. They were dumped ashore in ports from Boston to the Gulf of Mexico. The Louisiana term "cajuns" is a shortened form of Acadians. Ships went to France and England, others sailed to Bermuda, the West Indies, and even Corsica.[12] Some Frenchmen were slaves on their own land, pressed into service by the British to labor without compensation on projects like construction of seawalls and municipal buildings.

Henry Wadsworth Longfellow's famous poem, "Evangeline," is a tragedy involving a couple that gets separated on its wedding day by the King's orders to seize all the men in a small Acadian town. Gabriel is taken; Evangeline is heartbroken, and spends her life searching for him. She eventually finds him. But by then he is an old man on his death bed. Her shock at seeing him again, and under these circumstances, is so great that it kills her also.

An early portion of the poem follows: "You are convened this day," the narration goes, "by his Majesty's orders . . . painful the task is that I do, which I know to be grievous. Yet must I bow and obey, and deliver the will of our monarch; namely, that all your lands, and dwellings, and cattle of all kinds be forfeited to the crown, and that you yourselves from this province be transported to other lands . . . Prisoners I now declare you, for this is his Majesty's pleasure."[13]

The Acadian Dispersal was promulgated to neutralize Acadia. Some scholars, like Rhode Island College's Paul P. Chasse, contend that the plan, and its architect, Gov. Lawrence, embarrassed the English crown. Nevertheless, it stands out as a disgraceful chapter in the British treatment of the French on this continent.

The result of the Dispersal was the creation of a displaced people. Some settled in the regions where they debarked, but many returned to Acadia. Some wandered back alone. Others gathered together for the return, such as the 800 Acadians who left Boston in 1767, and by foot headed for their homeland through Massachusetts.[14]

Yet disappointment greeted all on their return. Loyalists fleeing the American Revolution descended on Acadia between 1775 and 1780 – estimates indicate as many as 30,000 headed toward New Brunswick and Nova Scotia. In need of land to offer the loyal colonists, the British again evicted the French.

Finally, in 1785, a group of Acadians convinced the British crown to grant them land in a heretofore unknown region in the St. John River Valley called the Madawaska Territory. The British gave approval, and hundreds of French slowly began making their way to what would become their homeland after so much hardship.

The Acadians stayed in this region, which was too remote to invite trouble. They were settlers here; their descendants were to be natives. Thus this Acadian colony differed from the many communities that those from Quebec were to join. The Acadians in the St. John Valley were there first; the Quebecois were newcomers to an established town or city. Franco-Americans in Fall River or Manchester might have a local heritage of several generations, but some Acadian families in northern Maine date back almost 200 years.

Not all Franco-Americans in the St. John Valley today are of Acadian heritage, for families from Quebec have since arrived. But those who do have Acadian blood stand out. They have survived a series of events unique to this continent, and will let their roots be known. It is said that Acadians even today are suspicious of strangers, because of past mistreatment. It is said they are bold and independent, because of their historic battle to survive. It is said they just want to be left alone.

And who could blame them?

The French-Canadian newcomers made communities like Biddeford, Maine, bustling places. In picture above, taken near the turn of the century, men and women scurry about Pepperell Square. The city remained a bustling area when the automobile arrived, as this picture taken in about 1924 shows.

# Chapter III

# The French-Canadians
# Come to New England

New England maintains a clean, healthy image. Illustrated texts for the coffee table focus on majestic windjammers and quaint Protestant churches. New England's rivers flow through small mountain towns, and if an urban dimension is introduced, it is often Boston's Charles River park, or its Freedom Trail.

Such representations capture only part of New England, however. There are towns and cities in the region which are dominated by massive red brick mills. Their presence awes those who are seeing mill complexes for the first time. It is, after all, a powerful sight to behold the mills of Lawrence, Mass., from Route 495.

The French-Canadians inhabited the mill towns and cities when they arrived here more than a century ago. Their cities had rivers, but on each bank were mills and machine shops greedily utilizing the cheap labor and hydro power.

The towns the French inhabited possessed churches, but instead of meticulously painted clapboard structures with trees and lawn, the buildings were massive gatherings of brick, granite or stone set squarely amidst the three and four-story tenements of the "Little Canadas."

Research has yielded little proof that the French were aware of the delights of a windjammer on a warm August afternoon. Theirs was a different life-style indeed.

Scores of towns and cities in New England were built around the mills. Several, like Lowell and Lawrence, Mass., were constructed as the mills were built. Remarkably, the towns were built to accommodate the mills. And it is said that Manchester, N. H., was little more than a municipal arm of the Amoskeag Manufacturing Co.

But it is not necessary to look to specific municipalities in the six-state region to find the French. Inhabiting almost every mill community was this quiet, hardworking people.

They came by the thousands in the late 19th century, accepting millwork willingly. Other nationalities also participated in this acceleration of the Industrial Revolution, but the French were a key cog, especially in textiles. Mills in Maine, New Hampshire, and Vermont were dominated by French workers. Firms in Massachusetts and Rhode Island had even greater numbers, though they did not maintain the same high percentage of French employees. In later years, Connecticut was also a recipient of the flow of immigrants. Indeed, because of the migration, New England is heavily populated with those of French-Canadian descent. The Irish are more visible, but the French are as populous. And though a retiring public posture has contributed to a lack of recognition, the French are very much a presence in this region.

In northern New England (Maine, New Hampshire, Vermont), those of French descent are the major minority ethnic group. Fifteen per cent of New Hampshire residents grew up in households where French was the first or second language. Maine counts 14 per cent of its residents (141,489 of 993,663) as French, while Vermont's figure is 9.5 per cent (42,193 or 444,330).

Massachusetts, though maintaining only a 6.4 percentage, nevertheless has 367,194 inhabitants of French upbringing. Rhode Island (10.7 per cent, 101,270) and Connecticut (4.7 per cent, 142,118), also possess appreciable numbers of Franco-Americans.

And certain cities in New England have highly concentrated populations. Lowell, Mass., counts nearly 20,000 of 94,000 residents as French. Pawtucket, R. I., hosts 13,409 French in a population of 76,992. Manchester, N. H., has even more (27,777 of 87,754) while Lewiston, Maine, has a 59.9 percentage of French residents (25,037 of 40,779). Aroostook County, Maine, communities run over 95 per cent French – Grand Isle 97.5 per cent, Frenchville, 96.9 and Eagle Lake, 95.3.

And such figures are only relating to persons in French-speaking homes. Those of French name only, or some French blood, number more than 2.5 million in this region.[15]

As interest in the French increases, questions are more often heard: What brought these people here? What factors prompted them to come in such great numbers? Why did they stay?

Harsh times in Quebec made many French-Canadian habitants consider alternatives to their lives on the farms. Another factor entered into the great continental migration: labor shortages.

The industrial revolution turned much of New England into a blaze of economic opportunity in the early years of the 19th century. New inventions to produce goods, new techniques to make goods marketable, new methods of corporate finance to underwrite ventures all contributed to the growth of industrial output. Mills and factories were constructed on rivers throughout the region in the early 1800's.

It was not long before they needed workers, and lots of them.

The timing was convenient for both parties, particularly after 1840. The French-Canadians, harassed by the British and hindered by antiquated farm practices, were seeking better opportunities. Yankee mill owners, in a state of rapid expansion, were prepared to welcome the French into their burgeoning brick empires.

Prior to industrialization, the French were a rarity in the New England states. Historians rarely record their presence before 1840. When they do, it appears to be an exception rather than rule. "A Proulx was known to live in Woonsocket in 1814," says one writer; "100 French were noted in Burlington in 1815," states another. The first French-Canadian was "spotted" in Worcester in 1820, while a Marois settled in Southbridge in 1832 and the Dorvals resided in Millbury in 1834.[16] Yet after 1840, a rough correlation of Papineau's Rebellion of 1837-38, the French began coming south. They were looking for jobs, and jobs they found.

Supplying many the chance for employment were the cotton mills. Though the immigrants also worked in wool factories, shoe shops, lumber mills and the open woods, the cotton industry claimed the largest number. The French were arriving as the industry was expanding, and they were instrumental in making it grow.

Indeed, from the production end, the French helped make "King Cotton" what it was. Most Americans identify cotton solely with southern blacks. But the contributors on the other end were the millworkers of New England. The migration supplied thousands of French-Canadians to the mills. The French, in fact, would dominate the mill population in many New England communities, making them a unique ingredient in the growth of cotton.

The arrival of the immigrants came just after developments in the technology of textiles, which made for an abundant number of jobs. The 18th century had witnessed the "golden age of invention" in textiles; the flying shuttle in 1733, the spinning jenny in 1767, the spinning mule in 1779. Two events, even more important, took place in 1792-93. Eli Whitney revolutionized the processing of cotton with his cotton gin, and Samuel Slater created the first mill in New England. All the mills needed after these developments were workers.

Initially, the concept of large-scale mill production was not a popular one. During colonial days, it was feared that the factory system would degrade the worker as it had done in England. Prospective manufacturers, pioneers like Pawtucket, R. I.'s, Samuel Slater, were on the defensive in their efforts to start mill operations. They were obligated to prove themselves to a skeptical community. Mills in the early part of the 19th century, because of the extra attention by mill owners, were clean, well-lit and relatively safe places. Frequently set at a river's edge, they possessed even a pastoral atmosphere.

Consider, if you will, the account in the Essex Gazette describing Lowell, Mass., in 1825: "It is indeed a fairy scene. Here we beheld an extensive city, busy, noisy, and thriving, with immense prospects for increasing and boundless wealth. Everything is fresh and green with the vigor of youth, yet perfect in all the strength of manhood. What cannot a combination of genius, wealth and industry produce!"[17]

Those who labored in Lowell mills a half-century later would hardly use such glowing terms to describe that mill city. But the early conditions in the mills were vastly different from those the French were to inherit.

The initial days of the mill industry in America (early 1800's) took place before the French had migratory notions. Mills such as Slater's, now a museum, employed just a few townspeople. The French began entering the mills as the industry itself expanded. Development of

Preceding the French-Canadians into the textile mills of New England were young women from nearby farms. Here is a narrow-fabric weaver winding bobbins beside her loom, pictured in a woodcut by Winslow Homer.

(Merrimack Valley Textile Museum)

the New England mills, in fact, is the story of industrialization in America. Those coming from Canada were to be a part of that.

During the early period of industrialization, the first advances in labor-saving machinery were made. Initial success in the deployment of workers was registered, which enabled American mills to forge ahead of foreign competition. And it was in the New England cotton mills that managers learned the rudiments of mass-production, and production with speed.

As mill owners built larger buildings and filled them with more machines, the first call for labor was put out. Those answering were Yankee farm girls from surrounding countryside. Lured by regular cash wages, assured of acceptable working conditions, and guaranteed a bed in a company boardinghouse, many young women left the farms for the mills. The "city" excited them. The adventure of being on one's own was appealing. Some worked to pay off the family debts, while others came to earn their first own money.

"Since I have wrote you, another pay day has arrived," reads a letter from a Yankee girl sent back to her family farm in New Hampshire. "I earned 14 dollars (per month) beside my board. The folks think I get along just first-rate, they say. I like it well as ever, and Sarah, don't I ever feel as independent of everyone; the thought that I am living on no one else is a happy one indeed to me."[18]

Working in the mills was no lark, though, even then. Agents demanded obedience and commitment. The weekly pay check of $2 to $4 per week was not the kind of money that would permit a radical change of lifestyle from frugal New England ways. From 1800 to about 1840, though, such conditions were attractive enough to lure a work force from the surrounding farm country. Many entered the mills in winter, and returned to the farm to bring the crops in during the summer.

Just how desirable the mills were at this point is a matter of contention. Some accounts reflect the splendor of the experience, pointing to poetry clubs and literary papers the girls put out in their spare time. Critics, on the other hand, note a high turnover rate from year to year. Very likely, conditions varied from mill to mill.

The American mill was not to remain a chaste retreat for farmers' daughters, however. Increased technology and greater markets created the need for more workers; sophisticated management practices stressed greater production. Spearheaded by capitalistic elites like the Boston Associates, comprised of names like Lawrence, Cabot and Lowell, major projects were initiated.

The Amoskeag Manufacturing Co. in Manchester, N. H., purchased by Boston Associates in 1836, developed into the largest mill of its kind in the world. The communities of Lawrence and Holyoke, Mass., were created from the drawing board. Mills came first, the development of the town second. Relying on cheap river power, ready capital, and an intellectual climate that endorsed the growth of the business sector, industrialists pushed ahead with major expansion.

Rapid development brought deteriorating conditions, however. Interest in profit began replacing concern for the workers. Life in the mills became a true task.

Millhands balked at greater demands, showing opposition to 12-hour days. A first generation of millhands might have accepted 60 to 70-hour weeks, but the second generation of Yankee workers was not willing to continue.

The mill expansion fostered a two-fold problem for management. Degenerating conditions discouraged prospective workers. In addition, machinists and mechanics with some experience felt their skills should be more justly rewarded.

The region's labor ran short of willing workers in the 1830's. So when roving agents passing out handbill advertisements failed to provide an adequate work force locally, management put out the call for immigrants.

Though the French were to hear the cries advertising work, the first ethnic group that made an impact on the New England landscape was the Irish.

Irish immigrants had first come to Lowell in about 1830 when a mill agent met a group of laborers who had walked from Boston to the Merrimack River in search of work. By 1835, Lowell's Irish numbered 600, including about 250 who worked inside factories at menial tasks.[19] The Irish entered other communities following 1846, as the potato famine sent many across the ocean.

Desperate, the Irish immigrants would take jobs at low wages. They would work long hours.

Such a willingness to work forced the remaining New Englanders out of the mills. Hardcore Yankees might have endured sub-par industrial conditions, but they evidently could not cope with immigrants "tainting" their workingplaces. "Of 7,000 women operatives in 1836, less than 4 per cent had been foreign-born," says an entry in the Lowell Offering. "By 1860, 61.8 per cent of Lowell's work force was Irish. The first generation of Lowell mill girls was also the last WASP labor force in America."[20]

As immigrants arrived in large numbers, working conditions deteriorated. The presence of the Irish enabled manufacturers to become lax. These workers weren't Americans, the practice implied, so why worry about the human factor? As the textile industry approached the mid-19th century, it faced a long, though slow, slide toward trouble.

It was in this transitional period, one moving from industrial integrity to creeping avarice, that the French appeared. The major flow did not begin until after 1860, but a trickle was noted in the 1840's. It is said that between 1844 and 1848, 20,000 left Quebec for the United States.[21] Most chose New England.

The first French-Canadians to sample the offerings in the south were usually young men with a sense of adventure. They would spend winters in the mills of New England, then return for the summer harvests on the farms. The material goods they were able to obtain were a major reason they later opted to remain. A gold watch, or a new suit of clothes, were unheard of for the sons of Canadian farmers. As mill workers, they could buy these. And to be able to carry cash in the pocket was an impressive accomplishment indeed.

A feeling for French-Canadian migration was conveyed by Quebec writer Luc Lacourciere, in his *Oral Tradition: New England and French Canada.* Though it was written many years after the first immigrants went south, it nevertheless gives a picture of those who left, and those who stayed.

"I still remember 'la visite des etats', which was the term used when referring to the occasional return of Canadian emigrants to visit

Women and children were employed with regularity in the earliest days of the industry.

(Merrimack Valley Textile Museum)

relatives in the rural and farming areas of Beauce County. And what a sensation they caused in my native village."

"Sunday at church and afterwards when everyone gathered at the local post office, the young ladies paraded about all dolled up in stylish pink dresses, fashions seldom seen by rural residents in a small town."

"As for the young men, they invariably returned from the states driving rumble-seat Whippit cars, smoking cigars and wearing new clothes, not to mention new gold teeth."

"These young visitors would assume an air of superiority, and scandalized some as much as fascinated others by their attitude and their language, which bore traces of the new influence."[22]

The French were not displeased with what they found in New England. The mill conditions were discouraging to second generation Yankees, but appeared to be adequate to those who had just left endless chores on the poor farmland of the Province of Quebec. At least a long day in the United States yielded cash.

As one J. N. Bosse, a Quebec attorney, remarked in a "Report on Emigration" in 1849, "all agree on congratulating themselves in having left Canada, and they invite, in a very pressing manner, their relatives and friends to their property and so join them."

Migration was noticeable in the 1840's, though more Canadians would have come if better methods of travel had been available. Horse and buggy was the prevailing form of transportation, and a trip from Quebec to Woonsocket, R. I. could take three to four weeks in good weather.

Such constraints do not suggest that some hardy souls wouldn't make the trip regardless of discomfort. Israel Shevenell, one of the first French-Canadians to settle permanently in Biddeford, Maine, hiked 200 miles to Biddeford in the spring of 1845. He left his home in Compton, Quebec, carrying one day's supply of food. He managed to subsist on meals given to him by settlers along the way. The hardships of the journey included having to snowshoe over the White Mountains and being robbed of what little cash he had by a traveling companion. Yet he succeeded in reaching the community.

Shevenell took up the trade of brickmaker and earned $12 a month. Not one to lose his spirit even in old age, he joined in the city's bicentennial parade in 1905 carrying a sign, "I was here in '55."[23]

Most French-Canadians weren't as durable as Shevenell, however, and avoided the trip. But the arrival of the railroad in the 1850's made travel more appealing. The French now came to New England in large numbers. The Grand Trunk Railroad reached Maine in 1853, for instance, which accelerated immigration there. It permitted thousands of Canadians to reach Brunswick, Biddeford and Sanford. Two decades later, an extension was connected to Lewiston. Until the railroad reached the Lewiston-Auburn area, that community had less than 100 French-Canadians. By 1880 it numbered 4,714 and by 1900, fully 13,300 French newcomers had chosen the Maine community.[24]

Other communities in New England observed remarkable growth patterns following the arrival of the railroad midway through the 19th century. Factors other than rail transportation influenced growth, of course. But few deny that the railroad made New England suddenly accessible.

The French-Canadian population of Fall River, Mass., for instance,

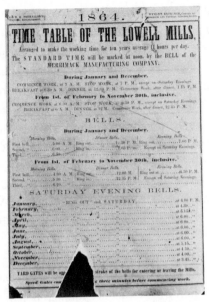

A poster from the Lowell Mills shows that the work hours were long — 12 hours long, and beginning at either 6:30 a.m. or 7 a.m., depending on season.

(Merrimack Valley Textile Museum)

was 10 in 1860. By 1880 it stood at 9,000, and by 1900, it had zoomed to 33,000.[25] Worcester, Mass., went from 386 in 1860, to 3,500 in 1880, and 15,300 by 1900.[26] Trains were full coming south. It was reported in L' Etenard National in 1870, in fact, that "in 1870, it was claimed one-half of the passenger traffic revenues of the Worcester and Nashua Railroad was derived from French-Canadian immigrants."

One characteristic of early French-Canadian migration was the tendency for those of a town or parish to stay together. If one family left for the New England states, it was likely that the next family to leave would also head for that community. Brothers followed brothers, and cousins would often move in the wake of cousins. But parish members would also tend to head for communities in which friends had settled. It wasn't unusual, therefore, to have a skeletal community of friends and relatives already established in some mill towns. And often was the case when a New England town would have a distinctive Canadian flavor. If six dozen habitants from Sherbrooke had settled in the same community, for instance, it was bound to take on a certain quality reflective of that back home.

As an overview, it could be said that the French heard about opportunity, saw means of transportation, and proceeded to relocate. Communities they settled in include the following: Connecticut: Danielson, Moosup, North Grosvenordale, Putnam and Willimantic; Maine: Auburn, Biddeford, Brunswick, Lewiston, Waterville; Massachusetts: Chicopee, Fall River, Holyoke, Lawrence, Lowell, New Bedford, Southbridge, Springfield, Worcester; New Hampshire: Berlin, Manchester, Nashua, Somersworth; Rhode Island: Arctic Centre (today West Warwick), Central Falls, Pawtucket, Warren, Woonsocket; Vermont: Barre, Burlington, Rutland, St. Albans, St. Johnsbury, Winooski.[27]

The immigrants came in increasing numbers during the Civil War. Mill closings and the army drafts created chaos with the region's work force. Many mill owners believe immigration would solve their employment needs, and they now looked toward Quebec for help. With the railroad capable of delivering workers in bulk, a new era in New England personnel practices began.

Statistics tabulated by the U. S. Census Bureau, and brought out in the Ph.D. thesis of Ralph D. Vicero (University of Wisconsin, 1968) underline the heavy flow of French-Canadians that did come forth.

The following population figures demonstrate the growth of French-Canadians in New England states during the period of 1860-1900:[28]

Number of French Canadian Residents:

| State | 1860 | 1870 | 1880 | 1890 | 1900 |
|---|---|---|---|---|---|
| Maine | 7,490 | 15,000 | 29,000 | 52,000 | 77,000 |
| New Hampshire | 1,780 | 7,300 | 26,200 | 49,000 | 76,000 |
| Vermont | 16,580 | 29,000 | 33,500 | 38,000 | 45,000 |
| Massachusetts | 7,780 | 34,600 | 81,100 | 162,000 | 275,000 |
| Rhode Island | 1,810 | 8,900 | 19,800 | 36,000 | 61,000 |
| Connecticut | 1,980 | 8,600 | 18,500 | 28,000 | 39,000 |
| New England | 37,420 | 103,500 | 208,100 | 365,000 | 573,000 |

Mill owners found the habitants suited to the textile work, which was reflected in their repeated efforts to recruit more and more French-Canadians. Provincial traditions and fervent Catholicism combined to make them effective servants of mill foremen. They arrived as the Yankees were leaving, and at the time the Irish were looking elsewhere for vocational endeavor. By 1860, the textile industry in New England favored the French.

"The French are much better than the Irish when learned," wrote one correspondent about female workers in the Dwight Manufacturing Papers, 1859. "They work steadier, and are much more ambitious."[29]

Another note salvaged from the Dwight papers, 1859, states that with "Irish girls . . . there is a strong disposition to run away to avoid paying their fares."[30]

And the Massachusetts Bureau of Labor Statistics (1890 report) said that businesses "prefer them (the French) in their mills; for they are industrious in the extreme, do not grumble about pay, are docile, and have nothing to do with labor agitations."

The relocation of the French brought immigrant families into a strange, English-speaking world but the newcomers soon adapted lifestyles very similar to those in Quebec. They established churches, parochial schools, societies and clubs. The new residents spoke French as if they were in Quebec; their warm family gatherings might have been in the living room of the old farmhouse they had just left. The immigrants showed a determination to stay together, to create an ethnic community similar to what they had always known.

Their neighborhood, often within the shadow of the mill, was called Le Petit Canada ("Little Canada"). French was the language heard on the street. Catholicism was the faith of the residents therein.

Growth of neighborhoods was rapid. If the tales are to be believed, as many as 20 persons, from two or three families, were temporarily housed together. It was rare for a French family not to extend help to fellow Francos.

Most French sections would soon have a church within its boundaries, as no other institution was more important. The French-Canadians had an unusually strong relationship with their parish priest, or curé, and that tie continued in the immigrants' world, through the late 19th and early 20th centuries.

The parish priest blessed, baptized, married and officiated at funerals of the French. In Canada, a curé was reputed to be strong enough for riding horseback from one mission to another, so two different communities could hear mass on a given holy day. He was also known to trade his Bible for a paint brush; if there was work to be done in raising a house, or painting a ceiling, the priest was enthusiastic enough to join right in. So close were the learned curés to their parishioners in Canada that some actually held a family's savings for them until the "proper time" to dispense it. He was a powerful man indeed in French Canada, using his greater education to be a leader in all aspects of community life.

# CHRONOLOGICAL LIST OF
# FRANCO AMERICAN PARISHES IN NEW ENGLAND
## by
## Dr. Paul P. Chassé

| | Date | Name (Nom) | City (Ville) | Diocese (Diocèse) |
|---|------|------------|--------------|-------------------|
| 1 | 1827 | Sainte Luce | Frenchville | Portland |
| 2 | 1832 | Saint Bruno | Van Buren | Portland |
| 3 | 1851 | Saint Joseph | Burlington | Burlington |
| 4 | 1856 | Nativité de la Sainte Vierge | Swanton | Burlington |
| 5 | 1858 | Notre Dame des Victoires | St. Johnsbury | Burlington |
| 6 | 1867 | Notre Dame de la Pitié | Pittsfield | Springfield |
| 7 | 1868 | Saint Joseph | Lowell | Boston |
| 8 | | Précieux-Sang | Holyoke | Springfield |
| 9 | 1869 | Sacré-Coeur de Jésus | East Rutland | Burlington |
| 10 | | Saint Coeur de Marie | West Rutland | Burlington |
| 11 | | Sainte Anne | Fall River | Fall River |
| 12 | | Notre Dame du Bon Conseil | West Boylston | Worcester |
| 13 | | Saint François de Sales | Waterville | Portland |
| 14 | 1870 | Notre Dame des Canadiens | Worcester | Worcester |
| 15 | | Sacré-Coeur | Webster | Worcester |
| 16 | | Saints Pierre et Paul | Lewiston | Portland |
| 17 | | Sainte Marie | Marlboro | Boston |
| 18 | | Sainte Anne | Lawrence | Boston |
| 19 | | Saint David | Madawaska | Portland |
| 20 | 1871 | Saint Louis de Gonzague | Nashua | Manchester |
| 21 | | Saint Augustin | Manchester | Manchester |
| 22 | | Notre Dame du Sacré-Coeur | North Adams | Springfield |
| 23 | 1872 | Notre Dame de Southbridge | Southbridge | Worcester |
| 24 | | Saint Amédée | Alburg | Burlington |
| 25 | | Saints Anges Gardiens | St. Albans | Burlington |
| 26 | | Saint Joseph | Biddeford | Portland |
| 27 | | Sacré-Coeur | New Bedford | Fall River |
| 28 | | Saint Jacques | Manville | Providence |
| 29 | | Sainte Marie de la Visitation | Putnam | Hartford |
| 30 | | Saint Joseph | Haverhill | Boston |
| 31 | | Saint François-Xavier | Winooski | Burlington |
| 32 | 1873 | L'Etoile de la Mer | Narragansett | Providence |
| 33 | | Saint Jean-Baptiste | Suncook | Manchester |
| 34 | | Saint Joseph | Springfield | Springfield |
| 35 | | Saint Louis | Indian Orchard | Springfield |
| 36 | | Notre Dame du Sacré-Coeur | Central Falls | Providence |
| 37 | | Saint Jean-Baptiste | West Warwick | Providence |
| 38 | 1874 | Notre Dame de Lourdes | Fall River | Fall River |
| 39 | 1875 | Précieux Sang | Woonsocket | Providence |
| 40 | 1877 | Saint Jean-Baptiste | Warren | Providence |
| 41 | 1878 | Saint Joseph | Salem | Boston |
| 42 | 1879 | Saint Hyacinthe | Westbrook | Portland |

40

| | Date | Name (Nom) | City (Ville) | Diocese (Diocèse) |
|---|---|---|---|---|
| 43 | 1880 | Saint Joseph | Old Town | Portland |
| 44 | | Notre Dame des Victoires | Boston | Boston |
| 45 | | Sainte Marie | Manchester | Manchester |
| 46 | | Saint Charles Borrommée | Providence | Providence |
| 47 | | Saint Laurent | Meriden | Hartford |
| 48 | 1882 | Saint Martin de Tours | Somersworth | Manchester |
| 49 | 1883 | Sainte Rosaire | Rochester | Manchester |
| 50 | 1884 | Notre Dame des Sept-Douleurs | Adams | Springfield |
| 51 | | Sainte Anne | Turner's Falls | Springfield |
| 52 | | Sainte Anne | Waterbury | Hartford |
| 53 | | Saint Rosaire | Gardner | Worcester |
| 54 | | Notre Dame de l'Assomption | Millbury | Worcester |
| 55 | 1886 | Saint Joseph | North Grosvernordale | Norwich |
| 56 | | Sainte Marie | Putnam | Norwich |
| 57 | | Saint Mathieu | Fall River | Fall River |
| 58 | | Sacré-Coeur | Taftville | Norwich |
| 59 | | Immaculée-Conception | Fitchburg | Worcester |
| 60 | 1887 | Saint Jean-Baptiste | Lynn | Boston |
| 61 | | Sainte Marie | Spencer | Worcester |
| 62 | 1888 | Saint Augustin | Augusta | Portland |
| 63 | 1889 | Sainte Anne | Hartford | Hartford |
| 64 | | Saint Louis | New Haven | Hartford |
| 65 | 1890 | Saint Georges | Manchester | Manchester |
| 66 | | Notre Dame du Perpétuel-Secours | Holyoke | Springfield |
| 67 | | Saint Joseph | Fitchburg | Worcester |
| 68 | | Saint Jean-Baptiste | Pawtucket | Providence |
| 69 | | Sainte Anne | Woonsocket | Providence |
| 70 | | Saint Hyacinthe | New Bedford | Fall River |
| 71 | 1891 | Saint Joseph | Worcester | Worcester |
| 72 | | Sacré-Coeur | Laconia | Manchester |
| 73 | | Sacré-Coeur | Brockton | Boston |
| 74 | | Coeur Immaculé de Marie | Fairfield | Portland |
| 75 | 1892 | Sacré-Coeur | Concord | Manchester |
| 76 | | Notre Dame de la Pitié | Cambridge | Boston |
| 77 | | Saint Dominique (1901 – Saint Sacrement) | Fall River | Fall River |
| 78 | | Saint Ignace | Sanford | Portland |
| 79 | 1893 | Saint Antoine | Bridgeport | Bridgeport |
| 80 | | Saint Charles Borrommée | Dover | Manchester |
| 81 | | Saint Georges | Chicopee Falls | Springfield |
| 82 | | Saint Nom-de-Jésus | Worcester | Worcester |
| 83 | 1894 | Saint Joseph | Waltham | Boston |
| 84 | | Saint André | Biddeford | Portland |
| 85 | 1895 | Notre Dame de la Consolation | Pawtucket | Providence |
| 86 | | Saint Antoine | New Bedford | Fall River |
| 87 | 1896 | Notre Dame du Perpétuel-Secours | Phoenix | Providence |

| | Date | Name (Nom) | City (Ville) | Diocese (Diocèse) |
|---|---|---|---|---|
| 88 | 1899 | Saint Antoine de Padoue | Manchester | Manchester |
| 89 | | Saint Roch | Fall River | Fall River |
| 90 | 1901 | Saint Louis | Auburn | Portland |
| 91 | | Saints Jean & Athanase | Rumford | Portland |
| 92 | 1902 | Sainte Anne | Salem | Boston |
| 93 | | Saint Louis de France | Lowell | Boston |
| 94 | | Saint Louis de Gonzague | Newburyport | Boston |
| 95 | | Sacré-Coeur | Amesbury | Boston |
| 96 | 1903 | Sainte Famille | Woonsocket | Providence |
| 97 | | Saint Louis de Gonzague | Woonsocket | Providence |
| 98 | | Saint Antoine | Burlington | Burlington |
| 99 | | Sainte Marie | Willimantic | Hartford |
| 100 | | Saint François d'Assise | Fitchburg | Worcester |
| 101 | 1904 | Saint Jacques | Taunton | Fall River |
| 102 | | Sacré-Coeur | North Attleboro | Fall River |
| 103 | | Notre Dame de Lourdes | Providence | Providence |
| 104 | | Bon Pasteur | Linwood | Worcester |
| 105 | | Saint Jean-Baptiste | Ludlow | Springfield |
| 106 | | Saint Antoine | Worcester | Worcester |
| 107 | 1905 | Sacré-Coeur | Lawrence | Boston |
| 108 | | Saint Antoine de Padoue | Shirley | Boston |
| 109 | | Saint Joseph | Attleboro | Fall River |
| 110 | | Immaculée Conception | Holyoke | Springfield |
| 111 | 1906 | Saint Mathieu | Central Falls | Providence |
| 112 | | Notre Dame du Bon Secours | Easthampton | Springfield |
| 113 | 1907 | Notre Dame de l'Assomption | Chelsea | Boston |
| 114 | | Sainte Anne | Bristol | Hartford |
| 115 | | Sainte Marie | Lewiston | Portland |
| 116 | | Saint Louis de France | Springfield | Springfield |
| 117 | | Notre Dame de Lourdes | Lowell | Boston |
| 118 | | Sainte Anne | New Bedford | Fall River |
| 119 | | Notre Dame du Rosaire | New Bedford | Fall River |
| 120 | 1908 | Sacré-Coeur | Southbridge | Worcester |
| 121 | | Saint Thomas d'Aquin | Springfield | Springfield |
| 122 | 1909 | L'Enfant-Jésus | Nashua | Manchester |
| 123 | | Notre Dame des Victoires | Woonsocket | Providence |
| 124 | | Sainte Rose de Lima | Aldenville | Springfield |
| 125 | | Saint Joseph | Everett | Boston |
| 126 | | Saint Stanislaus | Ipswich | Boston |
| 127 | | Notre Dame du Mont Carmel | Methuen | Boston |
| 128 | | Saint Joseph | New Bedford | Fall River |
| 129 | | Sainte Cécile | Pawtucket | Providence |
| 130 | 1911 | Saint Jean l'Evangéliste | Newton | Boston |
| 131 | | Sacré-Coeur de Jésus | Manchester | Manchester |
| 132 | | Notre Dame | Waterville | Portland |
| 133 | 1914 | Saint Jean Baptiste | Manchester | Manchester |
| 134 | | Saint Edmond | Manchester | Manchester |

| | Date | Name (Nom) | City (Ville) | Diocese (Diocèse) |
|---|---|---|---|---|
| 135 | 1917 | Saint Alphonse | Beverly | Boston |
| 136 | | Saint Ange Gardien | Berlin | Manchester |
| 137 | 1923 | Sainte Jeanne d'Arc | Lowell | Boston |
| 138 | | Sainte Famille* | Lewiston | Portland |
| 139 | | Sacré-Coeur* | Auburn | Portland |
| 140 | | Sainte Famille* | Sanford | Portland |
| 141 | | Sainte Croix* | Lewiston | Portland |
| 142 | 1926 | Sainte Thérèse de l'Enfant-Jésus | Mexico | Portland |
| 143 | | Saint Jean Baptiste | Winslow | Portland |
| 144 | 1927 | Sainte Thérèse | Dracut | Boston |
| 145 | | Le Christ-Roi | Hudson | Boston |
| 146 | | L'Assomption | Bellingham | Boston |
| 147 | 1928 | Notre Dame de Lourdes | Saco | Portland |
| 148 | 1929 | Saint Joseph | Woonsocket | Providence |
| 149 | | Sainte Thérèse de l'Enfant-Jésus | East Blackstone | Worcester |
| 150 | | Sainte Jeanne d'Arc | Cumberland | Providence |
| 151 | 1931 | Sainte Marie | Lowell | Boston |
| 152 | 1934 | Sainte Thérèse de l'Enfant-Jésus | Manchester | Manchester |
| 153 | 1953 | Notre Dame, Reine des Martyrs | Woonsocket | Providence |
| 154 | 1953 | Sainte Agathe | Woonsocket | Providence |

* Bishop Walsh did not establish these as "national" parishes though they have French clergy and French schools even today.

His influential role in community life continued as the immigrants settled in New England. His duties changed, of course. The newcomers often sought his aid in matters relating to naturalization procedures, or the availability of jobs. As one in a given community who could read, he informed his parish of the laws of the new country, and some of its practices and traditions.

The power of the parish priest could be stern, too. By the late 19th century, he would give pointed advice on suggested contributions to the church building fund, or he could deliver strong words on the proper pursuit of marriage. It was not unknown, for instance, for a priest to relegate a wedding ceremony to the basement of the church rather than the sanctuary. If he thought an unorthodox courtship, or pregnancy, were involved in the union, he could unilaterally take such action, and thereby mortify the wedding party.

The power of the Franco priest in New England was significant when exercised, but in some communities it was difficult for a French priest to get to the pulpit. For years Francos in different areas had to listen to their masses in English, and have their sacraments in the foreign English tongue.

"In the course of their stormy struggle for ethnic religious survival, Franco-Americans suffered in many instances untold mental and moral anguish due to the pressures brought against them by presiding clergy," writes Dr. Paul P. Chasse. "These clergy went as far as refusing to baptize their children, to allow them to attend mass inside non-French churches; to give them the sacraments or to bury their dead; by maintaining an uncompromising stand against allowing them to hear the word of God preached in French; and to censure French priests for having preached in French, and laymen excommunicated for having attended their mass . . . "[31]

Emotions ran high on this issue of French independence with the church. Often the anger was directed at the Irish. The French claimed Francos were not being represented in the circles of power, furthermore, they said, they had the right to be part of the decision-making process because of their heavy population.[32]

In Lawrence, Mass., for instance, the French newspaper Le Progrés carried articles around the turn of the century that complained about the power of the Irish. "Should the bishops be Irish in a predominantly Canadian district?" it asked. "Le Progrés protested that while Canadians comprised two-thirds of the diocese of Portland, and three-fifths of Manchester, N. H., they had no high church officials in those cities except a great vicar, who was part Irish at that. It warned that the clergy was driving Canadians to apostasy by tyrannically suppressing the French language," wrote Donald B. Cole in his *"Immigrant City."*[33]

The French were insistent that they be permitted to worship in their own style, and most immigrants eventually saw this desire become a reality. There were battles along the way, however. In 1911 many Franco-American parishioners in Maine rejected Bishop Walsh's system granting ownership of all Catholic property within the diocese to the bishop. And in 1924, many Rhode Island Catholics engaged in a heated confrontation with church authorities by refusing to support a major diocese fund-raising drive which promised few benefits for Franco-Americans. The rebellious Sentinellists eventually lost this battle, however.

Such battles are in the past now, but what remains has been the reverence for church and its priesthood. Today the role of priests has been reduced by greater social action by local, state and federal governments, but the entity that Franco-Americans turn to when in need is still often the church.

In addition to the church, an institution that helped the French-Canadians acclimate to New England was the societies. Though the ethnically-oriented fraternal groups are still prominent today, they were of paramount significance in the early years.

The first such organization in the United States was Societe Saint-Jean-Baptiste. The society was founded in 1850, but not in New England. Gabriel Franchère started the organization in New York City, where at the time a large contingent of French-Canadian immigrants lived. Burlington, Vt., had its first chapter in 1859; and these two were followed by one in Springfield, Mass., 1864, Pittsfield, Mass. 1864, and Meriden, Conn. 1865. Such was the interest in societies even at that time that a national convention was held in New York in 1865 where leaders vowed to "promote the welfare of

Early industrial development of the Biddeford-Saco area, when the mode of
transportation was still sail.

(McArthur Library, Biddeford, Maine)

French Canadian immigrants, provide quarters for social, cultural and religious gatherings, and try to obtain French-speaking priests and parishes."[34]

In 1896, the Association Canado-Americain was formed in New Hampshire from a group of smaller societies. The association issued life insurance, while earmarking a small percentage of the profits to promote Franco-American cultural activities. In addition to providing these activities, it now maintains in Manchester, N. H., one of the most complete libraries of Franco-American resources in this country.

Societies and clubs are not as active today as they were when the immigrants arrived. Television and automobiles, two components of "the good life," seem to be stiff competition with people who are deciding how to spend their leisure time. But societies continue to have influence in attempting to keep culture and language alive. A Societe Saint-Jean-Baptiste in Manchester may contribute to a cultural outing; the Rochambeau Snowshoe Club in Biddeford will host a snowshoers' convention for clubs from New England to Quebec.

French language newspapers existed in almost every industrial community in New England, which suggests the illiteracy was not as widespread as assumed. Many immigrants and their descendants understood French, but perhaps not English. This picture was taken in 1896, in front of Lewiston's famous Le Messager.

Journalists of French newspapers were among the prominent figures in Franco-American communities. Gathered here are among the most famous writers of their day. Seated, from left, are Wilfrid-J. Beaulieu, Adolphe Robert, and Philippe-Armand Lajoie. Standing, from left, are Paul Asselin, Georges Benard, and Louis-Philippe Gagne.

In addition to church and society, a key aspect of early Franco-American life was French newspapers. The first paper to be published in French in New England in the 19th century was Le Patriote of Burlington, Vt., in 1838. In the following years virtually every major industrial center had its own French newspapers, including towns like Salem, Mass., Norwich, Conn., Van Buren, Maine and Somersworth, N. H., communities of modest size. And in Woonsocket, R. I., which had but 300 French-speaking families in 1875, fully three French newspapers were there by 1875: the Courrier du Rhode Island, the Courrier Canadien, and Le Re'veil.[35] The papers that appeared in other towns and cities are literally too numerous to name. French newspapers leave a rich legacy, and many legendary names: Ferdinand Gagnon, Benjamin Lenthier, Jean-Georges LeBoutillier, Godfroy de Tonnancour, Louis A. Biron, Antione Clément and Louis-Phillipe Gagne. One veteran tying the old world of journalism with the new, Wilfred Beaulieu, died in the spring of 1979. Beaulieu, who served the Manchester, N. H. region for years, jokingly called himself "the last of the French Mohicans."[36]

The fact that so many French newspapers were able to flourish indicates that the early Franco-Americans were hearty readers. The image that seems to have been passed down by the Anglo press and historians is that the French were non-literate. Such vibrant publications could not have existed without readership. Perhaps many immigrants were slow to learn English. They evidently did not lack the ability to read and write in their own language.

Another characteristic of early Franco-American communities was the appearance of Catholic schools, though not all children attended these schools. French families were often in need of money, so many youngsters worked.

Though outsiders were to criticize parents' motives, their attitude to schooling was an outgrowth of their practices in Quebec. Children always worked on the farms. It was natural to expect them to continue working, in this case, in the mills. In the absence of child labor laws, children took jobs as doffers, batter hands, and bobbin boys. The inclination to leave school, however, was to be a detriment to the French for generations.

Employment, church, society, schools – the French reached for the institutions they knew. And probably the most visible example of their efforts to retain their culture was their use of the French language.

Some never learned English. It's not uncommon even today to encounter French-Canadians living here who speak no English. Perhaps this is what their early years in New England industry are remembered for: an insistence on retaining their heritage through use of their "native" language.

French was a problem at the beginning. Anglo store owners, bankers and professionals could not understand the newcomers. But soon immigrants began offering services. They entered the trades themselves.

Afix Marcotte, for instance, is remembered as the first merchant in Lewiston to give credit to the immigrants. He located his store across from the railroad station, and kept pots, pans, blankets, soap and flour right on the street. Those getting off the train could purchase immediately. Marcotte's faith in their willingness to repay was rewarded many times. His name today stands atop one of the largest stores in Lewiston.

A. H. Benoit started his retail career in Biddeford, where he was a salesman in a clothing store. He was the only French-speaking worker in the shop. After a reasonable period of "apprenticeship," he struck out on his own. He got virtually all the business from the French-speaking community, which in Biddeford meant he was on his way to a successful career. Today Benoit's is one of the largest stores in Portland, with branches in Augusta and Waterville.

More widely recognized has been the story of Frederic Dumaine. Dumaine quit school at 11 to help his widowed mother, and took a job as a clerk in Dedham, Mass., for $4 a week. He became a Franco-American Horatio Alger, as he rose to become president of the Eastern Steamship Co., the Mack Motor Truck Co., and the New York and New Haven Railroad. When he died, he left an estate of $90 million.[37]

Few immigrants became millionaires, of course. But as the French became more comfortable in their surroundings, individuals moved forward to open pharmacies, groceries, restaurants, law practices and doctors' offices. There was no wholesale defection from the mills, to be sure, but ambitious immigrants, or their offspring, were able to participate in local commerce in the early days of the 20th century.

Today one still sees evidence of French store owners serving French needs. Amidst the three and four-story wooden tenements in mill cities of New England are downtown pharmacies owned by Doyan or Belanger, and corner drug stores run by Cote and Dutremble. Though many young adult French have moved toward suburbs or farms, cities like Lowell, Fall River, Manchester, Biddeford and Lewiston still maintain highly concentrated French neighborhoods.

In the overview of the French Fact in New England, the French in the St. John Valley should not be overlooked. They did not go through such an "adjustment" process in the 19th century. The Acadians were the dominant ethnic group in the region. Though their numbers are small in comparison to the French in mill communities throughout the six states, their presence is nevertheless part of the Franco-American story. An Acadian will remind a speaker or writer about just this fact.

While the French were populating industrial communities in the 19th century, the Acadians were living in rural isolation in northern Maine. They cut and drove timber; they planted crops and raised animals to remain as self-sufficient as possible. Miles away from the nearest urban development, theirs was a quiet, complacent existence after the chaos their forefathers had endured in the 18th century.

It was almost as if they were in a world unto themselves, more an independent community than residents of a particular state or country. Indeed, until the Webster-Ashburton Treaty of 1842 defined the border separating Canada and the U. S. (the border line was the St. John River as far east as Grand Falls), the Valley was more a community of French than a matter of two countries. Even today, the national boundary is not of great significance to those in the area, for many residents cross the river daily to see relatives or carry out household chores.

The Valley had little or no communication with the mill cities throughout the 19th century. They were a different breed of French.

A major source of livelihood among those of Acadian descent in Aroostook County, then as now, was potatoes. Here the men of the family pause with some of their produce.

(Family photo courtesy of Marcel Mathieu)

Horse power helped in the potato fields of Aroostook County. But Franco-Americans in the Valley were like those in the urban communities of New England: they had to work hard for anything they got.

(Family photo courtesy of Marcel Mathieu)

Increased communication, vastly better transportation systems, and changing economic times have brought the Valley into closer relationships in the 20th century with those to the south. The descendants of the Acadians might not be squarely in the mainstream of New England activities, but certainly they are no longer isolated on the faraway tip of the region. They are more visible today than ever, thought it's likely they would just as soon keep some distance between themselves and the "other" world.

The migration that was filling New England mills in the 19th century was having an impact on Quebec as well; to wit, it was emptying a province.

From 1866 to 1875, according to historian Wilfrid Paradis, roughly 50,000 people left the province of Quebec annually. Many chose New England, for its proximity and its employment opportunities.

Steve Dunwell, in his comprehensive text, *The Run of The Mill*, says that "one-third of Quebec had moved to New England by the turn of the century, and most of these people went straight into the mills."

And Ralph D. Vicero has stated that Quebec experienced a loss of 600,000 persons to New England between 1840-1900, five-sixths after 1860. It's not hard to see, then, why many mill towns of New England were so French, so Canadian, in flavor!

Despite such statistics, it should not be assumed that the French-Canadian migration was the only movement underway. Other ethnic groups, some in greater numbers, came to America, too. Connecticut, Rhode Island and Massachusetts especially felt the inflow.

Foreign-born Italians in the U. S. numbered 484,027 in 1900, for instance, and by 1910 there were 1,343,125 in the United States. The Polish population was 14,407 in 1870, and by 1900, the total stood at 383,407. By 1910, there were 937,884 Poles in this country.

The Greeks, too, increased in number. There were 8,515 Greeks in the U. S., in 1900. After a decade of migration, Greeks stood at 101,282. By 1920, the total was 175,976.[38]

All eastern states noticed newcomers in their midst in the late 19th and early 20th Centuries.

Lower Pacific Mill in Lawrence, Mass., as another shift is about to begin.

(Lowell Museum)

Table.  Foreign-born Population of Massachusetts by
Country of Birth 1850 - 1910[2]

| | 1850. | 1860. | 1870. | 1880. | 1890. | 1900. | 1910. |
|---|---|---|---|---|---|---|---|
| Ireland, . . . | 115,917 | 185,434 | 216,120 | 226,700 | 259,902 | 249,916 | 222,867 |
| England, . . . | 16,685 | 23,848 | 34,099 | 47,263 | 76,400 | 82,346 | 92,658 |
| Scotland, . . . | 4,469 | 6,855 | 9,003 | 12,507 | 21,909 | 24,332 | 28,416 |
| Wales, . . . | 214 | 320 | 576 | 873 | 1,527 | 1,680 | 1,513 |
| Canada,[3] . . | 15,862 | 27,069 | 70,055 | 119,302 | 111,315 | 158,753 | 162,710 |
| Canada French, . | — | — | — | — | 96,286 | 134,416 | 134,659 |
| Atlantic Islands, . | — | 433 | 1,944 | 2,421 | 4,973 | 4,432 | [4]11,128 |
| Austria,[5] . . | 10 | — | 365 | 587 | 1,729 | 12,931 | 35,455 |
| Finland, . . . | — | — | — | — | — | 5,104 | 10,744 |
| France, . . . | 805 | 1,280 | 1,629 | 2,212 | 3,273 | 3,905 | 5,926 |
| Germany, . . . | 4,417 | 9,961 | 13,072 | 16,872 | 28,034 | 32,927 | 30,555 |
| Greece, . . . | 23 | 25 | 24 | 41 | 59 | 1,843 | 11,413 |
| Holland, . . . | 138 | 351 | 480 | 586 | 609 | 993 | 1,597 |
| Hungary, . . . | — | — | 14 | 82 | 389 | 926 | 1,996 |
| Italy, . . . | 196 | 371 | 454 | 2,116 | 8,066 | 28,785 | 85,056 |
| Poland,[6] . . | — | 81 | 272 | 681 | 3,341 | 849 | — |
| Portugal, . . . | 290 | 988 | 735 | 1,161 | 3,051 | 13,453 | 26,437 |
| Russia, . . . | 38 | 61 | 154 | 462 | 7,325 | 37,919 | 117,261 |
| Sweden, Norway and Denmark, . . . | 503 | 1,069 | 1,955 | 5,971 | 22,655 | 37,997 | 48,399 |
| Turkey, . . . | 14 | 16 | 50 | 102 | 310 | 2,896 | 16,138 |
| Others, . . . | 1,328 | 1,952 | 2,318 | 3,552 | 5,984 | 9,921 | 14,317 |
| Total, . . . | 160,909 | 260,114 | 353,319 | 443,491 | 657,137 | 846,324 | 1,059,245 |

[1] Compiled from the *U. S. Census* 1850 to 1910.
[2] *Ibid.*
[3] Canada French, not distinguished from Canada English until 1890.
[4] White population only.
[5] Includes Bohemia.
[6] Distributed under Austria, Germany and Russia in 1910, and so far as possible in 1900.
Source: U. S. Commission on Immigration, "Problem of Immigration in Massachusetts,"
(Washington: U. S. Government Printing Office, 1914), pg. 29.

# HISTORICAL SKETCH OF WOONSOCKET

## TABLE 65

Regional Derivation of Population in Woonsocket from 1846 to 1925
(Data Derived from Decennial State Censuses and Other Sources)

| Regional Derivation | 1846 | 1875 | 1885 | 1895 | 1905 | 1915 | 1925 |
|---|---|---|---|---|---|---|---|
| Armenian | — | — | — | — | — | — | 54 |
| Austrian | — | — | — | 1 | 42 | 220 | 396 |
| Belgian (Flemish) | — | 12 | 3 | 38 | 149 | 504 | 405 |
| British total | — | — | — | — | — | — | — |
| a) English | 349 | — | — | 652 | 785 | 755 | 643 |
| b) Scotch and Welsh | 29 | 97 | 102 | 157 | 124 | 144 | 105 |
| c) Scotch-Irish | — | — | — | — | — | — | — |
| d) Canadian English | — | 450 | 450 | 409 | 392 | 302 | — |
| e) Canadian Scotch | — | — | — | — | — | — | — |
| f) Canadian others | — | — | — | — | — | — | 185 |
| g) British mixed | — | — | — | — | — | — | — |
| h) British, others | — | — | — | — | — | — | — |
| Chinese/Colored | 3 | — | — | — | — | — | — |
| Czech | — | — | — | — | — | — | — |
| Dutch | — | — | — | — | — | — | — |
| Finnish | — | — | — | — | 82 | 58 | — |
| French Canadian | 250 | 3,376 | 4,366 | 7,481 | 8,939 | 8,484 | 11,695 |
| French, European total | — | — | — | — | — | — | — |
| a) French, France | — | 64 | 60 | 108 | 311 | 817 | 826 |
| b) Walloon | — | — | — | — | — | — | — |
| c) Alsatian | — | — | — | — | — | — | — |
| d) Swiss | — | — | — | — | — | — | — |
| e) French mixed | — | — | — | — | — | — | — |
| German | 1 | 37 | 33 | 45 | 76 | 170 | 55 |
| Greek | — | — | — | — | — | — | 85 |
| Irish | 666 | 2,218 | 2,081 | 2,032 | 1,369 | 937 | 645 |
| Italian | 1 | — | 5 | 11 | 158 | 773 | 859 |
| Jewish | — | — | — | — | — | — | — |
| Portuguese (white) | — | — | — | 5 | — | 17 | 149 |
| Roumanian | — | — | — | — | — | — | — |
| Scandinavian total | — | — | — | — | — | — | — |
| a) Swedish | — | — | 9 | 38 | 67 | 73 | 51 |
| b) Norwegian | — | — | — | — | — | — | 7 |
| c) Danish | — | — | — | — | — | — | — |
| Slavic Total | — | — | — | — | — | — | — |
| a) Polish | — | — | 5 | — | 793 | 2,167 | 909 |
| b) Ukrainian | — | — | — | — | — | — | — |
| c) Russian | — | — | — | 132 | 297 | 338 | 330 |
| d) Lithuanian | — | — | — | — | — | — | 2 |
| e) (Galician) | — | — | — | — | — | — | — |
| Spanish | — | — | — | — | — | — | — |
| Syrian | — | — | — | — | — | — | 68 |
| Turkish | — | — | — | 46 | 88 | 183 | — |
| All others | — | 9 | 9 | 29 | 62 | 244 | 403 |
| Total Foreign-born | 1,299 | 6,263 | 7,123 | 11,184 | 13,734 | 16,186 | 17,872 |
| Total Native-born | 3,557 | 7,313 | 9,076 | 13,284 | 18,462 | 23,889 | 31,809* |
| Grand Total | 4,856 | 13,576 | 16,199 | 24,468 | 32,196 | 40,075 | 49,681 |

* This includes 38 colored and 33 others, not white.
Source: Bessie Bloom Wessel, *An Ethnic Study of Woonsocket, R. I.*, (Chicago University of Chicago Press) pg. 225.

Certainly the history books used in American schools underline the migrations that ended in New York City. But while immigrants found their way to every state, the French-Canadians will remain unique to the New England states.

The figures relating to the Canadian migration indicate that both "Canadian" and "French-Canadian" residents were leaving their country in large numbers. The two groups were not separately delineated at first. In 1870, there were 493,464 Canadians living in the United States. By 1880, there were 717,157.

Separate figures kept in 1890 show that there were 302,496 French-Canadians here, and 678,442 "Canadians."

By 1930, there were 370,852 French-Canadians, and 915,537 "Canadians." When the numbers were mixed again, a total of 1,003,039 foreign-born Canadians were living throughout the country.[39]

It is evidence that not only other nationalities flocked to the United States, but a good many Canadians who were not of French-Canadian stock.

For a country of Canada's limited population, the 19th century exodus was large. So great was the movement south that the Canadian government took steps to have it stopped. Concern about a population drain had been registered as early as 1849. As the number of emigrants increased, action was proposed to stem the tide.

By 1873, the government launched an effort to bring immigrants back "home." And the time was on its side. An economic crisis that year caused many layoffs in the mills. If faith was to be shaken in the American dream, it was likely to have been in '73. Canadian politicians promised that those returning could get land inexpensively, and a Repatriation Act of 1875 was to make returning even more appealing. Ferdinand Gagnon, a French-Canadian journalist in Worcester, earned a lasting reputation for his efforts in attempting to convince immigrants to go back. Several hundred even availed themselves of free transportation to Quebec for a first-hand look at what was available.

Few decided to return to Canada, however. Their trip "home" was jokingly referred to as a free holiday. Mill work was not easy, but these new Americans were simply opposed to returning to the rigors of agrarian life. And with their close-knit Petits Canadas in almost every mill community, the French didn't think they were missing much by not going back.

More pressure was brought to bear in an effort to repopulate the countryside of Quebec. According to the publication Le Minerve, the House of Commons considered a law in 1881 to make American recruitment of Canadian labor a criminal offense. The measure failed to gain approval, but is indicative of the most fervent sentiment.

By today's standards, it is difficult to imagine how the French found conditions here favorable. Labor conditions were deteriorating toward the end of the century; wages ranging from $3.60 to $7 a week in the 1890's could not meet the increased costs of living. The newest immigrants were given the worst assignments, and were the first to go when economic cycles forced lay-offs. And mill owners, claiming they were threatened by competition in the south as well as other parts of New England, pushed for greater machine speeds. Seventy hour weeks, with increasing pressure to produce, were commonplace.

Yet the French kept working. They were intent on pursuing their "streets paved with gold." That avenue called for realization of cash wages, even if it meant endless hours in the mills. An 1872 report from the Massachusetts Bureau of Labor Statistics observed, "A Yankee with brains don't like day labor at present." The French didn't seem to object.

Because of their capacity for hard work, the immigrants were often ridiculed. They dressed differently; they spoke a "foreign" language. Often they did battle with the Irish, who themselves were trying to exit from the bottom of the labor heap. The reluctance of the French to embrace trade unionism was another reason they were sometimes the subject of scorn. Even their remarkable capacity for work, a factor in building industry in New England, was twisted into negative terms.

Col. Carrol Wright of the Massachusetts Bureau of Statistics called them the "Chinese of the East." In 1881, he wrote, "so sordid and low a people should awaken corresponding feelings in managers, and that these people should feel that, the longer the hours for such

Naturalization was important to many French-Canadians, though there were those who refrained from citizenship because they planned on returning to Quebec. Here is an 1892 poster that outlines the evening's entertainment for a Lowell, Mass., benefit of naturalization.

(Richard Santerre Collection)

Franco-Americans had their heroes, as this 1898 poster indicates. Lowell's George Charette, "the hero of the Merrimac," was feted in elaborate splendor by the French community following his actions in the Spanish-American War.

(Richard Santerre Collection)

people, the better; and that to work to the utmost is the only good use they can be put to."

That the French could endure a society that held attitudes like this is forever to their credit.

By the dawn of the 20th century, hard work had enabled the immigrants to get a foothold in the new land. They were hardly princes, but second and even third generations were finding greater flexibility in the new land. It was at this time, in fact, that the migration peaked.

Canada's economic situation was improving in the final decade of the 19th century. Habitants no longer left in such great numbers. The Canadian-Pacific Railroad was creating jobs and adventure in the West; industry was finally growing in the eastern sector of the province. The Quebecois was no longer desperate. After 1900, the growth of the French population in New England would have its greatest increase through self-perpetuation rather than immigration.

If the French slowed their assault on the borders of the United States, though, ethnic groups from Europe took up the slack. A poor economic climate, combined with political repression, inspired Russians, Poles, Lithuanians, Italians, Greeks and Portuguese to come to America. Immigrants of new nationalities were now seeking their own "streets paved with gold." The European migration dwarfed that of the French-Canadians – in 1907 alone, 2.7 million newcomers arrived in the port of New York.[40] The French concentration in New England mill towns, however, continued to have its impact.

Europeans who chose New England often went straight into the mills like the French-Canadians had done a generation earlier. They took low-paying jobs at long hours, without complaint. Stories are told of grown men sneaking past security guards so they could plead with foremen for jobs. Children's positions were filled with desperate, shaking men who had families to support and rents to pay. The arrival of a new wave of immigrants had the effect of pushing the French up the economic ladder. They became foremen and supervisors, drawing on their experience to direct the masses of newcomers.

Psychological impact of becoming "established" fostered changes, however indirectly. Merchants opted to move their shops from Le Petit Canada to Main Street. French with real estate became landlords to the recently arrived Europeans. For years the French had shared the bottom with the Irish. New immigration patterns in the late 19th and early 20th centuries enabled them to leave the basement for others to occupy.

Economic gains coincided with political progress. Though the French were notorious for their internal squabbles, they began electing their own to a variety of posts. In early years, many immigrants ignored naturalization processes thinking they would return to the farms. But as more stayed to become citizens and voters, the political power of this ethnic group grew.

Charles Fontaine was elected Congressman from Vermont in 1873. During the late 1880's, the New Hampshire State Legislature had 10 French-Canadians in its chambers. In 1884, Dr. Louis J. Martel was elected from Lewiston to the state legislature in Maine and turned out to be one of the community's top civic leaders in the era. And leading the movement in Rhode Island at this time was Aram J. Pothier, who became mayor of Woonsocket in 1894. In 1897, he emerged as lieutenant governor of the state.

Increased political consciousness helped elect municipal and state representatives, but it didn't seem to effect their activity in unions. While the Irish were pioneering labor organization at the turn of the 20th century, the French took little interest. They were called ignorant; they were harassed for being "strikebreakers." Some historians suggest that the complacence of the French was a factor in retarding labor organization in mill communities.

The immigrants from rural Quebec were not schooled in the philosophy of urban labor organization, but they would soon go to class. After 1900, a major theme of life in the new world was union vs. management.

The French had not arrived to the year 1900 without impressive gains made on their own. Industrial New England came of age in the 19th century, and the French were one of the major reasons. They took jobs as lumbermen, brickmakers, masons and furniture makers. Many New Englanders will swear there wasn't a house built in the region without at least one French carpenter on the job. Francos were active in the boot and shoe industries, too, making up as much

Franco-Americans have been known for their political divisiveness, but have on many occasions elected their peers to positions in government. Sitting at left is Mayor Charles P. Lemaire, Lewiston, Maine's first Franco-American mayor, at a March 4, 1918 gathering of local political figures.

(Heritage Center, Lewiston)

as 12 per cent of the personnel in 1900. Small businessmen, farmers, and a mix of white collar workers were of French heritage.

But providing labor for the cotton industry will probably be remembered as the key role of the Quebecois. By 1900, they made up fully 44 per cent of the cotton mills' personnel. In Maine and New Hampshire, they accounted for almost half of all textile labor. In other New England states, it was 25 per cent. Even their involvement in the wool and worsted fields (15 per cent of New England labor) did not compete with their involvement in cotton production.[41]

From 1860, when the United States produced 75 per cent of the world's cotton, New England mills were manned by Francos. If cotton were indeed king in the 19th century, it's worthwhile to note that the industrial subjects enabling the empire to continue were the French. Men and women (it was one of this country's first industries of equal percentage of employment) labored from 6 a. m. to 6 p. m.

Employes in the yard of Stark Mill, Amoskeag mill yard in Manchester, N.H., 1878. The Amoskeag was once the largest textile mill in the world, and many of its employes were French-Canadians.

(Courtesy, Manchester (N.H.) Historic Association)

Management during the 19th century was non-French, though the French-Canadians made up a majority in most textile mills. Franco-Americans did rise to foreman status in the 20th century. This 1895 photo captures management representatives of the Pepperell Manufacturing Co. in Biddeford, Maine, as well as the dreaded yard boss at far right.

(McArthur Public Library, Biddeford)

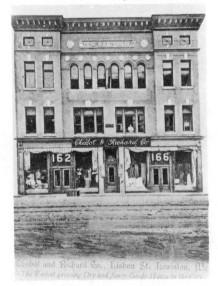

As French-Canadians got established in their communities, they opened their own shops and stores. Here is a "fancy goods house" by the Chabot and Richard Co. housed in a building owned by McGillicuddy.

(Lewiston Public Library)

June 24, 1897—"Allegorical float," in Lewiston celebrating the explorations of Jacques Cartier. French-Canadians had great pride in the achievements of France in North America.

(Joseph Dignuard photo, Heritage Center, Lewiston)

Painchaud's Band of Biddeford, Maine, pictured here in this turn of the century photo, was organized in the 19th century. It recently observed its 100th birthday, and shows that some French-Canadian institutions have been preserved.

(McArthur Public Library, Biddeford)

A French neighborhood off Ward Street in Lowell, one of many "Little Canadas"
throughout New England.

(Lowell Museum)

for year after year. In doing so, they were the foundation of an industry.

By the turn of the century, the immigrants from French Canada had helped build the textile business. They had also settled into a region. Many had learned to speak English. Some had become American citizens. There were now native born Americans of French-Canadian parents. The French had retained the language, religion, traditions and folklore of Quebec. Indeed, their resolution to remain French in character puzzled many American observers. However, their loyalty was to the United States; they revered their adopted country. Perhaps because of this, they became known as "Franco-Americans" in about 1900.

Indicative of increasing self-awareness was the establishment of Assumption College in 1904. The school was directed by Assumptionist Fathers. Its goal was to educate young Franco-American men for preparation for business and the professions. Though education remained a secondary priority with many working families, the creation of Assumption in Worcester, Mass., was an indication that an educated elite was being fostered in New England.

And by 1910, there were 133 Franco-American Catholic schools in New England, proof of the permanence of the newcomers.[42]

As Franco-Americans became more established in their new country, they met new problems. Just as the challenges of finding a job and creating a household were being met, other roadblocks to security were encountered. Included in the problems of the early 20th Century were the rise of the southern cotton mills, and labor turmoil in New England.

The textile industry had originally succeeded in the region for several reasons. A major one was that rivers provided inexpensive water power, and many powerful rivers, some with booming falls, were available throughout the six states. These rivers often flowed into the Atlantic Ocean, which enabled ships to pick up cargoes, and sail smoothly away to national and international markets. The natural humid climate of the North was also an asset, as it made all millwork bearable. If there was an unclaimed river, the 19th century businessman would soon be thinking about mill construction. It was as natural then as an investment in a roadside fast food stand today.

But technology took away the Northeast's natural advantage in the early 20th Century. And those benefiting from changes were aggressive manufacturers in the South.

One change in operations was the advent of steam power, which freed mill owners from a dependence on flowing rivers. Steam power was also used in railroad transportation. This meant that a mill didn't have to be located near a coastal port to move its finished product.

In addition, the South was aided by the invention of an automatic humidifier that enabled workers to work in the hot mill buildings. Ironically, the device was patented by a New England man, J. G. Garland of Biddeford in 1881.[43] One wonders how popular Garland was following the use of his discovery, but nevertheless, the South had erased another obstacle to greater production.

The South also possessed a large work force. Displaced white laborers, and later unemployed blacks, were available in quantity. Unschooled in the finer points of labor organization, they were willing workers.

Yet another drawback for the New England manufacturing interests was the fact that northern mill owners were not alert to new developments in the field. Complacent after a half-century of success, they were slow to recognize new needs. They were pennypinchers when it came to reinvesting.

Electrification was another great equalizer. Its impact was felt following the turn of the century. In 1840, when the cotton manufacturing industry got substantially underway, the North possessed 1,597,000 spindles. The South could count but 181,000. Yet the South just grew faster. Between 1890 and 1900 for instance, the number of spindles in the North grew from 243 million to 272 million, an increase of 12.1 per cent. But in the same period, the South increased its spindle quantity from 53 million to 124 million, a growth of 131 per cent. By 1925, the capacity of the South had exceeded that of the North.[44]

Cotton manufacturing was not the only field of endeavor the French were pursuing. They were also important cogs in the production of wool shoes, lumber and machinery. Cotton is the field in which they had the greatest impact, though. And it was in the subsequent loss of New England jobs in the cotton industry that later touched so many families.

Not the least of the problems for northern mills as the 20th century progressed was labor unrest. The South, with no tradition of manufacturing, was not susceptible to the arguments of union organizers. Those in many New England mill towns, however, had witnessed two or perhaps three, generations of mill labor.

Pressure for labor reform mounted in the late 19th century. Rhode Island and New Hampshire had passed weak labor laws in the 1840's but Massachusetts got serious in 1874 by setting a 10-hour maximum for women and children. The minimum age for child labor rose to 13 in the 1880's.

Labor, buttressed by a strong core of second generation Irish, wanted more. Dirty, dangerous work conditions needed improvement; low wages had to be raised if workers were to support families. Workers, even the traditionally docile Franco-Americans, were pushed to union activity. Fall River, Mass., was the scene of a strike in 1904. When the city's mills cut wages, employees refused to return to work. The strike closed 85 mills. Thousands were unemployed as it dragged on for six months.

The Lawrence, Mass., strike of 1912 gained international attention. It idled 23,000 workers, and in doing so was embraced by the Industrial Workers of the World (IWW). Organizers Joe Ettor and Bill Haywood came in to direct strike efforts, and the conflict grew to such proportions that it was receiving front-page headlines in newspapers around the world. Memorable about the strike was that families sent hungry children to relatives in other cities so they would at least have enough to eat.

The Lawrence strike is particularly memorable. The workers' eventual victory meant improvement in labor conditions throughout New England. In 1979, it sometimes appears that unionists make "unreasonable" demands. The desires of the Lawrence workers were modest indeed, as statistics relate. This is one reason why they prevailed.

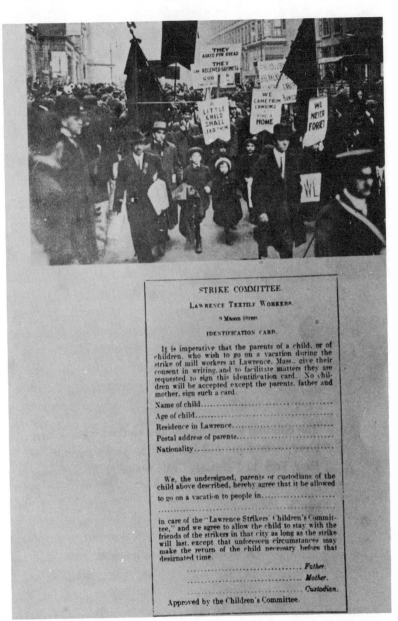

The strike of textile workers in Lawrence, Mass., in 1912 drew worldwide attention. So bitter was the confrontation that families sent their children to other communities until the trouble ended. Here a sign states that "a little child shall lead them" and below it, a consent form for children to leave the city.

(Merrimack Valley Textile Museum)

The Lawrence Strike Committee

(Merrimack Valley Textile Museum)

The immediate cause of the strike in Lawrence was a reduction in earnings growing out of a new state law that became effective Jan. 1, 1912. The number of hours was reduced from 56 to 54. In most cases, this meant a reduction in wages of only about three per cent. But to poorly paid workers, this loss was significant. Unwilling to take the cut, workers in several dozen mills went out.

What were these workers earning when they struck? The average rate of wages for 21,922 textile employees surveyed during 1911 was 16 cents an hour! The weekly wage when the mills were running full time was $8.76.[45] Management branded the strike as extreme, yet the wages they were paying did not ensure undying loyalty.

Even allowing for differences in living costs then, Lawrence wages made life difficult for the workers. Government statistics at that time stated that a suit cost $10 to $12, a cotton dress about $3. Milk was 8 cents a quart, while pork was to be purchased at 16 cents a pound.[46] Even though a family might have a half-dozen members bringing in paychecks, it was still difficult to make it from week to week.

The Lawrence strike is memorable not only for its size, but the result – the workers "won" the bitter walkout and this victory had a domino effect on other strikes in New England. It was a landmark triumph in textile union organization.

They had demanded a 15 per cent increase in wages, the abolition of all bonus systems, double pay for overtime and "no discrimination against the strikers for activity during the strike." The workers secured the following settlement from the American Woolen Co. and similar agreements at other mills: a 5 per cent flat increase, plus step raises that really meant raises from 5 to 20 per cent; bonuses or "premiums" to be given out every two weeks instead of every four; time and a quarter for overtime; and no discrimination to be shown to anyone.

Contrary to the mills' contentions, management was able to live with the increased wage package. According to figures that the American Woolen Co. supplied to the American Committee on War Finance, its net profits earned for stockholders rose each year following the strike. In 1913, net profits were $1,179,791; 1914, $2,788,602; in 1915, $4,080,865; and in 1916, $5,863,819.[47]

The following is a breakdown of wages paid at the time of the Lawrence strike in 1912. It comes from a 1912 report by the United States Commissioner of Labor, Charles P. Neill. It's noteworthy to remember that the strike did not occur over a desire for higher wages; it began as a protest to the reduction of the weekly paycheck.[48]

AVERAGE RATE OF WAGES AND AVERAGE AMOUNT EARNED AND HOURS WORKED DURING WEEK FOR WHICH DATA WERE SECURED, BY SEX AND AGE GROUPS—WOOLEN AND WORSTED MILLS AND COTTON MILLS.

[The rates, earnings, and hours worked shown in this table are based, respectively, on the hourly rates of time workers combined with the computed hourly rates of pieceworkers, the amounts earned during the week for which data were secured, regardless of hours worked, and the hours actually worked during the same week. See pages 75 to 78 as to amount of work available.]

| Sex and age groups. | Total number of employees. | Rate of wages per hour. | | | Amount earned during week. | | | Hours worked during week. | | | |
|---|---|---|---|---|---|---|---|---|---|---|---|
| | | Average. | Per cent of employees earning– | | Average. | Per cent of employees earning– | | Average. | Per cent of employees working– | | |
| | | | Under 12 cents. | 20 cents and over. | | Under $7. | $12 and over. | | Under 56. | 56. | Over 56. |
| MALES | | | | | | | | | | | |
| 18 years and over | 11,075 | $0.179 | 10.9 | 32.4 | $10.20 | 17.5 | 30.2 | 56.5 | 19.8 | 41.3 | 38.9 |
| Under 18 years | 1,075 | .114 | 72.8 | .4 | 6.02 | 80.2 | .3 | 52.5 | 20.8 | 76.7 | 2.4 |
| Total | 12,150 | .173 | 16.4 | 29.5 | 9.83 | 23.0 | 27.5 | 56.1 | 19.9 | 44.4 | 35.7 |
| FEMALES | | | | | | | | | | | |
| 18 years and over | 8,320 | .147 | 25.9 | 10.4 | 7.67 | 40.4 | 5.7 | 52.2 | 26.1 | 73.6 | .2 |
| Under 18 years | 1,452 | .117 | 66.3 | 1.7 | 6.02 | 77.1 | .3 | 51.5 | 29.8 | 69.7 | .6 |
| Total | 9,772 | .143 | 31.9 | 9.1 | 7.42 | 45.8 | 4.9 | 52.1 | 26.7 | 73.0 | .3 |
| Grand total | 21,922 | .160 | 23.3 | 20.4 | 8.76 | 33.2 | 17.5 | 54.4 | 22.9 | 57.2 | 19.9 |

In 1922, the Amoskeag Mill in Manchester announced a 20 per cent wage cut, coupled with an increase of the work week from 48 to 54 hours. Mill owners claimed restrictive labor laws and southern competition forced the move; workers cried out that "greedy" management was cruelly exploiting them. This strike lasted for nine months. Both the Lawrence and Manchester strikes were viewed as victories for labor, but the toll in wages lost and human suffering was high.

The French were not by nature interested in strikes. Ample proof can be cited to show they wanted to work for a day's wage. But the audacity of mill owners to cut already poor wages was too great an indignity.

A major effect of the strikes, however, was to create further financial insecurity for the Franco-Americans. Some were without work for months; there were those who found they could not return to work when the lockouts were lifted.

Observers today sometimes criticize Franco-Americans of past generations for financial conservatism. They "don't make the system work for them;" they don't "wheel and deal." Reflecting on the rocky times that mill workers encountered, however, gives one meaningful insight on how they obtained their "conservative" ways with money.

Financial challenges faced Francos at the onset of the Depression of the 1930's. "Last hired, first to be fired" was sometimes an apt description of their plight. Because many lacked formal education and sophisticated training, their "menial" positions were often eliminated. Families were often temporarily broken up when the father would leave one community to seek work in another whose mills were not laying off. Working class Frenchmen were not particularly mobile once they had settled in a town, but the Depression caused significant relocation throughout the region.

The Depression, it might be added, was influential in nudging Franco-Americans from the Republican to Democratic voting column. President Frankin D. Roosevelt's promises to create jobs was precisely the message this ethnic group wanted to hear. And mill communities like Lewiston, Biddeford, Fall River and Woonsocket have

**WARNING!**
Do not drink this canal water — it will make you sick.

**AVIS!**
Il est défendu de faire usage de l'eau du canal pour boire — elle pourrait vous rendre malade.

**OSTRZEŻENIE!**
Nie pijaj wody z kanalu tego, bo zachorujesz.

**ACAUTELEM-SE!**
Nao bebam a agua do Canal. Fas-te doente.

**ΠΡΟΣΟΧΗ**
ΜΗ ΠΙΝΕΤΕ ΝΕΡΟ ΑΠΟ ΤΟ ΚΑΝΑΛΙ:
Θ' ΑΡΡΩΣΤΗΣΕΤΕ.

E. H. WALKER, Agent

Massachusetts mills had a mixture of immigrants in their employ, so many that important notices had to be printed in five different languages. Following this warning in English are translations including French, Polish, Portuguese, and Greek.

(Merrimack Valley Textile Museum)

remained Democrat. Anyone who has seen a Kennedy come through a mill city can attest to this. One of Teddy Kennedy's favorite maneuvers is to mount the podium in an overflowing school gymnasium and loudly ask who will win Saturday's football game. In French! He rarely fails to receive a thundering response.

The Depression marked another watershed in the evolving of the Franco-Americans. Just as the turn of the century signified a subtle change from "immigrant" to "Franco-American," the post-Depression period ushered in the era of the "modern Franco-American."

Partly because of the economic crunch, which resulted in a keen competition for jobs, the nature of the Franco-American changed. For seven decades the French had been vigilant in maintaining their ethnic identity. They had protected their language, neighborhoods and societies. The 1930's, however, produced a tendency for younger Francos to shed "foreign" traits. They began seeing their ethnic background as hindering their chances on the job. They now wanted to appear American.

Perhaps the descendants of the French-Canadians could not live with their past indefinitely. Many wanted to leave the mills, leave Le Petit Canada, leave dismal jobs with little chance of improvement. They wanted better positions, with a house of their own and a future they could control.

As the second, third and even fourth generations of Franco-Americans emerged, they pursued goals unheard of in the past. An automobile purchased on borrowed money? A new house in the suburbs? The children in public schools? Such developments were revolutionary.

Another outgrowth of the desire to be part of the "American" community was a tendency to change one's surname to anglicize it for greater acceptance. A study of name changes in Woonsocket, R. I. reveals that Isai Berard became James Bell; Brindamour became Brown; Georginna Berard, Rossa Barre; Joseph Dubois, Joseph Wood; Paquin became Perkins; Phaneuf became Farnum; Provencher was now Moore.[49]

In Waterville, Maine, researchers Anne Kempers and Beatrice Maltais studied cemetery epitaphs. Their exploration into name changes indicated that Allain had been changed to Allen, Mercier to Marshall, Blais to Blair, Cartier to Carter.[50]

One case is on record of a man changing his name from Violette to Panzie. A floral rearrangement perhaps, but indicative that some French were compromising their Frenchness.

The results of such "Americanization" were clearly seen. French newspapers folded one by one, as younger Francos read English publications. Masses were celebrated in English because more parishioners were comfortable in this language. And the French language fell into disuse.

The decline of the use of French is probably the most disturbing of all to those in the Franco-American community. Even today, grandparents react with disappointment when facing the fact their grandchildren do not speak French – nor do they want to. One often hears that "my daughter can understand French, but she doesn't speak it." For those who fear that the cultural identity is waning, the fading use of the French language is a serious matter.

Yet opinion differs on the significance. Some Francos feel that the disappearance of the language is a natural development of modern times. It should not be feared, they argue.

Others, many representing the intellectual elite, decry the loss. They would have it taught not only at home, but in school in bilingual and bicultural programs.

The language issue is in actuality the trench in which the modern Franco intellectual battles are waged today. Such concerns are matters not dealt with years ago. Past generations would talk about openings at the mills, the shifts available, the arrival of new parish clergymen, the festivities planned for celebration of the day of St. Jean-Baptiste.

Today, however, the Franco-American fits into no such small box. Some remain in disappearing industries like fabric mills, shoe shops and tanneries. But Franco-Americans are no longer mill workers, per se. They cross all employment and educational lines. Doctors, dentists, teachers, businessmen, politicians, civil servants – Franco-Americans have spread into all corners of socio-economic life. It is of little wonder that they should be grappling with the issues of the day.

The demise of the mills as sole urban employment, in fact, has been a factor in the development of new economic horizons. For years it had been an unconscious calling to "go into the mill" following schooling. When the decay of the mill system, and its departure to the South, was underway in the 1950's, Franco-Americans by necessity had to look for other employment.

Older workers trained for jobs as mechanics, shipyard workers, carpenters and plumbers. Younger Franco-Americans evidently put a greater emphasis on schooling, and the results are evident. Many do control their own futures now.

Emergence from the mills has popularized the term "assimilation." Some Francos have rejected assimilation, or cultural absorption. Others have joined the American mainstream to such a degree they don't relate to their roots at all. In addition, there are those who choose to ignore their ancestral beginnings.

And a growing number don't know enough about their heritage to relate to it. As the French language is spoken in fewer New England homes, the parochial schools continue to show shrinking enrollment lists. The tie to the past through everyday experience is seriously weakened. The reality is a startling one: for years the French possessed a solidarity that was renowned. Yet assimilation, a concept that decades ago seemed to apply to every ethnic group except the French, appears to have arrived.

Efforts are being made to maintain the French culture, however. Aided by federal grants, cultural pockets in Providence R. I., New Bedford, Mass. and Manchester, N. H. are working to breathe life into French communities.

Programs are underway in selected New England school systems in bilingual education. Franco-American societies in many towns and cities present historical and cultural programs. And festivals, like the Franco-American Festival in Lewiston that drew 30,000 visitors in 1978, are helping a rebirth in interest.

In addition, some New England politicians have pressed the federal government to recognize Franco-Americans as a "legitimate" minority group. Federal grants would then be available for a variety of uses.[51]

It is not in the tradition of Franco-Americans to stand in line waiting for someone to pass out free money. Nevertheless, the more aggressive in the Franco-American camp have pushed for and achieved recognition. Grants, scholarship programs, and business opportunities will be forthcoming with federal aid, they say.

Characteristically, the Franco-Americans are the forgotten ethnic group in discussions of minority status. When the question of expanding the definition of "minority" was dealt with in a lengthy New York Times feature article July 30, 1978, Francos were not mentioned. The survey noted that blacks and Hispanics are entrenched as the recognized minorities. An enlarged definition, the article said, could include "Italians, Poles, Jews, Greeks, Arabs, eastern Europeans, southern Europeans, German-Americans, Italian-Americans, and Irish-Americans." Those of French descent were not included in the dialogue, not even in passing.

Efforts to resuscitate the French culture suggests that another watershed period is at hand. Franco-Americans, concerned that their rich heritage is being diluted, are seeking to strengthen ties to the past. They've come too far, been exposed to too much, to let the present spread a blanket of oblivion over the past.

The French heritage in New England is an admirable one. The landscape of the region will continue to be quiet, if depressing, testimony to it. Mills in countless towns and cities continue to stand. Symbolic by the emptiness, or partial utilization, they nevertheless reflect the life and times of the region's workers. Who can take interstate highways past Manchester, Lawrence or Lowell, and not feel admiration for those who spent their working lives in those mammoth caverns of mill buildings? Who can drop by a senior citizens' center in Springfield and Fall River, and not wonder how those elderly Franco-Americans were able to tackle drone-like jobs for 30 years at a stretch in order to support their families?

The massive brick monuments to a past of hard work are considered unattractive in most New England communities today. People say they are eyesores. They say they are unappealing relics of the past. You don't hear Lawrence touted as a glamour city, after all. And why live in hulking Manchester when you can skip off to suburban Amherst just minutes away? Lewiston, Chicopee and Pawtucket! They're not nearly as attractive as Portland, Hingham or Kingston, to say nothing of Greenwich or Brookline. What is their use?

Yet these mills took in thousands upon thousands of earnest, hardworking immigrants; those ever-present three and four-story wooden tenements hosted the largest continental migration in this region's history. Personal, poignant histories are worn into those structures as surely as they have been at chic Faneuil Hall, or the awesome mansions of coastal Newport. These vestiges of the French past deserve some credibility, too.

History has yet to discover such significance, however.

Such a past, a blue-collar past of non-Anglo origin, has not been adequately treated by scholars and historians. The creation of the mill communities, and the arrival of the immigrants, has not been publicized. It is difficult to imagine that the migration that resulted in the presence of more than two million New England residents of

French descent, and subsequently built the most successful industry (textiles) in the history of the region, has been overlooked. But it has.

As significant as the history of the Franco-Americans is, one of the remarkable aspects about the French presence has been its lack of recognition. It really has been a quiet presence. Quiet and unheralded. When Ralph Ellison wrote his prize-winning novel in the early 1950's about the anonymity of blacks, he entitled it *Invisible Man*. He was referring to frustration. Though blacks comprised a significant percentage of the population, they were virtually unnoticed. If there was a gas station stickup or a business failure involving blacks, attention would be focused. But the author noted that in a participatory sense, blacks were unnoticed or "invisible."

A similar situation seems to exist in Anglo circles about Franco-Americans. Their history is not known, their contributions unpublicized. The public is aware only of generalities about the Franco-Americans in New England, and often these are not positive. Some see massive mills, they see French. Finis.

One manifestation of the anonymous nature of Franco-Americans is their lack of visibility in major political circles. Franco-Americans do hold many municipal and state offices. But they are not at the forefront of politics when it comes to landing top state and national posts. New Hampshire has a high percentage of Francos, but the 1978 governor's race was between a Thomson and a Gallen. Maine's race for governor saw Joseph Brennan take on Linwood Palmer; they were seeking to replace a Lewiston native, whose name was Longley! And Maine is a state where one senator is named Muskie (Polish) and the other, Cohen (Jewish).

Franco-Americans do not command majority numbers in Massachusetts or Rhode Island. Yet it would seem that on occasion a Franco would come to the fore. What makes the Irish dominate Massachusetts national politics to such a degree? And why do the Italians have such leverage in Rhode Island, when the number of French is almost equal?

While Franco-Americans have found it difficult to break into the top political circles in present days, they also have had trouble earning a place in history. Few books have been written about the French in the United States, particularly in English. The immigration of European Jews has been well-documented; one could fill a coffee table the size of a soccer field with pictorial texts of the Irish in this country. But the French? Aside from a handful of books in praise of the New Orleans French, the shelves are quite bare. Even the standard historical textbooks by Morison and Commager contain no more than a few lines mentioning the migration of the French-Canadians. A people who fueled the Industrial Revolution, whose labor helped create "King Cotton," and who now compose the backbone of scores of towns and cities in the region would appear to merit more than two or three paragraphs in the history of New England.

Media coverage has also been minimal. During the era of French newspapers, Franco communities got all the coverage they could have wished. English newspapers did not report on their activities with precision, though, and still do not. At the 1979 national convention of Franco-Americans in Providence, R. I., barely a half-dozen reporters were present to follow the activities of some of the most influential Franco-Americans in the country. If New England blacks had been meeting instead, one guesses the coverage would have been greater. Public television in several states has been shedding light on the Franco-Americans in recent years; several programs in fact, have been in French. On the whole, however, the French have not been accorded a high profile.

If the Franco-Americans are somewhat anonymous, though, it is in part because of their nature. Resistance to assimilation has been a trait since the earliest days. When commentators mention their tendency to stay to themselves in their "little Canadas" the observation cannot be disputed.

John Gunther in his "Inside the U. S. A.," termed the Franco-Americans the "most tenacious" and "unique" minority group in the entire country, and said they "hold with the utmost stubbornness and obstinacy to its folklore, customs, language."[52] Quiet to a fault, the Franco-Americans have aided in the process of anonymity.

It has been a quiet presence because they clung to their language, they stayed within their own culture, and because the proximity to

Quebec permitted a continuous relationship with "the old country." They chose a French orientation in their new world.

Nevertheless, the story of the Franco-Americans does deserve airing. It is beneficial for young Francos to have knowledge, and subsequently pride, in their heritage. It is helpful for non-Francos to know something about the background of this group, in order to understand the challenges they have faced and overcome.

For in an era characterized by the search for personal and ethnic roots, the story of the Franco-Americans has no less significance than the history of the blacks, or Irish, or Poles, or for that matter, the Yankees.

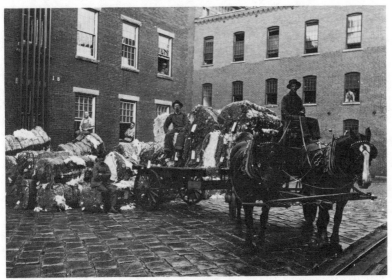

Unloading cotton at the Amoskeag Mills. Among the most cumbersome procedures in textiles was obtaining the raw cotton, and moving it into the building.

(Courtesy, Manchester, N.H., Historic Association)

French-Canadians and Franco-Americans rarely saw photographers in the cotton mills, but this turn of the century photo shows that a variety of age groups worked together in drawing rooms such as this one.

(Lewiston Public Library)

Photographers who did gain access to mills posed their pictures, but the shots nevertheless give some indication of working conditions at the turn of the century in spin rooms as the one pictured here.

(Lewiston Public Library)

The textile industry was one of America's first to be populated almost equally by women. This photograph indicates the number of women a warper room could accommodate, as well as showing that virtually all supervisors were male.

(Lewiston Public Library)

# Chapter IV

## *Stories of Franco-Americans*

To generalize is to invite misrepresentation. But most familiar with the Franco-Americans of New England would agree that they have been workers. Once called "the Chinese of the East" for their willingness to put in long hours without complaint, numerous sources document their diligence.

French-Canadians who came to New England, and the Franco-American descendants who followed, pursued a variety of occupations. They were woodsmen, farmers and fishermen; the French toiled in construction, shoeshops and woolen mills. Many are remembered for their work in the cotton mills that seemed to spring up on every river. They were doffers, spinners and weavers; they unloaded the raw cotton, they stacked the final product in cartons, they transported the cartons to a variety of destinations. It is estimated that almost half of the cotton industry at the turn of the 20th century was composed of those of French descent. French contribution to two aspects of history should be recognized, "the industrial revolution" and "King Cotton."

Thousands of French-Canadians populated the mills in the late 19th century, permitting mechanized mill systems to produce their storied profits, which in turn spawned such economic institutions as venture capital and corporate acquisition. And while the deep South deserves credit for its role in raising cotton, and developing the crop into one of the most powerful economic forces in the country, those who labored in the mills to produce the final product should not be forgotten. It was New England that enabled American cotton to dominate world markets in the late 19th century. And it was the French who were manning those mills.

Women were a major component of the cloth room, where final inspections of the product took place. Modest fire precautions can be seen attached to poles at left.

(Lewiston Public Library)

There are other memorable aspects to the manner in which the French utilized their hands in settling a new region.

The French were builders. Many were involved in making bricks, and then fashioning those bricks into the massive mills that still startle the uninitiated in cities like Manchester, Woonsocket and New Bedford. Many worked on the buildings that are now regional landmarks, including several statehouses.

Those of French descent, French-Canadians and Franco-Americans, toiled in raising large families. Mothers would often have 10, 15, or even 20 children. Their responsibility was awesome. Poor health care caused high infant mortality, and meager financial sources often deprived families of comfort. Sheer will was a factor in seeing the youngsters through childhood. And the French were leaders. Many professionals came from Quebec to assume the roles of doctors, lawyers, priests, nuns and merchants. Some historians have overlooked their role in the populating of New England communities. Presumably, if the French only stayed among their own people, they didn't count as civic leaders. But many older Francos relate the significant roles played by professionals within the French community.

Whether the ancestors of today's Franco-Americans worked in the woods, the textile mills, the home, the construction site or the law office, one characteristic cannot be obscured: THEY WORKED.

# 1. Roland Gosselin: Born to the mill

Was anyone more destined to enter the mills than Roland Gosselin? Gosselin, a 54-year-old resident of Lewiston, Maine, began working in the mills of that city in 1941. After 36 years as a weaver, he left the floor in 1977 to take the post of business agent with the Amalgamated Clothing Workers Union, serving central Maine.

His decision to enter the Bates Mills there was typical of many youngsters in mill communities. Few had planned specifically on such a vocation. It was just that the mills were there, they needed a job and . . . Gosselin followed thousands of Franco-American teenagers into the mills. He did, in fact, follow a long family line. When that day came in 1941 to take a job, it was natural that he responded as did his peers and parents.

"My grandparents on both sides worked at the Edwards mill in Augusta," recalled Gosselin. "Each one of them worked for 50 years in the mills. When you add it up, there is over 200 years of service there.

"I remember the company gave pins to employees for service. There was a pin with an emblem that you got after 10 years, and a pin with a diamond chip after 25. If you worked there for 50, the company offered a nice watch, for your wrist, or a pocketwatch. I still have my grandfather's pocketwatch with me.

"That was a long time to work in the mills, and not many people can put together 200 years like that.

"My parents started working in the mills when I was nine or 10. I remember taking them dinners at work, so I was a little familiar with the process by the time I got older. Eventually both my parents went on to other work, but the mill was always a thing close to our family.

"Was I excited about my first day of work when I left for the mill? Not really."

Intelligent, energetic and soon-to-be-cultured, Gosselin nevertheless left St. Dominic's High School before graduating. As the oldest of nine children, he was expected to make contributions to the family welfare. Today there are financial aid programs to help qualified students continue schooling; numerous social programs are available to families that require financial support. Teenagers today have the added luxury of guidance counselors to point them in an appropriate direction. But such vocational aids were not available to a young Franco-American in Lewiston four decades ago. For Gosselin, there was an unspoken destination to which he headed.

"I was not really excited about the mills," said the civic-minded labor official. "If my parents had had the money, I would have liked to have gone to college. But they didn't.

"My father started in the mills, and later managed a shoe store. My mother had been a millworker, then stayed home – there were nine children. When I started work in the weaving department, I was figuring I'd get into something better. But I never did."

Gosselin started in 1941 at $19 per week. He recalls the job provided security, spending money, and an adequate social standing. Single, he had the luxury of pursuing his deep-seated interest in the arts. He would travel to Boston, at the age of 17, to hear the opera. When theatrical productions came to town, he would not miss a performance. Later, he would become one of Lewiston's leaders in staging musical performances.

One does not hear regret in Gosselin's voice. Like earlier generations, he appears satisfied with the life he found. He does point out disappointments or dissatisfaction along the way, as anyone would, but his outlook appears to be that of ancestors who came seeking "streets paved with gold." It wasn't a bad job – and things could have been worse.

When looking back on 36 years in the weaving room, Gosselin doesn't talk about repetition or boredom. There is no mention of intellectual stimulation. It was a job, and life began once he left the building.

"I never got bored, because I was so involved with the work," he commented. "I was there to work my day, to do the best I could

Lewiston in the 1920's—a bustling community, which produced citizens like Roland Gosselin.

(Heritage Center, Lewiston)

while I was there. And don't forget, this is piece-work. You've got to hustle if you want to earn a good wage. I don't feel that working there was that bad – it was steady work at a good wage. Look at the shoe shops – they would rush, rush, rush, then the summer would come and they'd lay the workers off when they didn't have orders. I didn't want that."

Gosselin's tenure in the mills, like many other Francos, was an outgrowth of family movement. His grandparents on the Gosselin side were from Quebec, though the details of Alphonse Gosselin's migration here are sketchy at best. On the other side of the family, his grandparents had come from different directions. Joseph Hamel apparently had been a native of Lisbon, Maine, when he met Sophia Thibodeau, a newcomer from "somewhere in New Brunswick." Like other Francos, Roland Gosselin is making efforts at putting the family puzzle together. He has learned enough, though, to say that his French-Canadian grandparents put in long years in the mill system.

Grandfather Hamel was in the slasher room for most of his career in Augusta's Edwards mill; his wife worked as a spooler, then went to hand drawing. Alphonse Gosselin fixed looms in the weave room, while his wife, name uncertain, was a weaver. She later served as a room girl, repairing damage to the warp.

Gosselin is not one to complain about the mill conditions over the years. But a desire to improve wages and mill environment propelled him into union activity.

Union workers were making a matter of 10 cents an hour in the early 1900's. By 1941, when Roland took his first job, a newcomer earned but $19 a week. Wages are higher now.

The union official said minimum wage in 1979 for a first year worker is $3.42 cents. An experienced weaver will make $5.15 to $5.25 an hour, and some skilled weaving jobs pay as much as $5.87.

Old-timers recall the 72-hour weeks, with Sunday the only day of rest. Holidays were limited to Christmas. Now Gosselin can report that his union has negotiated 11 paid holidays, and up to three weeks vacation time. Blue Cross - Blue Shield health insurance is available.

"And there is a pension," the earnest official adds. "A retired worker gets $1.70 per month for each year he worked there. If he worked 20 years, he'd be earning about $34 per month.

"I got involved with the union long ago, starting at the bottom because I saw it as an honest chance for people to get a fair deal. This wasn't a union town over the years, and French workers haven't been organizers. They always worked. But the union is important now.

"I don't remember many strikes in Lewiston. There was one, I think in 1956 or 1957. It lasted seven to nine weeks. Personally, I didn't pay much attention to it – I wasn't married, and didn't worry too much. But there were men with families who were very upset.

"It didn't go that well. The community didn't really support the strike; the people at city hall would issue some food stamps, but then they'd say the workers shouldn't be so fussy, that they would lose more by striking. There's always been that attitude here."

Gosselin is not what one would call a historian of the union movement. As he explains, his bachelor status granted him an immunity of sorts to worrying about strikes. And he does not elaborate on Bates' withdrawal from mill ownership several years ago, leaving the community with the task of keeping the mills operating themselves.

The long-time millworker views life around him not so much a part of the big picture, but as a series of small events happening at his level only.

The pleasant Franco-American is a member of Lewiston's historic commission, as well as a planner with the annual Franco-American Festival there. He is on the forefront of the drama scene in the city, and recently counted 37 productions that he had either staged or acted in. And he is a long-time member of the Richelieu Club.

These middle years are good years for Roland Gosselin, for after decades of vocational and family commitments, he seems to be coming out of a cocoon of anonymity. His brothers and sisters hold positions of small business managers, social servants or clerks. He, the oldest who was obligated to enter the mill, is now an official (with a title) of the community's key union.

A man whose destiny seems to have subtly funneled him straight into the mills that his ancestors had worked is coming of age.

"I wasn't unhappy in the mills," he commented in his Lisbon Street office one winter day. "I spent a lot of years there. I would have liked to have been with the union years ago. But this is the way it's worked out.

"The union is good. My grandparents had stories about the mills before unions. There was discrimination, they said, not so much because they were French, but because there was no way to have a voice. If the working conditions were bad, who could you talk to? If a boss was harassing a woman, what could you do? Now the people have a voice, the company has to abide by certain conditions. Without the union, these things couldn't be helped. And the union has made the mills a better place."

Does Gosselin have any feelings on the career he chose? "I was happy in the mills," he said. "I felt it was the best place to be."

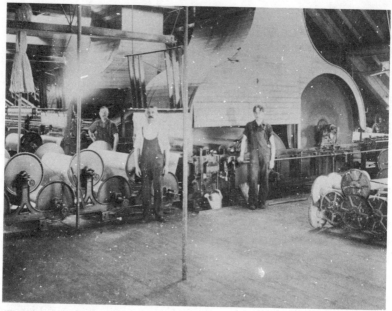

The French-Canadians, and succeeding generations of Franco-Americans, were found in every aspect of textile work. Pictured in this turn of the century picture are workers of the slasher room.

(Lewiston Public Library)

The weave room, and the many women who tended its machines.

(Lewiston Public Library)

# 2. Robert Lambert: Working man from Somersworth, N.H.

"My father was 18 when his family came down from Quebec. That was in 1896. Mills were recruiting in Canada then, so people had heard about the work that was available. My father and grandfather had been farmers on government-donated land near St. Frederick, but life was hard in that earth. They didn't have jobs when they came to Somersworth, but an uncle who had been here for two years helped them get work.

"I guess they planned to earn some money, then go back to the farms to buy better equipment, better tools. But they never did. They started roots here, and didn't give them up. They went back, and I've heard that my grandfather cried when he saw the old farm. But they were here to stay.

"My mother? She was two when her family moved down from St. Ferdinand, in Megantic County, about 60 miles southeast of Quebec City. They got to Somersworth in 1881. Her father was a woodsman in Quebec, and he stayed in that field. He never did work in the mills. No, grandfather Ruel started in Whitefield, N. H., with a team of horses. He farmed in summer, and went into the woods in winter.

"In 1883, there were enough French-Canadians in Somersworth to build a church. He worked as a supplier of materials. He had that team, and he hauled stone, and brick, and wood, to the site. After the church was built, he was able to buy a wood business – Ruel and Company, selling wood and coal. It operated from 1885 to 1945. If he had taken to distributing oil it would still be here, but when oil came in the 1920's and 30's, he wouldn't touch it. The family was pretty well off for Somersworth, though.

"My grandmothers, Ruel and Lambert, stayed at home. They had to. Grandmother Ruel had 12 children, and grandmother Lambert had 10.

"My parents went into the mills as a matter of course. They met there, they married, and then the children. I started in the mill myself, at the age of 14. I was the third of seven children – it was expected."

Robert Lambert is 73. Though his first days in the Great Falls Manufacturing Co. in Somersworth were close to 60 years ago, he recalls his youth quite clearly. He also remembers the progression he made following his arrival at the massive mill complex. From mill doffer, to shoe cutter, to Works Progress Administration (WPA) assignments, and finally to the Portsmouth Naval Shipyard, he is pleased to note his progress.

Not everyone made the step-by-step ascent that Lambert did. Thousands entered the mills as young teenagers, and exited only through death or retirement. Yet this soft-spoken Franco-American was interested in security. Not the can't-be-fired, can't-be-demoted type of job that some union shops have now developed, but simply an arrangement that insured a full work week, 52 weeks a year.

It's well that Robert Lambert thought ahead. When he began his career in 1920, he estimates the Great Falls Manufacturing Co. had a payroll of 3,000. Today that firm no longer exists. It, and scores like it, first lost ground to southern competitors, then went under to changing trends and technologies. Lambert stayed several steps ahead of economic disaster, and for this reason now lives a comfortable retirement on a navy yard pension.

"I never had a lot of schooling," he commented. "I started in public school, though, in 1911. My mother wanted me to take my first years in English, so I'd have a start. Then after two years, I went to the Catholic School, St. Martin Academy.

"I left school in 1920. That was what was done, because you had to help with the family. In Canada, my parents hadn't gone to school for long – I think my father went for two years, my mother for four, and that was just for religion.

"So I was about 14 when I started working, earning $11 a week. I was a doffer from 1920 to 1922. I might have stayed longer but there was the strike, the Great Strike, they called it. The Amoskeag in Manchester was out, but so were mills all over New Hampshire.

"I was 16, at an age where you didn't know much about politics. But even a person of 16 could understand what the companies were trying to do. The company was trying to increase the hours from 48 to 54 a week, and at the same time cut pay by 20 per cent. That was easy to understand.

"The mills had to close in February when we went out, and they stayed closed until October that year, 1922. There were a few strikebreakers, even some they brought from Quebec, but they went away. The mills stayed closed."

"Well, in the end the men went back at what the company offered. The company won, I guess, but no one won, because it never ran full-time again. It hurt management like it hurt the workers.

"Me? I started working in the shoeshop during the strike, and I never went back. That wasn't like doffing – it was skill, and it might take a year to really learn to be a good cutter. At that time, you see, you cut the hides by hand with a little knife. It was piece-work, so you had to be quick.

"The shoeshop paid better, but you couldn't plan on it because there was no security. You couldn't tell day to day what would happen, or if you'd head for work, and have someone tell you to just come back next week.

"We were jumpers, working from one shoeshop to the next, depending where the work was. I guess I worked in the shoeshops until 1939.

"I always had a job during the Depression. If the shoeshops weren't going, there was the WPA (Works Progress Administration) to keep you going. I remember it was 40 cents an hour, then 50 cents in later years. One job I did was going down to the University of New Hampshire in Durham, and building the fieldhouse, putting in ball diamonds, things like that. There were a lot of government jobs like that, and I took them when the shoeshops were quiet. I always worked."

Robert Lambert was typical of young Franco-Americans in many regards. He had a minimum of education, and went directly into the mills as his parents did before him. He worked in shoeshops, he toiled in make-work WPA programs. The hours in all jobs were long; the pay was not high. He was making $11 a week as a 14-year-old in 1920 and by 1940 was making but $35 a week.

But Lambert escaped from this treadmill in 1940 when he landed a job as a shipfitter at the Portsmouth Naval Shipyard. His destiny was finally in the hands of a stable governmental employer rather than the whims of dying dry goods industries. In this way he was different – he finally had a ticket to some kind of security.

"In a way my job at the shipyard wasn't so good," recalled Lambert, a soft-spoken bachelor with a very clear memory. "I was earning $35 a week at the shoeshops, and the shipyard was only $23 a week. But at Portsmouth there was some kind of security. My job was like a carpenter, but with steel – we did everything to fit the insides of ships. There was plenty of work, you see, so the future was always secure.

"I was able to work my way up at the shipyard, which wasn't really possible in the mills. I got to be a planner and estimator in my last years, making about $200 a week. You could get ahead, you know. People say the French were discriminated against there but I didn't see that. I'd say if you were a Mason, you'd get ahead faster, and the French weren't to be Masons because they were Catholic. But other than the thing about Masons getting first chances sometimes, I don't think the French were badly off."

Robert Lambert retired in 1964. He attempted a passive retirement, but for the past five years had been spending his time as a volunteer in the Somersworth school system. He has re-entered an arena that he left almost 60 years ago, a teacher aide, in the first, second, third, and fourth grade classes.

Lambert says he still wakes up at 6 a. m., perhaps a habit acquired during years of functioning on a strict work schedule. He is not obligated to work, yet years of toiling have left their mark. The difference is that now he works when he wants, and at the pace he wants.

Now that's some kind of security.

# 3. Henry Fredette: Loving the Life in the Pacific Mills of Lawrence, Mass.

"I remember the Great Strike of 1912," said Henry Fredette, an 81-year-old mill veteran who still lives in Lawrence, Mass. "I wasn't working in the mills then, I started just after. But I can see those strikers even today.

"They would be down at the common there, listening to the leaders like Joe Ettor, who was a real orator, and that woman, who they called the Red Flame.

"Thousands of people were out, because in those days there were five or six big mills. They went out for more money, but it was hard on them – they got hungry, and it was hard to hold out. They got mad, too.

"I remember one day on Essex Street when a crowd had stopped one of the electric cars. They were yelling and carrying on, and they almost turned it over right there. They didn't that day, but the strikers were frustrated, and felt like doing something.

"Our family didn't get as involved. My sister, for instance, worked in the mill but she didn't go out on strike. She stayed away because the mill was closed, but she wasn't one to strike herself.

"I was too young to understand much about it – I was 14. My parents wanted me to just stay away from what was happening. Mind our own business. My father didn't work in the mill; my mother had been a weaver, but didn't work regularly after the children started coming. I think my father was like other Frenchmen – he wanted to stay away, and make sure our family kept going. He wasn't looking at the whole."

Henry Fredette is one of a dwindling number of Franco-Americans who can remember the Great Strike in Lawrence, a bitter confronta-

Henry Fredette, retired from the Pacific Mills but active as a leading citizen of Lawrence. Fredette worked in the mills for 44 years and says he loved every minute of it.

tion between labor and management that is still recognized as the first major labor victory in the textile industry. Fredette doesn't live solely in the past, of course; he has earned numerous service awards from senior citizens councils, the Knights of Columbus, and St. Anne's Church. But as one who worked 44 years in the mills (Pacific Mills, mostly as a supervisor in the worsted division), his experience is a reflection of a Franco-American whose life was closely connected with the mill industry. And he was unique in that he ascended to the rung of supervisor, one of the first Francos to do so.

"My father was Frank Fredette, Francois Fredette, really. He was from Quebec, and I think the family came down in about 1890. He didn't work in a mill, though. He moved houses. He worked with a crew that would jack houses up, and with a team of horses pulling it, would take it from one side of town to another. It was a tricky job —they worked mostly at night, because they'd have to take down all the wires that kept the electric cars going. After the house had passed through, the wires would go back up. The most interesting to move was a brick house. They would put rope and wire around the whole thing, to make sure it stayed together. As I said, it was a tricky business.

"My mother was Georgiana Rancourt Fredette. She was from New Hampshire, though her family had come down from Quebec, too. She was a weaver. She stopped working to have children, but when hard times came she could always go back and get work again.

"We were a family of 10, so it was natural that I start working early. I went into the Pacific Mills in 1912, when I was 14. I had to go to work in order to help them. My first job was a backboy in the mule spinning room. What we did as boys was to keep the machines filled up with rovings for the spinners.

"I was a backboy for about two years. I earned $5.10 a week. Then I worked as a piecer, which is the job after backboy. The next thing up was a section hand, which I became when I was 19. That was young. And as a section hand I worked with the machines, repairing and making sure the machines ran. That was $35 a week, but it was good pay then.

"We're talking worsted here, not cotton. A mulespun yard was

Shift's end, a scene very familiar to career employees like Henry Fredette.

(Lowell Museum)

what you called a stretched yarn. When they made a piece of cloth out of that yarn, it was a very good piece of cloth. When you bought a suit, you knew it would be expensive. It was worsted, it lasted a long time.

"Then the war broke out. I tried to enlist but they were working on the draft. I signed up, passed; and I was to be sent to training on a Thursday. On a Tuesday, the Armistice was declared.

"At the mills again, I became a second hand, or second supervisor. Then I was named a general overseer in about 1930. That job paid about $75 or $80 a week. I was responsible for three different shifts, with at least 200 workers under me.

"I know that a lot of Franco-Americans in the mills stayed at one job all their lives, but in the mill I always looked ahead. I did my work; nothing was too hard for me. I didn't know too many like me who moved up – people are surprised I worked myself up without graduating from high school.

"I went to the Lowell Textile, though, and after one year the professor told me there was no need in going back. I knew my machines and there was nothing there they could tell me.

"I worked in the mills, the same mill, for 44 years, mostly as an overseer. I retired in 1958 – I had to retire because the mill was moving South. They offered me an opportunity to go with them, at another kind of job. But I didn't take it. I stayed in Lawrence.

"One thing I'm happy about is the new system that I started at the mule spinning room. It was a hot place, you know, getting to be 90 or 95 degrees. So I asked if we could install fans in the windows, and keep the department to a temperature of about 85, and keep humidity at about 65 per cent. They approved the idea, and we had fans. The department was better off after that.

"Most of the people under me were French. I had some Polish people, and some Italian people, and some Portuguese. The French worked hard, but so did everybody then. You had to then; everybody worked hard."

Fredette's retirement in 1958 did not mean inactivity. Through a connection at city hall, he landed a job as housing manager for a senior citizens apartment complex in the city. He held that post through 1968.

In 1968, "after another round of retirement parties," Henry Fredette went to the vocational sidelines again. But this time he was deeply engaged in working with local senior citizens groups. He has been an advocate for the elderly in Lawrence for the past 11 years, and some would say he has never retired.

Indeed, Fredette is among the most civic-minded citizens in the community. His living room wall in his duplex at 26 Washington Street reflects his commitment to years of contributions. The Knights of Columbus named him their Man of the Year several years ago. Numerous photos with high-ranking church officials document his position in the lay hierarchy at St. Anne's. His hours have also been directed to Alhambra, a society of Catholic men dedicated to helping retarded children.

And then there are the senior citizens. In addition to serving on numerous local and regional councils, he has been a guest at the White House when aging was the topic of the day.

Why, it might be asked, has this one Franco-American become such a visible achiever in the realm of community work when so many Francos have declined public service? What does Henry Fredette have in his background that pushed him into the local power structure when so many fellow French have remained isolated in their own little Canadas?

"I always loved to do things," the friendly gentleman said. "It wasn't my parents really – they never said I should do this or that. They let me make my own decisions. I'd say it was the Brothers at St. Anne's. They taught you how to participate, to get involved in anything. They encouraged you to try and that made a difference."

Among Fredette's endeavors was playing semi-pro football as a youth. An all-star halfback and tackle for the Tremonts, a club that won a state title, he took to a game that was all but unknown by his forefathers in Quebec. His mother, though not enthusiastic, quietly supported his play; his father would become enraged at the thought of his son wasting time on a strange game where players often left the field in ambulances. During some weeks, his mother would hide his football uniform behind the back door so as not to bring Henry's activities to his father's attention.

Henry Fredette remains a contributing force in the community today. He lives quietly within the shadows of the mills with his wife of 25 years, Alliette, who had been a mender in the textile trades. He is not wealthy. Happenstance finds him earning just $20 a month pension, plus social security, but he gets by. He could be healthier, but that doesn't mean he won't attend any of a half-dozen meetings of various organizations. Yet few senior citizens talk with such enthusiasm about their vocational lives.

"I loved the mills, I've got to say that. For 44 years I worked there, and I enjoyed it. I liked the housing job, too.

"In the early days, there was plenty of work for everyone. There were the Arlington Mills, and the Wood Mills, and Everett, and Duck, and Sutton-Methuen. If a guy didn't like his work, he'd tell the boss he was leaving, and he could go across town and find something else.

"You ask about the strike. Well, I don't know if the workers were right. I was too young, I hadn't even worked there yet. They were looking for more money, and in those days they weren't getting too much money. Prices weren't as high as today though, either.

"From my experience, looking over the years, I'd say the mills gave people a fair chance to make money. If the people didn't make it, it was their own hard luck. I went there, and if I had said that I don't want to do this, or I don't want to do that, I never would have gotten anywhere. I accepted everything that was offered to me. Many a time I didn't like it. But I said I have to do it, and that's all there is to it.

"But I'll tell you, I was tickled to death about what I had done when I retired. Overseer, that was something, because if I'm not mistaken, there were only two or three of us French in all the mills, in the mills in Lawrence with its thousands of people.

"I was proud when I left but I was sad. Because you know, I loved those mills."

Adelbert Plante, left, and Oliva Verrier. They worked together in the mills during the 1920's, and find themselves together again at a Mannville, R.I. nursing home 50 years later.

# 4. Adelbert Plante: Reflecting on life in Woonsocket

"I started working when I was 12 or 13," remembers Adelbert Plante, 78, of Woonsocket, R. I. "I was expected to go to work. But then, I wanted to work. I didn't like school – I wasn't learning anything and I couldn't wait to earn some money. So I went into the cotton mill in Woonsocket.

"I guess I worked there until I was 23. Then I went to the worsted mill. I worked there until I retired in 1962. Why did I leave? It paid better. When I was 15, I was making maybe $3 a week in cotton, and that's working 54 hours a week. When I went to worsted the money was better – $12 or $13. They told me it would be better, and it was.

"I was lucky during the Depression. I had the job of foreman and I never really felt the pinch. I was making about $25 a week in the 30's. What was I making when I retired? In 1962, I guess I was earning $80 to $90 a week."

Plante has been retired for almost two decades now. He lives in a nursing home with his second wife. He is partially paralyzed, but can cope. His wife is not so lucky – she needs constant medical attention.

In some ways, Adelbert Plante is an invisible man. His mobility is limited, so he spends virtually all his time at his home, the Hospice de St. Antoine outside of Providence, R. I. His remaining family is spread around the country, so close personal ties are limited. Even friends from years ago have trouble making contact with this retired mill foreman. The circle of friends is growing smaller by the year, and the extra effort to search out an old acquaintance is often lacking.

Plante is not unique in his position. Thousands of elderly Franco-Americans are in similar circumstances. They sit quietly in nursing homes or tenement apartments. If encountered by a passer-by on the street, the aged man might be ignored as if he no longer counts. They are easy to overlook now, despite the fact they put in energetic and useful lives.

But just because Adelbert Plante is older now, it doesn't mean he hasn't lived a meaningful life.

"There were 10 boys and two girls in our family," Plante commented. "I was number four.

"I spoke English before I spoke French, but shortly after I started working as a teen-ager I went to Quebec. I guess I did it backwards. First I worked on a farm, then I went and got a job in a Canadian worsted mill. When I left Woonsocket, I couldn't speak French. When I got back from Quebec, I had forgotten how to speak English.

"Oh, I had permission to be in Canada. My parents saw me off to the station, and I headed up to farmland of Quebec. I can't say just what made me do it – I just had an urge to, so I did.

"On my first job after I came back, the plant went on strike. Some mills were union, some weren't, but at this time (about 1915-1920) there was unrest among a lot of workers. I didn't pay too much attention – I was just a kid. And the strike wasn't hard on me. I could always live at home, so I didn't feel it like men with families."

Plante's family was French. His mother had been born in Lowell, his father "up in Quebec." Like many French families, the Plantes crossed the border several times before settling in Woonsocket. The parents, for instance, married in Woonsocket and returned to seek work in Quebec. They had two children there before deciding to return to the mills of Rhode Island.

Like his father, Adelbert Plante entered the mills. If the work was memorable, it is not reflected today in conversation. The retired Franco will talk about his wife, or his family (extended family only; his two daughters died years ago, one at seven months of unknown causes, one of appendicitis at eight years of age). But rarely does he talk about the years in the mills.

Passing time, by conversation or television, is a necessity these days, however. Retirement has brought him into contact with many Franco-Americans his age, but partial paralysis has limited his choices.

Sometimes he'll sit down with a former worker. On a cool, rainy day in the spring of 1979, he not only spoke with Oliva Verrier, but offered to translate a few notes from Verrier's background. Though he has been in Rhode Island since 1922, Verrier barely speaks English.

"He's 86 years old," smiled Plante, "I know, because he worked for me. I've known him for over 50 years, and here we are together.

"Oliva came here in 1922 to make some money. He was making 50 cents a day on a farm in Quebec. He already had five children, but two stayed in Canada with the grandparents. He wasn't scared to come down here, though. He wanted a better job.

"It wasn't hard for him to adjust to the new city, because everyone in his new neighborhood spoke French. For years he got by with the French, and even here in the retirement home he speaks French.

"His wife is at the home, but she's paralyzed. They're supposed to be getting a room they can share, but it takes a long time for one to open. But for now, things are okay. He's paying the bill for the home, so he must have done all right.

"He's a good worker, too. He put a lifetime in the mills, and when he retired in 1970, he was in good shape. He was respected."

Late that afternoon, the two sought support from each other as they hobbled down the hall to one of the few events they look forward to: dinner. Arm in arm – after 50 years.

RELIGION ET NATIONALITÉ

LOYAUX MAIS CANADIENS FRANÇAIS.

The banner of a Franco-American society sums up the loyalties that many have felt—
religion, nationality, and feelings toward both Canada and the United States.

(Heritage Center, Lewiston)

# 5. Maurice Roux: Company Man

The handsome white clapboard home of Maurice C. R. Roux, Sr., is technically in Biddeford, Maine, but residents of his section of town call it Biddeford Pool; the Pool.

The Pool is located on a peninsula jutting into the Atlantic Ocean. It has been noted that such geography makes it the coolest spot on the East Coast in the summertime, which is one reason the wealthy tourists choose the spot for the July/August retreats.

Roux's residence is about seven miles from the tenements of downtown Biddford, a mill town for over a century now. But Roux's home somehow seems more distant than just a handful of miles. The tranquility of the Pool, combined with its lush oceanside setting, makes Le Petit Canada seem worlds away. And the good life is possible for Maurice Roux because the 73-year-old Franco-American was a company man.

He was, in fact, the highest ranking Franco-American executive at the West Point Pepperell for many of the 28 years he worked there. He headed the personnel department there at a time when the mill employed between 1,600 and 2,200 workers. The oft-decorated executive administered training and safety programs, but he also recruited French-Canadians for the factory. He retired in 1969.

Roux knows, therefore, a bit about French-Canadians and the mills. "I can only speak of the time I spent here but I think down through the years, the French-Canadians were known as excellent workers," Roux will say.

"They are a responsible people – they go in with the idea of putting in a day's work for a day's pay.

"Oh, there were some exceptions of course, but technically you had people who wanted to work.

"They wanted to earn as much as they could. You offered them overtime, and they'd take it. They were excellent."

Roux's grandfather on the paternal side hailed from the south shore of the St. Lawrence River. The early ancestors were French soldiers who came to fight at Quebec in the battle against the British for New France. His grandmother also was from Quebec, though the family originally was from Acadia.

"They escaped the British in Nova Scotia, fleeing to New Brunswick," said Roux, who had been researching the family roots. "They finally got to Quebec, where they settled."

Roux's father was a molder in the Saco Lowell shops; his mother worked at Pepperell. But they had other things in mind for their son. He graduated from Thornton Academy (1923). Four years later he was awarded a diploma from the renowned Franco-American institution in Worcester, Mass., Assumption College.

If Roux was an exception in graduating from college in that era, he also proved to be unique in his ability to enter the Waspish circles of management. He was a seller of wholesale groceries until 1939, when he took a position with the Maine State Employment Service. Two years later, he joined Pepperell in the personnel division.

Roux rose to head the department.

"I guess it was unusual that I was where I was," said the former company man. "I was the highest in the plant, I know that.

"But I never approached the workers on the basis that they were Canadians, or Italians, or Franco-Americans. I treated people alike."

Roux's view of the immigration includes the fact that French-Canadians were just part of the flow of labor that came in to work the mills.

There were "Yankee girls" off the farms to first handle the work, he said. Then the Irish provided labor.

French-Canadians followed in great numbers. But there were Greeks too, the manager recalled. And in the case of the French-Canadians, they were not hard to bring here.

"In the early days, the late 1800's, there were no markets for produce in Quebec," Roux said. "There might have been farms that produced but there was nowhere to sell it.

"The French-Canadians were deprived of cash flow. They came to New England because there was cash, and for that time, a good wage.

"Many returned for the summer to be back on the farm. A lot just went back to live. I'd say 30 per cent of the mill workers returned to Quebec after working here."

Later 19th century methods of advertising were primarily word-of-mouth. There were some handbills and personal visits by mill agents, but families relaying satisfaction with the new life was the major persuasive tool.

In Roux's tenure as a recruiting officer, he used radio and newspaper advertising. But word-of-mouth was still important.

"During the war, we didn't recruit very much — not many people were moving. The 1950's were slow too, the mills were moving south. But in the 1960's we had a flow recruiting from Canada, at least 300.

"By this time we had to prove to the government that there was a need, so we could get them necessary visas. First we had to show there was a manpower shortage in Maine (through the state employment office), then in the region. The government was involved and there were immigration laws they didn't have a century ago. But there were still Canadians who came, because there was cash here, and not so much there."

Roux does not recall that French-Canadians or Franco-Americans were eager to unionize for more money.

"I don't think the Franco-Americans were interested in badgering management for more money," Roux said. "The Irish were interested in unions, but they were more political anyway, and that's part of unionizing. Franco-Americans didn't do much organizing until the 1930's. Then they felt the need to organize, but it was no great hoopla. In later years there were strikes, but again, I don't think that's a major trait."

Indeed, Roux suggests that management at Pepperell during his era was fair to workers.

"We had to compete in wages, and I think we were fair," declared Roux. "We had classes in English, sewing classes, things like that for workers. Yes, we treated the workers fairly – at least I know that's true during the time I was there."

Such is the view of Maurice C. R. Roux, retired personnel manager – and Company Man Emeritus.

# 6. Joseph Ruel:
## Over the border—and back again

One of the most difficult facts to document about the French-Canadian migration to New England is determining how many French returned to Canada. Historians suggest that there was some flow of return, but few have been able to determine just how many preferred to return to Canada.

Joseph Ruel lived in both worlds. Born of Canadian parents in Biddeford, Maine, in 1895, he and his family moved back to Quebec when he was six. He was to return to the United States twice; once in 1918 to serve in the United States Army and again, in 1945, to "settle down" in southern Maine where he could make a daily wage in the mills.

Today Ruel is an 84-year-old pensioner living in Biddeford, less than a half mile from downtown mills. Though he's been retired since 1965, he still wears "work clothes" around his immaculate tiny white house that is dwarfed by the wooden tenements that dominate the neighborhood. His hands, though, not his clothes, are what attract the eye. Thick, calloused and muscular, they seem to be an accurate reflection of the years this friendly gentleman has labored.

"My grandfather, Ephreme Ruel, came here in 1878," said Ruel. "He was from Wolftown, Quebec. His wife was Esther Therrien. I don't know very much about them, but he worked at the York Company in Saco, which became the Bates and then Saco Tannery.

"My father was Alfred Ruel, my mother Olivine Guay. I do know my father worked as a weaver first, then a loom fixer at several of the mills in Biddeford. My father and mother liked it in Biddeford, but they didn't stay. My father was sick and the doctor advised them to live in the country. It would be better for his breathing. They bought a farm in Beauce County, then later moved to another farm in St. Isidore, Compton County. That was about 1910 when they went to St. Isidore.

"I had just started public school in Biddeford when we moved. I didn't get much learning in Canada. I think I went to just fourth grade there. My father regained his health, and we stayed there, and the schooling wasn't very good. Why didn't we return? Well, my father's health was the reason, and most of my mother's family was nearby. I worked on the farm in summer and in the woods in winter. I went to my first logging camp when I was 16. That was 1911. It was in the United States, in northern New Hampshire. There were 125 men in the camp; everyone was French, except the boss, that is. They spoke French, but most were from New England.

"I could cross the border with no trouble, because I was an American citizen. A lot of loggers in Canada had trouble working in the woods in the U. S. though, because they couldn't get bond. That's the way it always was with me; I could come back to the U. S. because I was a citizen."

Ruel did return to this country in 1918 to join the U. S. Army. He had registered in Canada, but opted to actually enlist in America because "it was my country, and I felt patriotic."

He was trained at Ft. Devans, Mass. He did not go overseas though – the war was almost over. The action he saw was at the debarkation hospital in New York City. Despite the fact that his French was far better than his English, Franco-Americans such as Joseph Ruel did not stand out for being "foreign."

"Many people had come to America, you know," he commented. "The French-Canadians weren't the only ones. So in the army, there were Italians, Poles, men from eastern Europe, even boys who were of German heritage but born here. I didn't feel out of place."

Ruel returned to Canada in 1919, and that year was married to Arthemise Huot of Halifax. The family stayed in Canada, and if there was one word that characterized his life it was WORK.

"I worked on the farm, and in winter, in the woods," he said. "They both were difficult, but the woods was tougher. On the farm, you didn't work too much in the spring. In the summer, if it rained,

Joseph Ruel of Biddeford, Maine. He's lived in Quebec and he's lived in New England; the 84-year-old retiree has worked in the woods, and he has worked in the mills. He typifies those who lived in both worlds, splitting time between "home" in Canada and "home" in New England.

you couldn't hay or anything. In the woods, you worked every day, no matter what. I'd be in the woods for about four months. You'd leave the camp before light, and come home after dark. With an axe you'd bring the trees down, and with a big cross-cut saw, you cut them up. We loaded them on wagons drawn by four horses.

"I saw accidents in my day. Once two men were killed when a tree fell the wrong way. We were a long way from a hospital but it didn't matter – they died right away. I'd say we worked 10 or 11 hours a day. At night, the men would sing, or tell jokes, maybe dance. There was a very good tap dancer I remember. We went to bed at 9 p. m. though. You needed your sleep. About once a winter, a priest would come to the camp; there would be a mass and he'd listen to the men. You see, we weren't close enough for church.

"I worked in Pittsburgh, N. H., and Greenville, Maine, next to Moosehead, there. I was with St. Regis, Great Northern, at different times, the big companies. I made about $1 a day for my work –

maybe $35.00 a month most winters. It was hard work, and there were some very, very rugged men in the woods. You see, when I worked, there were no chain saws like today. You did the work yourself. I left in 1945. Chain saws were just starting to be used then. But you know, I never used one. They took too long to get working. In those days, not many men knew how to fix them. If a chain saw broke, it would lie around for two or three days before they got it running again."

Ruel left Canada with his family in 1945. He recalls he had $4,000 in his pocket, a substantial amount but "not very much for all the work I had done."

Among the reasons for leaving was the fact his sons did not want to work on the farm. Joseph Ruel thought he could make more money in Biddeford; his sons were sure of it.

"The boys couldn't speak English," he said. "But they had heard that this country was good. They went into the Army – they were U. S. citizens because I was, but the war was over. One boy was discharged after 90 days; he didn't speak a word of English and the Army didn't want to take the time to teach him at that point.

"Three of my boys worked in the Pepperell mills here – the two young ones learned trades, though, they didn't work in the mills. Three of my boys are living now – two died."

When Ruel returned to Biddeford in 1945, he obtained a job in the Saco-Lowell foundry. True to his history of hard work, the position was the exhausting task of cleaning the massive casting flasks. He earned 79 cents an hour. He worked at least three hours overtime every night, though, which enabled him to earn enough to get by on. After a brief time in the foundry, he got a job driving a truck for Saco-Lowell. He was clearing $58 per week when Saco-Lowell abruptly moved south in 1958. Joseph Ruel was not asked to move south with the firm, but was able to get odd jobs in carpentry and maintenance until he retired in 1965.

Though the hardworking Franco-American has carried many a burden since he began working as a child, the biggest one fell on him in October, 1978; his wife of 59 years, Arthemise Ruel, passed away. He now lives alone in that simple, but immaculate, home on Mt.

Vernon Street, Biddeford. "It's not so easy to come home in the afternoon now," he says. "It's very, very quiet now. It's hard after 59 years, you know."

So 84-year-old Joseph Ruel walks about Biddeford, the town in which he was born, avoiding as long as possible that moment when he must re-enter the empty cottage. It is remarkable commentary on the aging process that a man who lived such a full and vigorous life is passed on the street, and not noticed. The endless mill walls of Biddeford can show no friendliness; the packs of scampering school children rush by as if he were a moving whisper of the past. Aging is probably his greatest challenge ever, particularly now that he's alone.

The memories of a full lifetime of work, family and church must be of some comfort, though, for this man who lived in both Canadian and American worlds.

"This is my country," he said when asked where his allegiance lay. "America."

Emma Tourangeau, the oldest pensioner (91) of S.D. Warren in Westbrook, Maine. Her father was among the first French-Canadians hired by the paper company, and his excellent service was one reason firm officials hired more.

# 7. Emma Tourangeau: Early days in the Westbrook paper mills

Emma Tourangeau is a remarkably agile and independent woman of 91 who has the ability to recall in vivid detail much of what has happened to her since she was four.

She is a native of Westbrook, Maine, where her father was the first French-Canadian to be hired at S. D. Warren mill and her sister was the first Franco-American to break a similar barrier in the mill's finishing department. Emma Tourangeau lives now in Deering Pavilion, a church-supported apartment complex for the elderly in Portland.

Always a precise person, partly because much of her life was devoted to figures – she worked 46 years for Warren, mostly as a bookkeeper – she has lately been recording in a journal what it was like growing up in Maine as a Franco-American. She has been careful to make a duplicate of this ongoing work because an earlier manuscript she wrote about the evolution of Westbrook was lost by the family to whom she sent it for reaction.

"My mother worked in a mill in Westbrook when she was 10," Miss Tourangeau says. "She was so small they had to stand her on a box so she could reach her work. She married at 20, then she stayed home.

"My father and mother had both been born in Quebec. My father, he was Ludger Tourangeau, but people called him Gerry, arrived in 1881. He was 20.

"He and my mother, who had moved here with her family when she was a child, got married the following year. I was born two years later.

"The question of bigotry over religion and race was very noticeable at that time, the 1880's and 1890's, so much so that when father tried to get work, he was one year getting it. Mr. Warren, that was John

Warren, he was manager there, said he was hiring him because he was tired of seeing father each morning. Father was the first French-Canadian hired by S. D. Warren on account of the bigotry there was against the French, bigotry controlled by one bigot in each department.

"This condition remained for years and years. In 1906, my sister was the first French Catholic to get work in the finishing department of S. D. Warren Co. I also remember one year — it was in the early 1900's – that a petition was signed to remove two Catholic teachers from the school system – but to no success.

"My childhood wasn't very happy. My parents couldn't speak much English. My mother would tell me in English what to get at the store, but when I repeated that to the storekeeper, he said what I was saying wasn't a word. He would suggest my mother write it down. But she couldn't write. All the children of the early French-Canadians lived in ignorance and the Catholic religion and its teachings was the sole factor. I remember that our priest said we shouldn't be going to public schools so I was pulled out. I still remember crying, because I liked public school. I was sent to the convent at St. Hyacinth Church, Westbrook.

"When I graduated from the convent – there were just three of us to graduate – I had to take an exam with the public school department to receive a diploma.

"My father was injured at the plant in 1908. Mr. Warren asked him to sign a paper saying he wouldn't sue the company for any damages but my father felt badly that he was even asked. Of course he wouldn't sue. So Mr. Warren said then that Tourangeaus would always have jobs in the plant, and there have been many who have worked there since. I was there 46 years, in bookkeeping and accounting. I retired in 1952 and am one of the oldest pensioners. My father died in 1910 from the injury he suffered at the plant. He had worked up to a paper machine tender. What our father did with his life, amidst difficulties of all sorts – language, bigotry, hard times financially – is a great example of the stamina of the French-Canadian. He became an alderman, a Republican in a Democratic ward, so he had to work at it. And he bought a house. It took him 20 years to pay off a mortgage of $2,400.

"We had a wonderful family. There were nine children – I'm the last left. I'm writing a family journal of what I remember. There have been books that deal with the town or the company, but there's nothing about the human side of things that happened then. It was not a life of roses. I'm telling you. But we made it."

In 1967, Emma Tourangeau, who owned a cottage on Cushing's Island just off Portland, published "Aunt Emma's Island Cookbook, also featuring old French-Canadian recipes." This is one of the recipes that she recommends:

## MOTHER'S FRENCH OMELET

Dice into tiny cubes about one quarter pound regular fat salt pork of the kind found in supermarkets – do not use the type which contains meat.

Mix ¾ cup flour with half teaspoon baking powder, sift and add ¾ cup milk, five eggs dropped in singly, stirring lightly after each. Fry pork cubes slowly so fat does not burn. When cubes are crisp they can be removed or left in the egg mixture, depending on preference.

Before dropping egg mixture into the slow-heating fat, give it a quick stir to mix well.

Watch the cooking and with a spatula lift it up here and there. As it browns, and when it seems all cooked on top, turn it over or cut it in the portions needed to serve. Cutting in four gives generous portions.

Finally, cover tightly and simmer five minutes then serve, with or without the fried cubes.

Marie Breton Gilbert—Things got worse before they got better after she migrated from Quebec, but her family succeeded nevertheless.

# 8. Marie Breton Gilbert:
# ". . . but we made it."

Marie Breton was 18 when she left Quebec for Waterville, Maine in 1923. Her family was trying to rise above a broken life. Far worse was to happen, however, as this French-Canadian family was put to supreme tests in the new country.

"My mother was from St. Just de Bretonnaire – my mother's father's family had founded the town. You can tell by the name. My father was from St. George. We were a poor family — my father was a farmer. But when I was a child, the government was giving land to big families, so they could settle it. My father went to see about it, and ended up by getting land for a saw mill operation. I don't remember exactly where it was – I was a child. But it was well in the woods, on a river. There were no roads to where we were, so the only transportation there was boats.

"We moved several times, then the saw mill was ready. I couldn't go to school because there weren't any. I helped out the family. When I was 16, I cooked for the loggers in the woods. We were burned out in 1923. I was in the main house, and we woke up one night and saw the mill on fire. It didn't take the house; we weren't hurt. But everything was gone at the sawmill. It was terrible losing our whole means of making money. There weren't any jobs in the area. My parents knew people in Waterville, so we decided to leave Canada for the United States. I cried when we left; I was scared."

French-Canadians migrated for many reasons, but rarely were they as discouraged or destitute as the Bretons. The Bretons and their nine children took a horse cart, then a train for the new life they had heard much about.

But disaster struck again. Though 52-year-old Alfred Breton was successful in landing a job upon arrival in October, 1923, he was dead by July.

"My father got a job with Central Maine Railroad," said Marie Breton Gilbert, 75, now living in Augusta, Maine. "It wasn't a big job. He was a sweeper, I think. Or someone who cleans up, but it was work. He hadn't even been there a year when he was killed in an accident. A big crane hook in the yard let go, smashing him as he worked down below in the yards.

"The company, they didn't pay anything, really. They offered $3,000 for us to settle, to agree we wouldn't try to get damages. Well, there was a mother and nine children in the house and no social security or any federal money then. We took it. From then on, it was different. We had always been poor, but after my father's death it was living from week to week. The children got jobs, though. We stayed together. That's one thing about the French – we work."

It's difficult to imagine a family in more difficult circumstances: strangers in a strange town, unable to speak the language, the bread-winner dead. But one of the remarkable traits of the French has been their ability to function in the face of adversity. With the moral support of other Francos in Waterville, the Bretons faced the task of simply surviving. In an era before welfare, food stamps or social workers, they turned to hard work. The Bretons, in fact, are a study of a French-Canadian family not only surviving, but achieving notable success.

"I guess everyone started at the bottom," she said. "Most of the boys went to the mills, where they were doffers. That's one of the lowest jobs. The sisters worked too, and we all paid family expenses.

"We had faith, we worked. Everybody stayed together, everybody contributed. I started out in a cotton mill – I made $12.75 for a 54-hour week."

Marie Breton married Romeo Gilbert, a carpenter, in 1926. Soon after, she left work to have children. Other Bretons continued their efforts to keep the family functioning. Brother Louis Breton went directly into the mills, but he and brother Joseph returned to Quebec to learn trades.

"They couldn't read English, so they couldn't learn here," she said. "The boys learned up there, then came back here to work," recalled their sister. "Joseph became a barber; Louis achieved his goal as a mechanic. He succeeded because he could deal in two languages."

Louis Breton eventually opened Breton's garage on Kennebec Street in Waterville. Son Donald took it over following Louis' departure. Though the building has been replaced by municipal redevelopment, Donald continues in the field.

Another brother, Cyrille Breton worked in the woolen mills in the Waterville area. He was a "lifer." Going in as a maintenance man, after 40 years he rose to a low-level supervisory position. The mills was the only job Cyrille Breton ever knew – he entered at 16 and labored there until retirement.

Rose Breton married a Lefebvre after working in the Winslow pulp mill, and had three children. Julienne Breton married Rene LaChance and ran a grocery business. It is said Winslow's first post office was situated in her store.

Moses Breton was another long-time mill worker, putting his life service as a machinist-mechanic at a Winslow pulp mill.

Just Breton was remembered as the "operator" of the family. The Breton's youngest, he was seven when the entourage arrived. Evidently young enough to get an early grasp of the "American Way," Just came to own a grocery store, a catering service, apartments, wood lots and a trailer park. The ambitious Franco also obtained the position of selectman of Winslow, a most notable achievement for himself and family. His election was another example of the ability of the French to achieve respectable position in just one generation's time.

Rosaire Breton was the only family member to return to Quebec. He left to maintain what was left of the family property, casting his lot with the traditional vocation of farming. Evidently farming was no more lucrative in the 1920's than it was in the 1820's. He returned "sometime in the 40's" to run a farm in nearby Fairfield.

And Marie Breton? After putting in her "obligatory" time in the mills, she left to raise two sons. Fernand Joseph is a postal official in Connecticut, while Valmont is a Catholic priest serving St. Augustine's Church in Augusta.

Today she lives in Augusta with her son, working part-time at St. Augustine's. Her lot is like many older Francos – through the support of her family, she has achieved some security in her later years. She is proud to be the mother of a priest, "it was a benediction for God to have a priest in the family," she says. She stays close to the institution that has been a part of so many displaced French: the church. It has been painful to see brothers and sisters pass on; it is of some discomfort that she knows that her three grandchildren do not speak French.

Despite a difficult life, however, Marie Breton Gilbert does not dwell on it with bitterness. She's not even unhappy about it. Like others who have defeated the elements of hardship and poverty, she reflects without ill feeling.

"It was never easy," she commented one fall day in the comfortable rectory of St. Augustine Church. "After my father died especially, there was no money, no security. But we stayed together, behind my mother we kept up as a family. No one did any drinking; there wasn't any going out. The thing was to get a job, find a good wife or husband and work.

"We all worked hard, in the mills or wherever. We didn't feel sorry for ourselves, we didn't want a handout. The brothers and sisters knew what we had to do.

"It's different now, things are better. The men get jobs and their children go to college and have opportunity. We didn't have that when I came here; there was no chance for school in Quebec, and there was nothing but work when we got here.

"But we made it. I can say we worked and we made it."

# 9. Flavie Michaud Wilds Fitzgerald: Logger's Life in Northern Maine

When the great New England log drives were halted several years ago, some newspaper and magazine articles mourned the loss of the traditional means of transporting timber to the mills. Writers were saying that a beautiful institution was disappearing, and with it, a beautiful style of life.

But to hear 91-year-old Flavie Michaud Wilds Fitzgerald recall her life as the wife of a woodsman, one would hardly think the woodsmen themselves missed the annual spring drive.

Flavie says the men were glad that the drives were over.

"I remember when the drives ended," said Flavie, a resident of Fort Kent, Maine, "the men felt such relief.

"They would work so hard, and in the old days, make $20 a month. It was awful. My husband, Charlie Wilds, was a woodsman. He wasn't French but he lived in an area where everybody was French. He spoke French.

"The woods was the only place a man could work in those days, and I'm talking about what I remember, from 1900, or a little before. Charlie's father took him to the woods when he was 12, and so he never got much of a chance to go to school. That's the way it was in those days. When you were old enough, you went to the woods.

"In the winter, you went to down the timber. But you couldn't stay in the forest all winter. The snow got to be seven or eight feet in the country, you couldn't work there – you couldn't move the logs. So the men would come home.

"They'd stay until spring, then the log drives would begin. They'd drive it from the Allagash to the St. John, as far as Van Buren.

"My husband Charlie was never hurt but men were injured or drowned. And in the old days, they just buried them right on the shore.

The life of a logger, as remembered by Flavie Michaud Wilds Fitzgerald, involved annual log drives such as this one. Flavie recalls that her husband, Charlie Wilds, used to ride the logs with his dog several feet behind him for company.

(Avery Collection, Maine State Library, Augusta)

Logging in northern New England was dangerous—and it was rugged. These early 20th century pictures were taken in early spring, when the water was terribly cold.

(Avery Collection, Maine State Library, Augusta)

Many French-Canadians and Franco-Americans of New England worked not in urban mills, but in the vast wilderness as woodsmen. This early 20th century photo shows a woodsman bringing logs into the main camp.

(Avery Collection, Maine State Library, Augusta)

Modern skidders carry massive loads, but this photograph indicates that horses were capable of pulling power too, as they prepare to move this hefty sledload.

(Avery Collection, Maine State Library, Augusta)

"I never worried about Charlie, though, he was an awfully brave man. He was smart as a driver, too. He'd get on top of the log with his dog, Jim, and he'd be all set. He may have fallen, but he was never in bad trouble."

Flavie Michaud Wilds Fitzgerald is among the oldest residents of the northern Aroostook community. At the age of 87 she was married to long-time friend Henry Fitzgerald. She and Henry live in a small single family house in Fort Kent, one they bought but have been unable to obtain the title to. They don't worry about that, though. Their view is that time will take care of it.

Flavie is French. Her first husband, Charlie Wilds, was one of the few Anglos in the area. She herself spoke French as a child, and though she was married to Anglos, has always been able to communicate in both languages.

She is not one that apologizes for her long and colorful life. She was the majority ethnic group, and it was Charlie Wilds who had to learn the language.

Indeed, for a young woman at the turn of the century, Flavie Michaud was successful and active. She began her career as a school teacher, then managed sporting camps with Charlie. Flavie did not have children of her own, but raised two.

At 91, she has a remarkable memory. Her eyesight is failing, and her station in life is that of a modest pensioner. Indeed, one wonders whether this elderly couple can last through another Fort Kent winter.

But Flavie is not a quitter. She has come through too much not to appreciate the December days of her life.

"My people were French, so I learned to speak English at school," the articulate lady said. "I went to Madawaska Training School. I graduated. My father was Fred Michaud. I used to know my grandpa, because he lived with us. I can't remember everything about him, but I do know he had worked on a farm and in the woods. I remember even now, he had a long beard, long and white. But I couldn't say where my grandfather was from. We never talked about that.

"I remember, I missed my father when I was a little girl. He would go into the woods to work for two or three months, and we'd miss him. It was hard on the mothers. There was enough food, because there had been a big garden in the summer, but mother would have to milk the cow, make the maple suger – they had the responsibility until father came home.

"I taught school after that. I think I was 19, teaching in Eagle Lake. I didn't go to college, you didn't have to. I taught and the youngsters learned. We didn't have that many qualified teachers up here, you know. The family was happy I was a teacher. I taught the little kids in a private home. I got $10 a week. But in the winter, I didn't teach. You see, the town was too poor to keep the school open in winter. They couldn't pay the teachers. So it was quiet in the winter – no school, not much transportation. The men were in the woods, so it was a lonely time.

"I didn't teach after I got married. I helped Charlie."

Flavie recalls the past with unusual ability, considering the turn of the century was eight decades ago. When she can't remember a specific, Henry might put it in. Henry knew Flavie many years ago, and despite the fact he's returned only in the past half dozen years to his native Fort Kent, he can put a word in about the past.

They exist in a small cottage walking distance from town. Their simple home is a resting spot after years in the woods or lake country. Flavie spent most of her time outdoors, particularly in the era when she and Charlie owned sporting camps. Charlie and Flavie Wilds ran the tourist facility for years, perhaps another example of the independence and ownership possibilities of those independent descendants of the Acadians.

"We called them Lake View Camps," recalled Flavie. "Now they're the Acadian Camps. We built some cottages near Eagle Lake, and guests came from New York, New Jersey, Pennsylvania to fish and hunt. I did the cooking and cleaning; Charlie took the people out to fish and hunt. But I did some hunting myself when I was young.

"Once I was surprised by a bear. I was shooting partridge alone one day – I had a 20-gauge shotgun with me. I parted the bushes to look for birds, and I surprised him. So there he was. About 10 - 15 feet away. He was startled but he didn't run away. He charged.

"Well, I was so scared I didn't know what to do. I guess I didn't think, I raised the gun and shot him right in the face. He stopped, then he ran away. I didn't watch – it happened so fast I really couldn't keep up with it. Well, I told Charlie, and he and his brother went to look for it. But they couldn't find him. That was my only bear."

Flavie's marriage to Charlie Wilds did not raise eyebrows, she said. It did not cause problems for a French girl to marry an Anglo or vice-versa in Fort Kent, even back in 1912. The elderly Aroostook native said she rarely saw problems between French and Anglos in her life.

"The French weren't discriminated against," she stated. "Remember, we were the majority. Most people were French, and they had lived here many years. We hadn't just come in to look for jobs – this was our home. I spoke French all my life; Charlie, he spoke it too. He didn't go to school, so he couldn't read or write when I met him. I'm proud – so proud because I taught Charlie Wilds to read and to write a little. He worked on it and I taught him. Most men in those days couldn't though; they went to work early in those days, 1900, 1905, 1910."

To hear Flavie Michaud Wilds Fitzgerald reflect on her life, one does not hear complaint or misgivings. Even the harsh reaches of northern Aroostook County have not tainted her voice with resignation. It has been a full life, at home with both French and English.

"It got cold and there was snow, seven to eight feet in the woods sometime, but we got by," she said. "We lived all right. What was hard was that there were no jobs there for awhile. Before the saw-mills came in, I think around 1900 or 1910, there was no work. I mean, you could farm or cut wood, but there was nothing where you could earn wages.

"Before the saw mills, it was just about all French up here. After that, everybody came. But that was okay. The French were the natives, it was our home."

# 10. *Father Clement Thibodeau: Seeing both sides*

Though Father Clement Thibodeau was transferred from Springvale, Maine to the remote reaches of Eagle Lake, Maine, three years ago, the cultural distance he travelled was not as lengthy as the 350 miles would imply.

Father Thibodeau, after 17 years in the mill town community of Sanford, was going home. He was returning to a rural community in northern Maine close to his childhood home in Caribou. In some ways, the wheel had come full circle.

Clement Thibodeau, a cultured priest who speaks both languages without accent, is one of the few clerics to have lived in "both" worlds of Franco-Americans. He knows of the rural, independent French high in the "wilderness" of Aroostook County, and he knows of the Francos who have toiled in the mills of southern Maine.

To have grown up on a family potato farm in the shadow of the "Madawaska settlement" was to know a life of self-employment, independence. It meant no tiers of supervisors directing one's work day, it meant plenty of home grown food on the hardwood harvest table. Such a life also meant cash money was a scarce commodity, that salaried jobs just were not to be had in the area.

And to have served in Springvale, a mill city itself and near mills of Biddeford and Saco, Maine, Somersworth and Rochester, New Hampshire, was to be exposed to an element of workers who knew cash wages but little independence. They stacked cotton cloth, they cut leather soles, at hours prescribed by a foreman or a yard boss.

"I think there was a big difference in the French of say, Caribou, and those of a mill area like Sanford-Springvale," Thibodeau said. "Their backgrounds are so different.

"The French in the mill towns were a more subservient people, with no dignity, no pride, none of the independence that we rural farmers had. Those who worked in the mills were drones in a mechanical society that was foreign to them. They were not less of people for it, but the contrast was there."

Father Thibodeau, 45, today lives in a solid, roomy rectory above St. Mary's Church in Eagle Lake. The town is among the most northerly in Maine, just 20 miles south of the St. John River. The entire sector, Eagle Lake, Fort Kent, Madawaska, St. Agatha, Frenchville, Van Buren, Caribou contains the highest percentage of French-speaking residents in New England. In these rural areas that once hosted the Acadian immigrants, the French are dominant. The percentage, for instance, of those whose mother tongue is French is quoted at 95.3 in Eagle Lake, 96.9 in Frenchville and 97.5 in Grand Isle. "Minority" status cannot be attributed to Franco-Americans in this region of New England.

The northern Maine community in which Clement was raised, Caribou, is marked by characteristics lacking in other New England areas, especially those of mill or factory emphasis. The French were first here. Dispersed from Acadia (Nova Scotia) in 1755, turned out again in favor of fleeing American Tories in 1775, French families of Acadian ancestry began arriving in the unpeopled Madawaska Territory in 1785. They remained. And if they didn't actually prosper in the harsh wilderness, at least they survived to spawn new generations in northern Aroostook. Thus while many French families migrated to existing communities, such as Woonsocket, Fall River, Lewiston, etc., the French in the Eagle Lake, Fort Kent, Madawaska, Van Buren, Caribou region were there first. They were natives.

Northern Aroostook communities are different, too, in the sense that much of the working force is independently employed. Unlike mill communities, tiny villages in the area offered few jobs. Men would farm, or they would log. Usually, they were involved in a combination of tasks to keep the family going. They faced, cold, harsh environments but they were their own bosses.

"My father and grandfather worked the same farm in Caribou," Thibodeau said. "The family was originally from Van Buren and research places the family there in the 1830's, so we've been part of the area. My father was Paul Thibodeau – my mother is Caroline

The Rev. Clement Thibodeau, during his tenure in Springvale, Maine. Father Thibodeau served the Quebecois in Springvale and an Acadian community in Eagle Lake, Maine, where he is presently located.

King. She wasn't French, though she learned the language and spoke it. In our culture, it was a prestigious thing to have an English-speaking wife.

"I was the second oldest. None of the others in the family has gone into the church. They don't even go to church. We were poor. Oh, we had food and clothing, but no cash money. There just wasn't that much to be made on the farm. I enjoyed the life on the farm – I thought I would continue in it."

Clement Thibodeau chose St. Francis College, Biddeford, Maine, after graduation from Caribou High (1954). St. Francis, run by Franciscan monks, was an influential institution as it turned out.

"My family was against my going into the priesthood," he recalled. "It was an old Acadian trait – anticlerical, distrust of the clergy, or anything, really. They were suspicious. My father said, 'I don't mind you being a priest but I don't want any scandals in our family.' You see, he was talking about sexual infidelity. The French who came to the area after the deportation got Quebec priests, and there were many cases where these priests were not upstanding men."

Clement Thibodeau, who chose St. Francis partly to avoid the "discriminatory" University of Maine campus, graduated from the

University of Montreal School of Theology in 1958. He was ordained the same year, and assigned to St. Ignatius in Springvale, a small town adjacent to Sanford. Much of his clerical work in the next 17 years involved counseling and teaching at Nasson College, a small coeducational liberal arts school that, in actuality, enrolls far more Wasps and Jews from New York and New Jersey than Franco-Americans from New England. Yet 17 years of even peripheral service to parish fosters feelings and reactions.

"I think that some parishioners in Springvale felt they were a minority people," he remarked. "But oppressed, no. I know that some of the intellectual elite of Franco-Americans in Maine raise the question of oppression, but these working people were not conscious of being oppressed. They were glad of the opportunities — they wanted to work.

"The French are hard workers – it seems that there is a Catholic equivalent to Calvinism. You know, there is the Calvinism of Protestants that stressed the work ethic. Well, the Jansenism of Ireland and France, was similar to this Puritanism. Perhaps the French have it. The harder you work, the more you merit. Eastern Catholics may have had the theological and religious imperative about working hard. It was more acceptable to God. It's well known how hard the French worked.

"The French in the mills worked hard. The French on the farms worked hard. The point that my experience has brought out, though, is that in the rural community they are independent, self-sufficient and self-determining. They don't work for others, which isn't the case at all in the mill towns and cities to the south."

Father Thibodeau's experiences in a mill community are over now. There are certainly no textile mills on the edge of Eagle Lake offering pay-by-the-hour positions. Instead there is a sturdy rectory upon a hill in Eagle Lake that serves a rural population. And that's fine with him, one who has known "both worlds."

"It's like going back to childhood. I chose to come back to northern Maine, and plan to immerse myself in the lives of the locals here."

# 11. Ernest Chasse:
# The product was potatoes

"I didn't start out as a potato farmer," recalls 69-year-old Ernest Chasse of Madawaska, Maine. "But the government was supporting the spud prices in 1943, so I got into it then. Oh, I had been exposed to the farming – in northern Aroostook just about everyone was. I remember seeing oxen pull potato wagons when I was 10 or 12. Then horses pulled them, and along about 1935 the tractors came, first with the steel wheel, then with the rubber tires two or three years later. It was in 1943 that I bought the farm from Dad, and got started. Prices were good because of the war.

"They were good years, those during the war. In 1943, for instance, you might be guaranteed $2 for 100 pounds – and you would be sure of selling what you raised. The price started slipping and by 1948, with government support, it was down to about $1.35 per hundred. After that, it was a tricky business. But it was good when I started."

Ernest Chasse lives on the St. John River. Canada (New Brunswick) is just across the water. He reflects with the perspective of one who succeeded in the ever-changing potato industry. For 34 years he farmed, and when none of his five boys wanted to follow him in spud farming, he sold 900 acres of his farmland to a long-time assistant.

In addition to being a veteran of the potato industry, Ernest Chasse is of French heritage. He did not speak English until he was 12, and throughout his years in the north country he used French as his primary tongue.

But being a French potato farmer in Aroostook County is not unique. On the contrary, it is like being a mill worker in Manchester, or a fisherman in Kennebunkport. In this northernmost section of

New England, up to 95 per cent of small Valley communities are French. Ernest Chasse is, in the end, a prototype of a local resident.

"There's a cross along the river at the end of our property," he said. "That marks the spot where the French landed after they had come up the river in 1785. They were Acadians, you know, and they were here because they were kicked out of Nova Scotia by the English. Finally they found that they could live in the St. John Valley, and up they came. My family was with that group, so it really goes back.

"Potatoes have been important here for as long as I remember. When I was a kid the children didn't have shoes. Oh, they'd wear a pair to school, but they'd take them off when they got back to work in the fields. There were many children helping with the harvest. School started after the potatoes came in, maybe in October. In the old days, kids were paid maybe 20 cents a barrel, and a barrel was a lot to fill. Today they're getting $20 a day. Kids were always a problem, too – they'd start play, or just sit on a basket and watch. Still, they were awfully helpful.

"Everything in the fields was in French; I was 12 before I could understand English. The French and potatoes went together – they're both fixtures in the Valley."

Chasse has left the potato business for semi-retirement. He and two sons are in the heavy machinery business that includes trucking, bulldozing, laying driveways and winter plowing. After buying his first farm in the 40's, he acquired over 1,000 acres before selling in the mid-70's. Today it appears he lives a good life.

His property that holds the seasoned farmhouse is on the banks of the historic St. John River. Married to the energetic Geraldine Chasse, he now takes an active interest in the heritage of his community, and its people. On the forefront of their property is the tiny museum created by the Madawaska Historical Society. Inside are many true relics, dating back hundreds of years. Most displays relate to old farm tools and household goods, but there are personal effects, too, from the early Acadian arrivals.

Chasse's past has been noteworthy enough to have been recorded in the Maine State Library in Augusta. Several dozen Franco-Americans from the Valley told their stories on tape several years ago during a government-funded project about people in Aroostook County. The French in Aroostook have lived a different life than those in New England mill cities, and Ernest Chasse is an example of one such challenging, yet successful, individual.

"Life was difficult in northern Maine, but I don't think anyone complained much about it," he stated. "During my first years, I was at the Fraser, but later I was in farming. That was in the growing months. In winter, it was different. We spent a lot of time in the warehouses, loading those 100 pound bags. Four men working all day could load a freight car, and then off it went. Some of the guys would sleep in the freight cars as they headed south. They had to keep stoves going inside the car, or the potatoes would be frozen solid, and spoiled.

"We also plowed snow. In the early days, a man would use his team of horses to pull big rollers. That would pack the snow down. I think the first year they started keeping the road from Caribou to Houlton open was 1931.

"I started snowplowing on a truck in about 1936. The town gave me $1.50 an hour to do it, but you had to buy your gas. It was something like 17 cents a gallon then, but still, that took away from your pay. And I'll tell you, some nights plowing those roads was murder. You couldn't see hardly anything, and the snow would be two or three feet deep, and much higher in drifts.

"Potatoes was the big job, though. Most people in the Valley had some connection with the potato business. At first you didn't have to be very smart with the support prices of the 40's but that changed when the supports changed later. And there were times when farmers weren't using the system right. It became known the farmers were taking money from the government for potatoes they couldn't sell anyway. It was a real mess."

Chasse's retirement from the potato trade has enabled him to spend time on more leisurely pursuits. He sometimes reflects on the French in the area.

"The Valley is French of course," he commented. "I wouldn't say there was any resentment to the English, though. They made it rough for the French when they banished them from Acadia, and those people were under great hardship to find their way up here, but I don't hear many bad words about the English. The English have had more education up here, and often were decision makers, but we let them be that way. 'Let Charlie do it' was our attitude.

"Things changed. We were always the majority up here, but now we might benefit by being recognized as a minority in other places. My son recently applied to law school. He was accepted at Suffolk in Boston, but he was trying for Northeastern. Well, he got a letter after he applied asking him to confirm that he was a Franco-American. They said that it would strengthen his application if he was from this 'minority.' So people are saying it helps to be French.

"After all these years, that seems so funny now."

# 12. Maurice Violette: "Let me tell you about the Acadians . . ."

When Arthur Maurice Violette goes out on the lecture circuit, he takes with him a childhood picture of himself and two brothers posing with an older sister. He points to the background of the picture, where another brother is barely discernible through a screened door.

"See, my brother didn't have his own pair of pants," Violette says. "He had to wait inside until someone came in to lend him a pair. Either that, or he was scared of the photographer. That's the way the French were – suspicious, wary of any stranger who came around because strangers could bring trouble."

Violette is a Franco-American whose roots are in Acadia, now Nova Scotia. While many people relate to the migration of the French-Canadians in terms of the province of Quebec, Violette is forceful in stressing the Acadian role in Maine. As the author of two histories of Franco-Americans in Maine, Violette is generally regarded as one of the relatively few experts in this field in the state.

His first text traced the history of the Calumet Club in Augusta, his home. His second, *The Franco-Americans*, told the tale of the Franco-American experience as it occurred in Augusta. His is among the most recent research on Franco-Americans, a subject about which there is a dearth of resources available in English.

A member of the marketing department at Central Maine Power Company after careers in the oil business and the Navy, Violette is a vocal resource on the subject of Franco-Americans.

"A lot of people talk about the Franco-Americans coming from Quebec but my family came from Acadia," he says. "My ancestors were in Louisbourg in Acadia, now Nova Scotia, when the English began their persecutions. The French Acadians wouldn't accept the

Maurice Violette, author in Augusta, Maine. One of his preoccupations is seeing to it that Acadian chapter of Franco-American history is brought out.

British, and the British responded by trying to wipe them out. They forced some to flee and actually carried others off to faraway territories – families were broken up. The Acadians ended up all over the place but eventually some began drifting back to what was called the Madawaska territory, in the upper St. John Valley: Madawaska, Fort Kent, Eagle Lake. The word went out that they could live there with their own customs without being bothered.

"My parents lived in Drummond Station, across the border in New Brunswick, near Van Buren. The name Van Buren came from the family name: Violette Brook, later Van Buren. When I was four months old, though, the family moved to Augusta, where my father heard there was a better job. That was in 1922.

"We were strong and hardy – I weighed 16 pounds at birth and a sister weighed 14 pounds. We didn't have much money, though. I have pictures from the old days that I take to lectures where you see that we didn't have store-bought clothes or sometimes even shoes. We were poor, like so many other French-Canadians.

"But 50 years later things were different. My brother Anthony was elected Mayor of Augusta in 1968. What a thing! In just 50 years, we had come that far. I try to give my children everything that I didn't have. Maybe I give them too much.

"People ask why there isn't more written about the past, books like I've done. Well, no one could write. The French-Canadians were illiterate, they had no time for schooling, they had to work. Histories were handed down from mouth to mouth, but there was never anyone to write them down. Even now, people have a lackadaisical approach to history. Some try to write about the Franco-Americans but you can't write the history if you haven't lived every minute of it.

"I got into research when I worked on a history of the Calumet Club. That's the French men's club in Augusta. It took a lot of research into church records to get the names of people. Then the priest called me to write a history of the St. Augustine Church. It took hours and hours, because nothing had been written down before. You might call it Acadian stubbornness that made me write *The Franco-Americans*. I said, 'They say I can't do it, so I'm going to.' But I won't touch another publication until I retire.

"It was an act of fate that I wrote the book. I believe that, it's my fatalist philosophy. During the Navy and afterward, there were at least four times when I could have been killed, should have been killed. I lived and I feel I was chosen to write this book on Francos. Franco-American heritage, and the use of language, is getting thinner, but that's good. Heritage will never disappear, it will change. Eventually, the language will be lost but there will be impressions, customs, feelings still there. That's okay with me. I believe in progress, not regressing. If losing the language is the way forward, that's good.

"The Franco-Americans have had such a life, such difficulty, that it's hard for people to imagine. Someday they will and when they do, they will be proud to be French and proud to be Americans."

# 13. Rita Violette Lippe: Keeping the family together

When Rita Violette Lippe was planning a family reunion of the Violette clan, she projected an attendance of 50.

No, her husband said, there'll be at least 75.

As it turned out, her reunion July 16, 1978 in Methuen, Mass., drew 350. Few family gatherings have exceeded such a number – but then, few amateur genealogists take their family as seriously as Rita Violette Lippe.

The 45-year-old Methuen resident has been pursuing her family past for five years. Like many Franco-Americans, she has become intrigued with where she came from, and who were her forebears. She has been aided by the fact that French-Canadian roots are among the best to trace, because of accurate church and municipal records; this wife and working mother has been helped, too, by numerous genealogical groups that have been born in recent years.

Mostly, though, the credit for her success in tracking down the past goes directly to her. Here is one tireless student of the past.

"I got interested in genealogy through my husband," Mrs. Lippe said. "Robert had been one of those fortunate youngsters to have lived most of his early years a few houses down the road from his grandparents. His grandfather told him when he was about eight that there was royalty in the family. It didn't mean much to Robert then, but in the mid-60's he began to search out the Lippe name.

"Well, he discovered that the Lippe family, though French, actually began as a German family that had come to Quebec years ago. The Lippe name had been influential in Germany, and the family had played a fairly significant role in German history. There had been royalty.

"My husband's findings began to interest me, and in 1973 I began to share his interests in genealogy. I started going to meetings in

Rita Violette Lippe, behind a stack of correspondence intended for the many Violettes scattered around New England. The Methuen, Mass., resident says the next reunion of the Violettes will be in 1981 in Van Buren, Maine.

Manchester, N. H., and this group eventually came to be known as the American-Canadian Genealogical Society of New Hampshire. We looked into his family some more, and found we could trace it all the way back to 1113 in Europe.

"Then I started working on the Violettes."

Though Mrs. Lippe has not yet been able to return as far back as the 12th century, she and those working with her have been able to draw a clear line back to 1751.

The finding is significant not only because it means good reunion parties in summertime. The calculations indicate that just about anyone in the Northeast who is named Violette comes from this ancestry. The genealogical search has meaning to any Violette, inasmuch as they all hail from this Acadian stock. In addition, such research sheds light on early origins of Aroostook County. The town of Van Buren, Maine, on the St. John River, was settled by the Violette family. When they entered the area they lived on what was called Violette Brook. This site was renamed, Violette Settlement, then Van Buren.

The story that Mrs. Violette, and her cousin in Augusta, Maine, writer of *The Franco-Americans*, Maurice Violette, have uncovered stretches back to one Charles Violet. Charles arrived from France in 1751 in Louisbourg, Nova Scotia (then known as Isle Royale, Acadia). He apparently was the only individual named Violet to emigrate from Villejesus (Aigre), France.

Though Charles, a Huguenot, reportedly returned to LaRochelle, France in 1759 following the fall of Louisbourg, his son Francois, was left in the new world. (Through a complicated settlement involving Charles' petition for bankruptcy, Francois was given over to "friends and neighbors" in Louisbourg through a Royal Court decree.) Thus Francois became the leading light of the Violette family (note new spelling of name.)

Francois eventually married an Acadian, and converted to Catholicism. He was, in fact, married three times, as he outlived his first two wives. These marital circumstances enabled him to sire 23 children, which is partly why the family has become so large.

In his quest to find a place far removed from the harassment of the

British, Francois and his clan traveled from Acadia up the St. John River, to Violette Brook. Francois died there in 1824, at the age of 84. The farmer-woodsman had gotten the family off to a prolific start.

Maurice Violette contends that the Violette name has never been found elsewhere in North America, and therefore all Violettes are related. Rita Violette Lippe suggests that others may have settled in the Virginia region. They agree, however, that those in New England are all descendants of the same family. If they were all alive today, there would be more than 150,000, Maurice asserts.

"The reunion that summer was really an amazing experience," said Mrs. Violette. "I had been corresponding with Violettes all over the country for several years. And there are a lot of Violettes. One relative of mine is a pilot, so every time he's in a new city, he goes to a phone book, gets names, and sends them to me. I've followed everything up, and believe me, there are a lot.

"I was surprised so many showed up. We had a priest from Rome, and there were Violettes of Ontario, Quebec and New Brunswick. We had family members from California, Arizona, Indiana, Illinois, West Virginia, Florida, New Hampshire, Maine, Connecticut, New York, Rhode Island, and from at least 25 cities in Massachusetts.

"It was really thrilling, to see all the group together. Most had never met – I didn't know Maurice a few years ago, and now we correspond frequently. Some weren't even Catholic, because I guess when that branch went to the Midwest years ago, there weren't any Catholic churches in the community they settled in.

"There are more Violettes who did not come, or we haven't been able to get in touch with. We'll try to get to them for our next one."

The reunion itself included registration, buffet, historical discussion and exhibits. It also featured a mass.

The following is the Homily at Mass by the Rev. Chanel Violette, S.M. It is indicative of the spirit of the day.

"Above me, you see the motto that has been chosen for this reunion; 'We Are One!' I would add just one word to that motto: 'We Are One Bunch!' Violettes, like bananas, come in bunches, or to be a little more artistic, Violettes come in bouquets. From where I stand, you make a very pretty picture of wall-to-wall Violettes!

After so many years, we finally meet, thanks to the indefatigable efforts of Mrs. Rita Violette Lippe.

"It is my great privilege today as a Violette to offer the Holy Sacrifice of the Mass. When I was ordained, Archbishop Cushing said to me, 'Receive the power to offer the sacrifice of the Mass for the living and for the dead.' I would like to offer this mass for all the living Violettes, for you who are here, and for the Violettes who cannot be here. I would also like to include the deceased Violettes, the latest of whom is Brother Patrick Violette, a Marist Coadjutor Brother, son of Laurent (a Basile) Violette from Van Buren, Maine, who died last Friday.

"This Mass is also said in Thanksgiving for all the graces with which God has blessed the Violettes. He has given us many good qualities, which have been enhanced by the excellent families into which the Violettes have married. No Violette has ever died in the electric chair, maybe because there was not electricity at the time. No Violette has ever been hanged, though I have known some who were at the end of their rope. No Violette has ever been murdered, though the desire has been expressed now and then that a few of us should be. All in all, we come from good stock and we should be thankful. It would be well here to enumerate some of the qualities that we have, so that we may appreciate our heritage more deeply. Noblesse oblige! If God has blessed us with good parents and grandparents, we are all the more obligated to see to it that we live up to those qualities we have inherited.

"First, a Violette is honest. Honesty has always been a characteristic of the Acadian nature. A Violette would never dream of taking something that did not belong to him. It is a good trait, especially in this age of continual rip-offs. Because we are honest, people trust us and our word is our bond.

"A Violette is sincere. Sincerity is a charming thing in a person and one that makes people attracted to us.

"A Violette is also sensitive. He feels things very deeply. He will take joy in a beautiful sunrise or sunset, and his heart will respond well to the beauty that surrounds him. This is a quality that make some of us dreamers, and some of us poets.

"Because we are sensitive, we are also compassionate, sensitive to others' needs. We can never turn away from someone in distress. Violettes have a good heart, and that quality alone makes up for some of the qualities that we may lack.

"Because of the above good points, most Violettes are very lovable, a rare breed of people who can charm their way into many lives.

"One thing that we have which is more precious than all the above qualities is our faith. It is solid and firm. We believe in God, we believe in our church and we believe in eternal life. We may fail in our love of God once in a while, because we are human, but never because we have ceased to believe.

"We have our defects, too. We are stubborn in our ideas, quick to anger at any real or apparent injustice, bossy and resentful. We do not raise our voice often, even in anger, but we do indulge in self-pity and infuriate people by our silent treatment. That is why I have heard my in-laws say, 'Those doggone Violettes! They are so charming that you can't live without them, and so infuriating that it is hard to live with them.'

"And this brings us finally to the Gospel of today's Mass, which tells us about the farmer that went out to sow his seed: 'Some fell on good soil and yielded grain at a hundred, or sixty, or thirty-fold.' And I as I look at you today, I thank God that the Violette seed has fallen on good soil and brought forth a beautiful harvest."

Certainly the reunion was a crowning point for a dedicated genealogist like Mrs. Lippe. Yet her interest in the field has not been life-long. She suggests it may be an unconscious attraction, but it has not always been one of her interests. The daughter of Albertine Baron Violette of Lawrence, and Joseph Violette of Drummond, N.B., near Van Buren, she was not a student of the past while attending St. Theresa's High School in Methuen (she graduated in 1951).

She went to French schools, but this did not create an immediate interest in the past; both her parents worked in Lawrence area mills, but such a background did not stimulate research. But in the mid-70's, heritage was an idea whose time had come.

"Maybe the French-Canadians in the past were guilty of not being proud," she commented. "In the old days, a lot of French were not educated, people tended to look down on them. And our French wasn't 'good French' like they teach in schools.

"But all of a sudden, there's been a new feeling, like 'Roots' or something. The French are saying 'that's our heritage, so let's be proud of it.'

"I was never involved. But now, it takes a lot of my time. I talk French with people again, I have French records, I belong to several genealogy clubs. I even left my job (bookkeeper, the Christian Formation Center) to allow more time.

"It's been important not only to me but to my parents. I've worked on my mother's genealogy — she was an orphan when she was four, so it wasn't easy. But we found an uncle of hers in Quebec City and an aunt in Edmunston. We went on a trip through the provinces in connection with her family and the ties were there right away. She learned about her mother, and about her family for the first time. We went to an aunt's and we talked. Finally the aunt pointed to a sewing machine in the corner of the room. She said, 'That was your mother's sewing machine.' Well, you see. My mother had not even been aware of her family but all of a sudden she was brought very close to it. Genealogy starts with names and dates, but then there's a new perspective.

"My father came down here from Drummond, New Brunswick, when he was 17 or 18. He'd never been back. Well, you'd have to know my father to appreciate this, but we asked him if he wanted to go on a vacation. He never goes anywhere. Anywhere. But we said we were going to New Brunswick, to see if there were any relatives there. He seemed surprised, he asked why, but he went.

"We got there, and even though he hadn't been there in 57 or 58 years, he started recognizing things. He knew a house, then a small store. Finally, he was directing us through backroads and telling us where so-and-so lived, or where an old family had worked. There were times when he was so overcome, so emotional, he couldn't say anything.

"And we'd stop at just about any house that said Violette, and knock on the door. Well, we were all related — it just took us awhile to figure out just how. All the families in the Valley were very warm, very open. It was wonderful, especially for my father. All of a sudden, it meant a great deal for him to meet Violettes."

# 14. Lucille Caron Lagasse: Tracing family roots

It took just a $6 genealogy course at the local YMCA to get Lucille Caron Lagasse started in the absorbing field of genealogy. And from that initial interest, she has gone on to co-found one of the largest societies in New England, the American-Canadian Genealogical Society of New Hampshire.

The group started in 1974, numbering just a handful of members. By 1976, it had a membership of 150, and two years in 1978 it counted a total of 500. By 1979, the Society had expanded to 1,000 members, with the likelihood of a great deal more recruits.

Either they offer a very stimulating course at the Manchester, N. H., Y, or Lucille is a dynamic founder and officer. Inquiry into the roots of this group indicates that the latter is true.

"One of my children was in college," recalled Lucille Caron Lagasse, a widow who lives in Goffstown, N. H., outside of Manchester. "One professor was doing genealogy, and my daughter said that 'hey, my mother does that.'

"Not many people were doing it then, this was about 13 years ago, and she said that maybe my mother could help. Well, the professor, Roger Lawrence of St. Anselm's College got in touch. I had never met a professor – but we started it.

"At first it didn't seem like there would be time to do all the work, but you make time. We grew, and as more people became interested, the society took a more active role.

"I speak in other cities and states now, helping to set up a genealogical society. More people are interested all the time now. We direct people, we get them started, we handle correspondence. It's a much bigger operation than we had ever planned."

Lucille Lagasse, with her leadership position in one of the region's most active genealogical orders, is a product of the mill society of Manchester. Her parents were both from Quebec, and each spent time with the Amoskeag. Though Mrs. Lagasse herself never worked in the mills, her background is one that was intertwined with that institution.

Her mother, Anna Ducasse Caron, was from the Gaspe Peninsula region. The family came south in 1903, first settling in Fall River, Mass., then moving on to Manchester. Young Anna Ducasse was working in the mills at the age of 12.

Her father, Athanase Lagasse, was brought down in 1910 by his family, natives of Skewanigan, northeast of Montreal. Sketchy stories traded at family reunions indicate that Athanase's father had worked on the Canadian Pacific Railroad.

Anna and Athanase met in the mills, where both were weavers. Coincidentally, both came from families that numbered 10 children. The two were married, and they themselves proceeded to have 10 children. Their vocations changed as the years went by: Anna spent most of her time at home, supervising the family, and Athanase became a carpenter.

"We lived in what they called the 'Flats' in Manchester," Lucille recalls. "It was a French area, and most worked in the mills. Some writers are saying that life was so hard, that the people complained, but I don't remember it that way. We did all right.

"The mills allotted large areas for workers to grow vegetables; they were at the end of town, and families raised a lot of their food for the winter. We raised chickens and even pigeons – squab under glass," she laughed. "There were no taxes then and things didn't cost much. We got along okay. My father built tenements and single family dwellings, which we lived in. He was very skilled, and used to help the millworkers with their building.

"Me? I never worked in the mills, but I went there all the time to take my sister her dinner. Actually, I was the first one in my family to graduate from high school – St. Marie, in 1940. Everyone was so proud, because it meant a lot for one of us to go all the way through."

Lucille Lagasse is 56, a widow since 1977 when her husband Armand, an executive whose own roots were in the mills, passed away. Environments, by definition, have an effect on behavior, and the background that produced Mrs. Lagasse has turned out a vibrant, intelligent and even controversial Franco-American.

For Lucille Lagasse is not one who just talks; she exclaims, she elaborates, she persuades. This enthusiastic woman doesn't sit in a chair; she stirs, she changes position, she remains poised ready to pounce with a statement or a response. Though the loss of her husband was a cruel blow, this is one woman who is not easily crippled.

Mrs. Lagasse is capable of the strongest of feelings: she is very careful to eat only the healthiest of foods ("drugs will kill you – by eating right, I was able to cure myself of leukemia") and is outspoken about her politics, which drift toward the right.

"They told Armand at the company that if I didn't quiet down, he'd be in trouble. I said that the day we have to shut our mouths, it's not America. Well, I was working for Reagan and he won every single ward. That was on Tuesday. On Thursday, Armand had lost his job."

Perhaps it is this tenacity, this fearlessness, that has enabled her to not only endure obstacles in life, but prevail with distinction.

A survivor of leukemia, a mother who lost three children, and now a widow, Lucille Lagasse, like other Franco-Americans, has been put to the test.

"I've never been one to stand still," she said. "Time takes care of everything, and every day is a new day for me.

"Even when my husband died, people said, oh, how you must cry at night. But I never cried at night. In the day, yes, but not at night. Then I would hold Armand's cross and dog tags, and think about when we would get close to stay warm, and it wasn't so bad.

"Our family never believed in complaining. Why, my father lost an eye when he was a carpenter. But if there was any resentment, I wasn't aware of it. Today you'd have law suits back and forth, but we've taken life as it was dealt to us. That's been our attitude."

Mrs. Lagasse, who now works in the state liquor store down the street to meet the steep mortgage on her house overlooking Lake Glen, has demonstrated her flexibility as she has become active in a variety of fields.

In 1970-71, she served as a representative in the New Hampshire House of Representatives, and was a Republican elected out of a Democrat stronghold at that. She served as a delegate to the state constitutional convention in 1974, and in recent years has served as a library trustee and a member of the Goffstown Budget Committee.

It is difficult to say where the bulk of her energy is directed, for there is so much energy involved. But certainly genealogy takes part of her time. She has completed the fan charts of her own family, and now helps others with theirs. She has ventured to Quebec and even France; the lively official has traveled to numerous New England communities to lecture and instruct. She was once the talk of the family for graduating from high school. Now Mrs. Lagasse is a college professor, teaching at St. Anselm's and Merrimack Colleges. What began as a casual investigation into family roots has developed into a role of significant proportions.

"When I started genealogy 13 years ago, I did it when I could find time," said Mrs. Lagasse, who has traced her ancestry back to 1630. "The children would go to bed, and I'd plan to get to my correspondence between 9 and 11.

"Then we got more active, and for awhile my home served as a library for the society. People would come by, we'd direct them, and they'd use the materials that we had.

"The genealogy has given us a lot. I remember we went to Canada to look up a great aunt. We arrived there and called, and her daughter said that they were home but were going out. We said we'd make it the following day. But no, the daughter said that wouldn't be good. Now the relative we wanted to see was 85, so we thought perhaps she hadn't been feeling well. We asked if Sunday would be better. When she said no to that, we didn't know what to think, because we had come all the way from New Hampshire.

"Well, the phone rang 20 minutes later, and the daughter said we could come over for a few minutes. When we did, we saw that she and her husband, who was about 92, were scared, they didn't know what to expect because we were from America. They asked if we wanted a beer, and somehow that broke the tension. We started talking, and when they realized we talked French, and had such an interest in our Canadian family, they were very warm. In fact, we got to talking about the family, and about the ties, and we were crying with the closeness we felt. We stayed until 3 a. m.

"Those who stayed in Canada, I might add, never regretted not coming down like so many of their friends and family. And I have my own theory on that, too. The French in Canada grew with the land – they are physically big people, the men are over six feet tall. Those who came to New England and worked in the mills, they're short.

"Another time, when we were in Canada, we took my mother-in-law to the area where she grew up. We were there to trace heritage, and we went to her old church. Now she was 85 years old, and hadn't been back for 30 years. She certainly hadn't seen some of her neighborhood friends since she was 16. But after church, an old man came up and asked, 'Aren't you Eugenie Charest? I'm your neighbor so-and-so Belanger.' Well, they hadn't seen each other since school days, and didn't the old men enjoy seeing her again. They said she looked great, and she was glowing all the time just like a 16-year-old. So genealogy isn't just writing letters and drawing charts.

"I've been to France, too, to trace records. I went to Larochelle, France, in 1977 for about 10 days. The French-Canadians have very good records in churches and city halls, probably second only to the Mormons, and they say that the records in France aren't as good. In tracing Armand's ancestry, though, I found plenty of records. They just weren't compiled. You'd go to a church or municipal hall, and they'd hand you a shoebox full of little papers and notes, and you'd have to go through them yourself, reconstruct, sift through to find something about your family. If you have the time, you can make progress."

Lucille Lagasse has strong feelings on many subjects. Two came to the forefront during a lengthy interview in her Goffstown home. One is that the French were not exploited in the mills. They were not unhappy despite conditions that today appear to have bordered on poverty.

"I've had speakers at my meetings talk about the terrible times," she remarked. "After they talk, I point out the good things, and how valuable parts of their discussion were. But, and I have one case in mind, I'll tell them I disagree with them on the 'downtrodden French.'

"The French did better in New England than they were doing on the farms back in Quebec. It was work in the mills, but it was harder, backbreaking labor on the farm. Some writers now are talking about the discontent and hard times of the French-Canadians here, but I disagree. The French were satisfied because things were better."

Another leaning that this forceful Franco-American possesses is toward the return to the roots. She is adamant in discounting the effect of the television blockbuster ("Roots," I & II). It is, rather, the soul that will determine a person's inclination to explore one's past.

"It's hard to explain exactly what kind of people trace their roots," she stated. "It's not one group, not necessarily those interested in history, or on the other hand, those who worked all their lives in the mills. It's in the soul, you just want to do it. I've started literally hundreds of people, clipping out a family obituary, tracing several generations, then sending it to a friend as a starter. But not everyone continues; it takes that certain something.

"Oh, free time is important – you don't get so many young people looking, because they have to work. But middle-aged or older Francos who do have time get involved. You learn about history, you learn about civilization. Genealogy isn't just charts.

"I'm interested in more things, of course – my mother told me there was no end to education. I don't even read some books about Franco-Americans because I have so many other things to read, so much to study. But the study has been so important to me and my family.

"Just think, out of a $6 course came one of the greatest avenues that's ever been open to me."

# 15. Ronald Couturier: Living the Franco life in Lewiston, Maine

Ronald Couturier is a French teacher at Lewiston High School who has traced his heritage back through nine generations, mostly in the province of Quebec. His next task will be to visit France to continue his task of digging for the roots of the family tree.

Raised in a tenement in Lewiston, Couturier is the son of a shoe shop worker who later became a carpenter.

Couturier grew up in a bilingual home here and spoke French long before he learned English. He attended St. Peter's parochial school and like many of his peers, went on to St. Dominic High School, transferring to Lewiston High School for his senior year to take advantage of their French department. When he graduated from the University of Maine, Portland-Gorham in 1966, he was the first generation of his family to have achieved such an education.

Few Franco-Americans live their heritage as fully as Couturier. He is a teacher of the language by profession and he is a tracer of his past by avocation.

"I didn't start looking into my family history until several years ago," says Couturier. "I had always had an interest, but when I received a brochure in the mail from a company that traced coats of arms, I got started in it. The more I discovered, the more I wanted to know. It takes work, but it's been very meaningful."

Couturier has traced his family from its brief time in Maine through numerous generations in Quebec. He has found that one Pierre Aucouturier was married in 1736, evidently the first of his clan in Canada. In 1825 Canadian officials seemed to have shortened the name to Couturier.

It was difficult to learn much about his ancestors because birth, marriage and church documents rarely included details about the individuals. He has, however, been able to determine that since the mid-19th Century, most were farmers.

"The farther back you go, the harder it gets," he says. "Many records have been lost or burned. The documents you do find are often limited to names and dates. In two years I've traced the family through Canada. I'll now be looking into the origins in France – I already know that we came from the Lyon region. It's time-consuming but I do it because I'm interested in where we came from, how the family evolved."

As a teacher at Lewiston High, Couturier sees much of the youth of the city. Many of his students are of French-Canadian heritage, but few, he says, now speak the language.

"The young people don't speak the language like they used to even when I was in school," says Couturier, who graduated from Lewiston High in 1962. "It's a fact. What are you going to say? When I was a boy we spoke French at home and French in the neighborhood among friends. Not now. It used to be that parents would speak French.

"The language is falling out of use, and I think that's sad. Knowing two languages, any two languages, is a valuable thing."

With the exception of several years of schooling, Ronald Couturier has spent all his years in Lewiston. Among his milestones was a term as alderman at the time his brother, Robert L. Couturier, was serving as the nation's youngest mayor.

His has been a life lived fully as a Franco-American, both on the job and at home. He considers himself, he says, "a Franco-American but also an American. I live two cultures, but that doesn't mean I'm different than any other American."

Since this story was written, Ronald Couturier has continued his search. He writes: "In July, 1978, my wife and I set out for France . . we were most fortunate to peruse original documents dating back to the 1600's . . We learned that my ancestors living in France in the 1600's and 1700's owned a grain mill which is still standing; they had servants; some relatives made wooden shoes. Their church is still there. We had lunch with a family in the village and during lunch I discovered that one of their relatives married one of mine in 1736."

# 16. Annie Chasse Boucher: The girl who wrote the letters

"In my neighborhood in Somersworth, N. H., I was the girl who wrote letters," 71-year-old Annie Curran Chasse Boucher recalls. "A lot of the families couldn't read or write, so they asked me to. I was about 11 or 12 when I started – I was writing for people until I was at least 15. Most of the letters were from families writing back to their relatives in Quebec, but I remember I wrote love letters for one young man. That was exciting.

"I remember one family I wrote for sent back simple news about their new life in Somersworth. They'd say they had a big yard, a cow, a pig, a well, basic things like that. There would be times the well ran dry, so that was big news.

"They told about jobs, about working in the mills. Generally, they said the work was good – they were paid in cash and it was steady work. They liked to visit, too, and wrote about their plans. But they didn't want to stay in Canada. I don't remember anyone wanting to go back. Look at my mother's family – they came from the Gaspe area, and there was no work. Not many returned for good.

"The love letters came from a young man about 22 or 23. He was sort of sickly, and his parents had been able to buy a small store, where he worked. He was in Somersworth – the girl he wrote, who must have been about 19, was in Manchester. She worked in the mill there.

"Well, this young man would tell her he loved her, that he missed her, and things like that. He was very serious about it, you know, and while he was telling me to write these things I was dying to hear more. I was 15, and thought I was so smart. I wasn't embarrassed – I wanted to hear more. He never felt funny about telling me these things; he gave me a quarter after I would finish the letter. But you know, I don't think he married her. I think he ended up with a girl who came to Somersworth from Canada.

"I remember another family, too. They had a son working in Manchester. In the winter, when I was walking to school, I would hear a tap at the window of the house I was passing. The woman would motion to me, and that would mean they had received a letter. So I would go in and read the son's letter for them. They didn't pay me – I was happy to do it. It meant a lot to them."

Mrs. Boucher lives in Rochester, N. H., with her second husband, but her memories revolve around her native Somersworth. Her first husband Noel Chasse, a barber and deputy sheriff, passed away in 1963. For five years she worked in the shoeshops of Somersworth, and only in recent years has she moved to Rochester.

Like the young Annie Curran who would read and write for the French-Canadians who could not, Mrs. Boucher remains strong of heart. Had she been born in this era, she likely would have been an independent professional career woman of great achievement: she was an officer in a half-dozen community organizations, while having what appeared to be the singing potential of an opera star. She assumed the role of wife and mother in deference to her husband, though, and was one of the most popular and accomplished home-makers in the community.

Young Annie Curran believed that if you were "polite, humbled and smiled," one would get everything that was desired. It would be difficult to assess the success of this outlook, but it would be accurate to say that it served Annie well through her years in the mill community in eastern New Hampshire. Descended from Irish and French ancestors, she has lived a full and fruitful life.

"My grandfather on my father's side was Irish – Patrick Curran. My grandmother, Adele Lavertue, was French. When they met, he didn't speak French and she didn't speak English. But they had 14 children, so they were a success, eh?

"I think my grandfather came over from Ireland during the potato famine, about 1856. Parents were dying there in those days, and the priests in Ireland were appealing to the priests in North America to take in some of the orphans. My grandfather was brought up by the French, but they didn't change his name. They could have.

"My grandfather was a blacksmith; my grandmother raised the

family. They were from St. Romuald in Quebec Province, and came down in 1882.

"My grandparents on the other side were from the Gaspe region – they came down the same year. My grandfather, Paul Thivierge, was a widower. He had seven children, and when he remarried, he married Arthimise Michaud, who was much younger. She was two years younger than his oldest daughter.

"He worked in the woods, rolling logs in the winter. In the summer he was a fisherman, selling his catch of salmon and cod. He lived a hard life. He died of something they didn't know much about then: appendicitis. They called it twisted intestines then. It was logging season and he was away from home, but they got him back. But they didn't know enough about it, so he died there.

"My parents are Henry Curran and Marie Thivierge. They had nine children, but four died, one of appendicitis, one of meningitis, one was premature, and I think the fourth had the fever. My mother watched as the fourth died while she was carrying me, and people say she cried the whole time she carried me.

"Both my parents worked in the mills. My father was a mechanic in the woolen mill – my mother was a weaver. She worked for 20 years while the kids were growing up. My grandmother stayed with us, and we loved her. Our family was close to the mills – my parents, my brother, my sister, they all worked there. When we were kids, we thought the mill belonged to us.

"I started school at St. Martin's Academy in 1914 when I was six. I graduated from grammar school in 1923, and the family was so proud. 'She graduated from eighth grade,' they said. I wanted to become a nurse but that didn't work out. One of my sisters asked why I shouldn't work in the mills like they were doing.

"I didn't go into the mills. Because my grandmother wasn't feeling well, I stayed home with her. I watched some of my friends start high school, and I wished I could be with them. But someone had to help grandmother.

"I did eventually get work. I started as a salesgirl in a dry goods store. I worked for two old maids – Misses Laverdiere and Plante.

I sold dresses to the women who came in, and the idea was not to let people out without them buying something.

"I was there about three years, until I was 17. The man I was dating was 10 years older, and he didn't want to wait any longer, so we got married. I had my first child 10 months and three weeks after we were married. I didn't go back to work."

If Annie Chasse did not return to a salaried position, she didn't vegetate inside the house. For the following four decades she dedicated herself to bearing three children, and acting as a leader in the Somersworth community. Recalling the past one spring morning in the Somersworth summer home of her son, Dr. Paul P. Chasse, a professor and nationally recognized authority on Franco-Americans at Rhode Island College, Mrs. Chasse recalled many of her activities through the years.

"In politics, I first started to seek voters to come to vote, especially within the Franco community. Then, I became ward clerk for three years, and became a member of the city committee whose duty it was to advise the mayor and provide him a slate of candidates for positions before he made his recommendations to the council, which then voted on the appointments. Then, I was elected to be one of the supervisors for 11 years, which gave me 16 years of this work.

"For my church, I was vice-president of the Saint Martin's Alumni (called la reunion des Anciens in French) for four years. And I was secretary-treasurer of Saint-Anne's Sodality for 18 years. I was also vice-president of the National Council of Catholic Women of the Strafford County Dreary for four years.

"In education, I was a member of the University Extension (UNH) for 20 years, and chairman for four of these years."

Annie's husband, Noel Chasse, was a barber, and a good one, townspeople say. He cut the hair of Somersworth's leading citizens, and when he had to bolt out of the shop to fight a nearby fire (he was assistant fire chief), it's said the patrons would simply wait until he returned.

The position of barber yielded an adequate wage, which was later supplemented by mill earnings of the oldest children. Still, the family had its difficult days, especially during the Depression.

"We had less during those hard years," Annie recalled. "Money was scarce, so wives would cut the husband's hair. And the fathers would cut that of the children. We were hoping we wouldn't have to shut the barbershop — somehow we made it through."

While managing to provide for his family, Noel Chasse was a minor cog in community activity. For eight years he was assistant fire chief; for four years he was chairman of his ward. Noel was also president of the Saint Jean Baptiste in Somersworth, served as a bail commissioner, and for 16 years was a deputy sheriff.

When he passed away suddenly in 1963, Annie Chasse wasn't sure she would be able to cope with the loss. But a job in the shoeshop sustained her for five years, and marriage to Arthur Boucher, nine years her senior, has been another positive force.

Alert and vivacious, Mrs. Boucher today revels in stories of days gone by. In one breath she relates how Arthur Boucher attempted to relocate from Quebec to Ontario.

"He was 20 then, and got in a freight train to Ontario. There he was, with his two horses and a plow in the middle of a freight car. But he was lucky, because without the horses he might have froze. It was winter, and he stayed warm from the body heat of the animals. He didn't stay in Ontario, though, and went eventually to work in the mills in Newmarket, N. H. He's worked in mills in New Hampshire, Massachusetts, Vermont and Rhode Island."

In another burst of memory, she'll recall a pilgrimage to Quebec.

"We were in a church, and a woman came in looking tired and hungry. We offered to help this poor woman, and later found out she was actually a wealthy hotel owner. She just had walked 27 miles, like she did every year, as part of a personal sacrifice on this pilgrimage. And there was this colored man in the church who we talked with. He questioned me as to why I would talk to him, a Negro. I said I talk to anyone, color does not matter. He smiled, and was very kind. We later found out he had been the president of Haiti, and he kept up a correspondence with me for long after."

Though in her senior years, Annie Curran Chasse Boucher has not stopped glowing. Memories provide meaningful moments as the December days dawn.

"I've lived in a French community but I'm part Irish, too," she commented. "There were three other families like that in Somersworth, that is, with Irish and French blood.

"My father, Henry Curran, spoke French. Sometimes he went to the Irish church, though when he got older he came with us to the French church. He rarely said anything about the family mix – only when he had had a nip, and he'd ask why we didn't speak American. My last name was Irish, but I was as French as anyone. I felt I was wanted by the Irish, and felt I was wanted by the French as much, if not more.

"There wasn't any discrimination that I could see. It always seemed that if you got there, then you had worked for it. You had to work. . I will say that some people, some Irish, used pull. The French were proud, they didn't want to thank anyone for what they got. The Irish, maybe they used other means sometime.

"Discrimination at the mill? I don't know. The foremen were hard, but sometimes they were French foremen."

In the late afternoons now, Annie often reads her newspaper by the fading sunlight. She will be sitting quietly when Arthur comes by. Arthur cannot read very well and Annie therefore must read several paragraphs, mentally digest them, and relate them to Arthur. "He can't read, but he wants to know," she smiled wistfully. "So this is the way we read the papers."

It's really a very touching scene.

# 17. The Mondors: Thankful for 17 children

One of the aspects of French-Canadian heritage that historians have marveled at is the high birth rate that was recorded in Canada, and later, in New England. The French took their Catholicism seriously, and spawned many offspring. Families with 12 or 14 children were not uncommon as the great migration to New England was about to begin; to sire at least a half-dozen was not just commonplace – it was anticipated!

French families, both in Quebec and Acadia, thought in terms of practicality as well as religious considerations when "planning" large households. Farm work needed many hands for completion; later an extra paycheck in the mill, modest as it was, helped make ends meet.

The first awareness of the prolific ways of the French was in the late 19th century. A dynamic increase in the number of French in Canada was observed between the Conquest in 1759, and the Migration, roughly a century later. The rapid growth of population on the small farms of Quebec was one of the major reasons the habitants moved to new communities to the south.

The American Antiquarian Society reviewed the situation as early as 1891. The report was included under the general heading of "The French-Canadians in New England." It sought some frame of reference for the increase of French-Canadians that were flooding the New England mill cities.

The report pointed out that at the time of the conquest, the Canadian population was about 60,000. By 1881, according to the census, the provinces of Quebec and Ontario numbered 1,176,563.

Breaking down the population race in several eastern townships of Quebec, it forwarded the following statistics: "In 1831, the eastern townships contained 37,964 Protestants (English) and about 3,000 French Canadians. In 1844, the figures were 48,398 British and 14,622 French; in 1861, 76,317 British and 60,199 French; in 1871, 72,591 British and now 83,705 French."

In 1881, a year that was very much in the period of habitants leaving Quebec, the French nevertheless outnumbered their English counterparts 109,042 to 77,805 in the townships studied.

It's doubtful the habitants were consciously trying to outnumber their Protestant rivals. But their inclination to reproduce has challenged the English in numbers, if not on the battlefield.

Their descendants, the Franco-Americans, continued high birth rates for several generations, but the trend today is quite the opposite. Better educated Francos are more independent of the church's teachings and no longer seek the earnings of their children. Smaller families seem more appropriate, and the days when a mother would produce more than 10 youngsters are gone. It is rare to find young women today who are considering more than three.

But there are bridges to the past – there are families of size despite the new trend. Occasionally a couple's enthusiasm for children stretches back into the 19th century. Their birth rate defies the Zero Population Growth advocates, underlining instead the simple attitudes that must have characterized past generations of the French.

You can tell one of these "old world" New England homes by the 10 pairs of Levi's on the clothesline; you know you've arrived because there are four cars and two dozen bicycles surrounding the roomy, old-fashioned dwellings. Dirt paths may criss-cross across the lawn – badly worn wooden steps may greet a visitor in place of a plastic welcome mat. They are the evidence of numbers.

Robert and Alice Lecharite Mondor of Saco, Maine, have full clotheslines and a lot full of vehicles. They also have 17 children.

School teachers know the family well now, because they have educated the entire flock. The youngest, 10, is an indication that the procession has not ended.

Neighbors in the quiet residential section are familiar with the Mondors, because each child has canvassed the area selling cookies, or magazine subscriptions, or chances.

Robert and Alice Mondor, citizens of Saco, Maine, and parents of 17 children. "The church didn't push us to have children," Mrs. Mondor says. "It's my belief it was God's will."

Certainly those in the mills of Biddeford and Saco know the Mondors. Robert Mondor worked in the mills for almost 30 years. And at the conclusion of his shift would head for his second full-time job: grave digger. He has been viewed as not only the man who sired 17 children, but the guy who had to work 16 hours a day to support them.

But work they did, Robert and Alice Mondor.

"I was born in St. Paul Chester," said Mrs. Mondor, 53. "My father was an American, though – he went to St. Johnsbury in Vermont to work, and he came back and forth. I had a choice of being a Canadian or an American citizen when I turned 21. I chose American.

"I had to work when I was young. I went to the local school through the sixth grade, and I wanted to go to Sherbrooke to study to be a teacher. But it cost $300 and I didn't have $300. So I worked.

"I got a job as a housecleaner. I got $5 every two weeks. It wasn't much money but there was no work in the area. So when I was 16, my sister and I came to Biddeford to work. They were making $13 a week in some places – that was good money, so in 1942 we came here."

Robert Mondor is of French descent, by way of American mill towns. His mother worked in Lawrence, Mass., his father in Saco, Maine. Young Robert Mondor reached his sophomore year at Thornton Academy before dropping out to join the Navy. Discharged in 1946, he went into the mills.

"I went to work in the York Mills when I came back – it was the Bates Mill then, though. I was an oiler – I went around the mill and oiled the different machines. A year later (1947) I started working at the Pepperell. I was in the finishing department – I put the blankets into the boxes to be shipped out.

"I was making about $42 a week, but I always had another job. When I was married I dug ditches up at St. Mary's Cemetery, in Biddeford. I got 50 cents an hour. But I remember, I hit Father Driscoll for a raise. So I think I was earning a dollar an hour. It was hard work – but I had to work."

The Mondors had 11 boys and six girls. One child died at the age of four days. So considering that the youngest Mondor is 10, the oldest 33, it does appear the children came fast and furiously. Many Franco-Americans have stories of large families in past generations, but few have produced 17 in the past few decades.

Several of the children have graduated from college, paying their expenses as they went. Others have found attractive positions in business or the armed forces outside of the state. Though most have worked part-time or summers in the mills, the Mondor children have not opted for careers in the crumbling textile trade. Perhaps they have seen the toll it takes on one who spends his working life there.

Worth noting about the children, too, is the warmth they feel for their parents. Cruising through the kitchen in mid-afternoon, a 16-year-old son puts his arm affectionately around his father and then asks him with a smile for a cigarette, which he receives. A 27-year-old daughter takes time off from work to be present during an interview with a non-Franco. She shows no sign of embarrassment when they don't understand a question, or answer in heavily accented English. There's just respect – and a good deal of love as she listens to the story of their life together once again.

Pictures of their children, whom they shyly decline to name out of concern for their privacy, are present in the living room. One might say photographs "dot" a wall, but in the Mondors' case, they blanket it. The children are smiling; the inscriptions to their parents, loving.

Family pictures are the main decor of the house; that and religious artifacts, such as crosses, pictures and words of Christ. This is a large, and very Catholic household.

"We just took things as they came," said Mrs. Mondor, who left the mill after the children started coming. "There wasn't the birth control of today. The church didn't push us to have children, though. To say that isn't true. It's my belief that it was God's will . . . if that's what happens, then that's what happened. If I can have children, if I can care for them, then I'll have the children. We'll sacrifice for our children.

"I worked hard for my family over the years," said Robert Mondor, who likely could have pursued just one job had the family been smaller. "We had good children, we loved the children. It was a thing that happened; if there was a birth, there was a birth. We took it as it came, it was God's will.

"The work – I had to work. I worked 13 years at the Pepperell, from 1947 to 1960, then from 1960 to now at Saco Tannery. I dug graves, painted houses, did odd jobs on the side. I always had another job. At Pepperell it wasn't hard – you worked at your own rate, and they respected a man for putting in a full day. Maurice Roux, Francis Spencer, Bernard Brady, Sr. they were men who respected a worker. And you know, I only lost four hours of work at the Pepperell in 12 years. I worked for the family – my wife didn't work after the children were born.

"What job did I like best? I'll tell you. I liked my job in the Navy best. I was a cook. I had control over everybody – if they didn't take orders from me, they didn't eat."

The Mondors, who look older than their 53 years, flirt often for a couple married 33 years. Robert howls when he divulges for the first time that in 1942 he bet a friend $5 that he could get a date with Alice. She, a bit later, cajoles him for forgetting how much he earned his first year in the mills. "You made more than $18 a week," she prodded him. "You were making a lot – $42 a week."

There is no joking involved when they discuss their children, though. Both were from fairly small families – each one of five. With 17 offspring, they have been a visible symbol of the old French ways. And they're happy.

"I want you to say that I don't regret the children at all," Alice Mondor stated. "I'd do it again – the children have been good children, good to us."

"Yep, don't regret it at all," Robert Mondor echoes. "What was to be was to be. There are no regrets."

# 18. Gilbert Boucher: A Franco-American mayor fights back

"The rich are on the run at Biddeford Pool."

That's the way a newspaper article described a set of circumstances in Biddeford, Maine, in 1973. A Franco-American mayor, Gilbert R. Boucher, was dissatisfied with the manner in which a seven acre beach property on the ocean outside of the mill city of Biddeford was being administered. It was owned by the wealthy Pool Beach Association. Though the law stated that the local citizenry had a right-of-way to the beach, the haughty, out-of-state summer residents were not permitting the local workers and their families to enter the area.

Therefore, Mayor Gilbert R. Boucher suddenly announced at a city council meeting that the city was "taking" the property by eminent domain.

The action was surprising. But there was Boucher, a self-educated contractor, saying that it's about time the mill workers get to enjoy summer recreation on their own seashore.

Franco-Americans have been as political as the next ethnic group, to be sure. Their squabbles and backbiting, as well as their election campaigns and reform packages, are well documented. But they have not been known as a group to right the wrongs of the past. Gil Boucher, therefore, was an exception. The mayor of Biddeford from 1969 to 1973, he was a controversial, maverick politician. Yet it's likely he'll be remembered in that mill community. His reclamation of prime beachfront acreage in what served as a private enclave for those from Boston to Baltimore was a major, if controversial, accomplishment.

Once he started, the 45-year-old Democrat didn't stop. He said he had history on his side.

Gilbert R. Boucher, former mayor of Biddeford, Maine. During his administration, he "took" beachfront acreage from a private beach association so the children and grandchildren of millworkers would have a place to enjoy.

"My parents were both from Quebec," said Boucher. "They were from St. Ferdinand in Quebec, where my father was a sheet metal worker. But there are just so many sheet metal jobs in a small town, so they came to the U. S. about 55 years ago looking for work. His first stop was Fall River, then Fitchburg and Amesbury. I was born in Fitchburg, but we came to Biddeford when I was about eight.

"I grew up as a Franco-American. I spoke French first. There was a French elementary school in Amesbury with French spoken – I went there but didn't learn much French grammar. When I got to St. Andre's School in Biddeford, I didn't know much French grammar – but the nuns will teach you that, believe me.

"My father, Emile Boucher was one of 17 children, I think 13 or 14 lived. My mother, Adelia Huot, was in a family of about 10 or 11 children. But when my parents married and left, their parents didn't protest. Today we're more selfish, we want our children to live near us. But it was a mode of life then. If there was a better life by moving, then you moved.

"My parents didn't have much education in Quebec. Their parents were farmers. My father had about two weeks of schooling, and my mother, about the same. They had good sense, though. And they had courage. They left Quebec with two small children, heading into a country where they didn't speak the language, didn't have a job. They stayed in French neighborhoods, though, and made a life.

"There was work in New England. My father got sheet metal work. He followed the jobs, because Ford Motor Company had different divisions. He followed the work, from Fall River, to Fitchburg, to Amesbury. Then the crash came, and the Depression meant a loss of jobs.

"He had to give up sheet metal work, because there wasn't any. He did hear of mill work in Biddeford, so the family came up. My father fell from being a skilled sheet metal man to a mill worker – hey, what a step down that was for him. He did it, though. In later years, he got a job at the Bates mill in sheet metal, and kept it until his retirement.

"My parents weren't wealthy but they were proud. You were as good as the next guy. And the French had a respect for private property. If a neighbor came over to my father and said we weren't to be on his lawn, hey, we didn't go there. We respected the property of others.

"The move to get the beach property at Biddeford Pool was against my upbringing, against the nature of the French. The French have been shy. They don't go out and make trouble. But here was this beautiful land at the beach. The city had a right-of-way to the water, but if the people of Biddeford tried to use it, they'd be chased off by the summer people. I didn't see how the injustice could continue.

"I started the move to get the land, and it was an outgrowth of my French background. Our ancestors worked hard in the mills, for years going in every day and every week. But when they wanted to come down to their own beachfront, it was off-limits. The summer people didn't want the French there, they just wanted their own.

"And how could the mill people ever use the oceanfront? Our ancestors never had a chance to enjoy it – they couldn't afford to buy it, and they weren't wanted there. I remembered that.

"Now I don't think I would have taken the land if it had belonged to an individual. That was certainly against what we learned, to take another's belongings. But it was an association, and even then, they seemed to be selling a little more ocean property each year. If we didn't take it, I'm sure it would eventually have been sold to private, wealthy people for houses.

"After the law suit got started, and the courts showed that we did have the right to take it by eminent domain, I got more determined to follow through. The Beach Association representatives looked down their noses at us, they acted like they didn't want any part of us.

"About halfway through, when the association realized we weren't just going to go away, they offered a plan. They said that we could use the beach; but we couldn't enter the beachhouse to use the facilities. Now, you can be making $20 or $20 million, but you still have to use a bathroom. You can have $10 or $10 million, but you still have to change. And they're saying we can walk onto the beach but we have to stay away from the beachhouse. That was insulting. That I wouldn't say to anyone.

"I think that if those people (the Pool Beach Association members) could have closed the sun to us (Biddeford residents), they'd do it. That's how they felt about us. But we were right. Even people who didn't think we should do that then have told me since they're happy we went ahead.

"And look, some officials are talking about changing the ocean access line from high tide to the low tide mark. If that happens, how could people who didn't own land use a beach. If they didn't have a beach of their own, they couldn't get to the water."

Despite the action to "reclaim" oceanfront, or perhaps because of it, Boucher was defeated by fellow Democrat Babe Dutremble. He has since run (1976) for the Democratic nomination for Congress, and lost that too.

Defeat followed him out of office, as did colorful anecdotes about his tenure: the time he not only fired his economic adviser, but changed the locks on the man's doors; his support of Republican Margaret Chase Smith over party candidate William Hathaway in the 1972 Senate election; his trip to Europe and Russia on city money, to "learn how the elderly are treated in other countries."

But one achievement will likely stand out about his administration. When the "amusing" asides of his tenure are forgotten, and petty political battles put into the past, one result will still remain. The city of Biddeford, indeed the public, will have an ocean beach. As available land on New England's coast diminishes each year, mill workers of Biddeford at least will have some measure of their own perimeter to enjoy.

"It was against my upbringing," Boucher commented. "The French just aren't like that. But we had the right of way that they weren't letting us use it.

"Hey, I checked it out myself. I was in my work clothes long before we started legal action, and I walked down to the beach along the deeded right-of-way. Some guy from one of the private houses comes out and he yells, 'get off my goddamned property, you son of a bitch.' I said I thought there was a right of way here, but the guy, I don't know who he was, he said there's no right of way.

"Finally, I said, that I was the mayor of Biddeford, and I had a right to be on the right-of-way. Well, he turned green. He walked away, and I didn't see him again. But it was then that I got the message.

"People were shocked but they appreciate it now. They don't like being looked down on. It's instilled in Francos that you can be poor, but be clean; you can be poor, but be proud; you're a person, you're as good as anyone.

"The French have not been aggressive in politics, and I don't understand that. And I don't know if it was the times, or the man, that created our situation in Biddeford.

"But we did it, we fought for that property we had a right to. And I'm proud we did."

# 19. Lorraine Pomerleau Doyon: Adjusting to "English only"

When 13-year-old Lorraine Pomerleau left St. Augustine Grammar School for Cony High School more than two decades ago, her English vocabulary was as follows: "hi" and "goodbye."

She was one of hundreds of youngsters raised on Sand Hill in Augusta, Maine. Her family was French and French was the language in the streets and at the dinner table. But like many Franco-American youngsters raised in New England, this monolingual upbringing did not help on her first day of public school.

"I remember I was scared," said Lorraine, now 37, and known as Mrs. Lorraine Pomerleau Doyon. "I could say 'hi' and 'goodbye' in English but that was about all. Everybody in the neighborhood was French and, at that time we didn't have television. And the kids, they didn't have cars like they do today, so if you were brought up on Sand Hill, that's about all you knew. Sand Hill was 100 per cent French in those days."

The Pomerleau family of which Lorraine is a part is among the older names in the Augusta area. Joseph Pomerleau, her great-grandfather, had a bakery on the old Washington Street, while grandfather Ovid Pomerleau had a grocery store in the same area. Lorraine's father, Arthur, worked at a bakery until it closed, then got work at the paper mill.

Not much is known about family roots beyond great-grandfather Joseph Pomerleau. It is said though, that the family's original name was Vachon de Pomerleau.

"How would you use that whole name?" Lorraine asks. "They ended up dropping the Vachon at some point."

Lorraine's enrollment at nearby St. Augustine's school was a natural development of her heritage, church ties and a desire for a good

Catholic education. It also improved her French. Parochial school 25 years ago, including St. Augustine's, was conducted in French. Math was in French, geography in French, and even the teaching of English was in French. Students got perhaps an hour a day in English, which naturally produced monolingual graduates.

To learn in French is a concept that some Franco-American educators favor. Certainly romantics who miss the old days would like their children schooled in that language. But to hear a graduate like Lorraine Pomerleau Doyon relate her experience suggests that there are difficulties as well as benefits. "When we got to high school," she recalls, "many of us couldn't speak English. Some couldn't understand it even. Most of us tried immediately to learn it, yet it was hard because everything around you was in a foreign language.

"The French would stay together. Sometimes they'd just remain in groups and speak French among themselves. My husband Val, he's seven and a half years older, had friends who were talking French in the hall. The principal of Cony High School came up and told them to stop. It was like a threat. He said they were at Cony now, and English was spoken at Cony, not French.

"I worked at my English. I studied, I joined clubs, I'd talk to people. I wanted to learn, but there was definitely a language barrier at school. Some students couldn't pick up English, and they'd turn away from their studies. So then they'd just wait until they were 16 and they'd quit school. Everyone knew kids like that.

"There weren't many Franco-American teachers there to help with language problems. Sure, there were guidance counselors, but we were shy. We didn't want people to know we were confused and having problems. I guess we just hoped people wouldn't find out about our situation.

"I remember I was at the blackboard my first year, and the teacher asked me to count some numbers on the board. I did the whole thing in French and everyone laughed. I was so embarrassed. You had to adjust. You had to change your language or be miserable. A lot of students eventually dropped out."

Lorraine's study paid off. She mastered English, graduated from Cony and after a year in the working world, married Val Doyon, a wage worker. Today, still a resident of Sand Hill, she is church secretary of St. Augustine's Catholic Church.

It amazes her that French was the sole language in parochial schools up to just 15 years ago. But the energetic worker, wife and mother does not mourn the introduction of English. Unlike some who would have French returned, she gives approval to English.

"Let's face it," she says. "We live in America. English is the language and English is what people speak in the colleges, on the jobs, and, more and more, in the streets of Augusta. I know what my generation went through in growing up with French and changing to English. Believe me, I'm all for the change. These kids today won't have the same problems.

"French is still spoken on Sand Hill. But things change. The church masses, all but two in the early morning for the older people, are in English. There was no big complaint when they were said in English. The young people grow up with English. That's what they want.

"It's funny though. Television has brought the English language to the youngsters in French homes. We still speak French in the house, but everything on TV is English, except once in a while, on cable television, there will be Canadian programs in French.

"But do you know, I have heard children in French homes laughing at what they hear on French TV. They don't know it but they're laughing at their ancestors. Things have happened so fast. When I was in school everything was French . . . "

Lorraine Pomerleau Doyon has three children. One is attending the University of Maine, Augusta. Upon graduation, he will be the first of the family to earn a college diploma. His entire academic life has been in English.

As Lorraine Pomerleau Doyon says, things happen fast.

The Most Rev. Amedee Proulx, auxiliary bishop of the Portland Diocese. His elevation to the post in 1975 was overdue in the eyes of many Franco-Americans. We are the majority group in the diocese, they reasoned. Why shouldn't one of ours hold a major position?

# 20. Bishop Amedee Proulx: The boy who grew up to be Bishop

There are two portraits on a wall of diocesan headquarters in Portland, Maine; one of the Most Rev. Edward C. O'Leary, Bishop of Portland, and the other of the Most Rev. Amedee W. Proulx, Auxiliary Bishop.

Bishop O'Leary's portrait is set slightly higher than Bishop Proulx's, yet few Franco-Americans are likely to raise issue with the placement. It wasn't until recently that the Franco-Americans were able to get a bishop into the Maine diocese at all.

Although Franco-Americans have traditionally made up a majority of the membership of the Catholic Church in Maine, the administration of the church, until the appointment of Bishop Proulx (pronounced Prew) had remained firmly in the hands of Irish clergymen.

When Bishop Proulx was elevated to Auxiliary Bishop in 1975, it symbolized to many Franco-Americans an overdue recognition of their existence. Indeed, Bishop Proulx is a visible example of a Franco-American brought up in the most modest surroundings, rising to a revered and responsible position.

"My father came from Quebec when he was seven, my mother came down when she was 14," Bishop Proulx says. "My father worked in several cities before the family settled in the Sanford area. He went to work in the shoeshops in Springvale. My mother worked off and on in the mills.

"I grew up in a French neighborhood. That's the language I first spoke but as I got older I lived in a bilingual environment. I attended elementary school in town at Holy Family, and then went to St. Hyacinthe in Canada for high school and college. We had family there and my brothers had gone.

"The priesthood had been an option I thought about throughout high school and college, and the decision was made during my senior year at college. I then went to St. Paul's Seminary at the University of Ottawa. My reading of church history is that the French in North America, in Canada and the United States, felt threatened at being a minority. They identified the English as threatening the faith and a great effort was made to keep the language and to keep the faith. It was felt that to lose the language would mean losing the heritage and the faith. The Catholic Church and Catholic schools felt it necessary to stress the language and faith, as a reaction to what they felt was an effort to wipe them out."

Bishop Proulx is somewhat circumspect when discussing the split between Irish and Catholic French as the organized church developed in Maine.

"Much of the tension was before my time," he said. "I don't know too much about it first hand, only what I've been told. I will say that the tensions were real, however. I personally have not experienced any great ethnic tensions. There have been traditions and values, yes. I am more comfortable with the traditions of the Francos and my brother priests of Irish descent are more comfortable with their heritage.

"But I can say this: I have seen a growing ability to live in peace. People on both sides don't seem eager to go back to the hurts of the past. The needs are different today, the aspirations are different. The life of the church today is not so closely allied to ethnic heritage."

Such a change notwithstanding, Bishop Proulx's early assignments were reflective of his French heritage. As an assistant priest, he was assigned to parishes with French-speaking members.

"At Holy Rosary in Caribou there was a mixed group of English and French. At St. Louis in Fort Kent, where I also served, it was 95 per cent French-speaking. During my time there, English was introduced in the mass. At St. Louis in Auburn, too, the liturgy was in French and there was during that period agonizing over whether to change to English. They did go to English, but after I left."

Following his departure from Auburn, he studied for two years at Catholic University. Returning to Portland in 1968, he was appointed

Secretary and Advocate of the Diocesan Matrimonial Tribunal. His subsequent work continued to be administrative and his elevation has been rapid. With a maximum of pomp and publicity, the clergyman was ordained as an auxiliary bishop in November, 1975. The post of auxiliary bishop was not created for him, but it was not unusual for it to be vacant for years.

"I see my background as having some bearing on my selection, but I'm confident it wasn't the only factor involved," Proulx says. "It was a beautiful experience. It represented the achievement of an aspiration of a people. Whether it was overdue is a difficult question. Given the number of Catholics of French heritage and the number of priests of French heritage in the diocese over the years, I'd say an earlier appointment to such a post would have been welcomed and justified."

Bishop Proulx said he doesn't see his duty in the church as working specifically to bring change for Franco-Americans. He does state that his role is to function within his own framework.

"I think any person has a right to be proud of his or her heritage. All positive ethnic values have to be respected, and that should be true in church circles, too."

The Rev. Msgr. Ronaldo L. Gadoury of Woonsocket, R.I. He celebrated mass on the floor of a mill, and the national publicity it generated enabled him to create a French parish in Woonsocket.

# 21. Father Ronaldo Gadoury: A Franco church is created

In 1953, the Rev. Ronaldo L. Gadoury had a dream of forming a French parish in Woonsocket, R. I. He had no people, no church, and no money. But he had a commitment to his church and a dream that would not go away.

Father Gadoury, therefore, embarked on one of the most rudimentary game plans in Franco-American history. It was as simple as it was appealing: he began saying masses among the weaving machines at the Airedale Mills. The unusual action inspired potential parishioners, and it also created national publicity that resulted in a modest building fund. Our Lady Queen of Martyrs Church, Park Square, Woonsocket, was born.

Today, Father Gadoury is the Rev. Msgr. Ronald L. Gadoury. He retired from formal duties in 1972, but has remained active in the community since. In the spring of 1979, the bilingual clergyman celebrated his 50th anniversary of ordination. But despite the passing of years, the Monsignor remains one of the most vital of clergymen. He is called a living legend in the Woonsocket area, with the emphasis on "living."

"I thanked God for two things when Our Lady was starting," Msgr. Gadoury commented shortly before his 50th anniversary of ordination. "I thanked God because I was a witness to a foundation. And I was thankful it came one year before the 100th anniversary of the announcement of the Blessed Virgin, and it would be a parish for the great jubilee."

The church that Father Gadoury built was one of the last French churches in New England. The early years of the arrival of the French-Canadian immigrants were full of new church building, and new church schools. By the 1950's, the church was seeing a decline in numbers. Thus Msgr. Gadoury's feat of organizing a parish, and constructing a new church, is a unique accomplishment.

"It was daring, it was challenging to start the church," recalled the lively clergyman. "We were starting from nothing. We felt there was a need, though, so we went ahead as we could.

"We had a sacred purpose – the church was for the welfare and well-being of the people, for the uplifting and salvation of their souls. It was also for the many people of French descent in the neighborhood. There were French churches in the region, but none nearby.

"It was an international parish. There were Poles, and Irish, and Italians, too. But I'd say members were 85 per cent French, so the question came up about which language would be used. The predominant language was said to be English, but there was an interpretation that permitted a vote. It turned out that parishioners felt that half of the masses would be English, half French. We continued that for the first 10 years at least, and of course in later years, English was the primary language. But when we started, there was a great need for French."

Msgr. Gadoury is remembered not only for pioneering one of the last French churches in New England, but building much of it with his own hands. He recalls he was a carpenter, architect, builder and union man all merged into one. At times his frail physical form did not permit him to complete the varied tasks, but just the sight of him struggling was enough to inspire others to pitch in and help.

"I may have seemed frail or inept," he said. "But that got other people working."

The man who built Our Lady Queen of Martyrs came from St. Damien de Brandon, Quebec, as a youth. His mother died at age 37, and he was raised by sisters and brothers already in the area. His older sister, Vercheres, was a preceptor, and like a mother, he said.

He spent six years at Precious Blood Church, then was assistant pastor of St. Matthew's in Central Falls, R. I. In Central Falls, he was known to don overalls when working for the Boy Scouts and Girl Scouts. He established Camp Ker Anna in Cumberland, R. I. for scouts. His activities also include his annual fundraising carnivals for his parishes, considered among the largest in Rhode Island. One of his skills was pressing parishioners into service at the various functions. He also had a way with machines, though. One of his most reliable aids was a clamcake machine that, with remarkable efficiency, could make "70 clamcakes at every shot. They were beautiful."

Once, he recalled, he wrote a children's play for a parish program. Not one to shirk the most trying roles, Father Gadoury took the part of a clown for himself.

Characterized by a rush-rush manner, a thick French accent, and a tendency to leave sentences unfinished, the durable cleric has evolved as somewhat of a legend in the Woonsocket area. He touched people's lives by not only building a church, but by remaining a vibrant force in the community as a whole.

"He's the most unusual character I've ever met," the Rev. Donat A. Barrette, pastor of Our Lady of Good Counsel Church, West Warwick, R. I., told Woonsocket Call staff writer Tony Aquino.

"He's the hardest working person I have ever known. He's always a priest first . . . but at the same time he's also a carpenter, electrician, plumber.

"He could be the gruffest, grumpiest, most cantankerous person. At the same time you were never offended. You knew he always cared. I don't think it was ever a pastor-curate relationship. It was always two people working together."

A different perspective, also respectful, was supplied by Ruth E. Jellison, wife of the Rev. Frederick N. Jellison, rector of St. James Episcopal Church. "He was an ecumenicist long before it became official, long before Pope John." His openness toward clergy in other faiths was "a radical departure for Woonsocket." Twenty-five years ago, she added, such actions were unheard of.

The hardworking character and dynamic presence of Father Gadoury evidently paid off. Not only was Our Lady Queen of Martyrs Church built, but a rectory followed in 1955, and a church school of 16 classrooms was constructed in 1960. He proudly points out that the debts were paid in 1968: $80,000 for the church, $48,000 for the rectory and $380,000 for the school.

Father Gadoury does not live totally by memory, of course. He says mass several days a week, is on hand for weddings and baptisms, and is available to parishioners and neighbors on a regular basis. But when he does think back, the creation of our Lady Queen of Martyrs Church is one of his most pleasant reminiscences.

"We had great participation at the church," he said. "The building of the church was embracing the Catholic action principle. I think that is one of the most important things for any Catholic parish — involve the people.

"I was always an organizer, I organized picnics and events in high school and college. I wanted everybody to get up and get involved. That to me has been the key."

# 22. Sister Aldea:
# A Quiet Life of Dedication

Sister Aldea, a member of the Sisters of Charity of St. Hyacinthe, Quebec, is the administrator of the largest hospital for the elderly in Rhode Island, Hospice de Antoine. Though born in Quebec, she has spent most of her professional life in New England. In many ways she typifies the women of the church who have served in the region's French institutions: quiet, competent, and exceedingly modest. Sister Aldea, for instance, declined to give her full name when interviewed at her facility in Mannville R. I.

"Just put Sister Aldea," she requested. "That's enough."

Much of her life has been spent providing service to health care facilities in New England cities. Her early days were on a farm, however. Like generations before her, she is from farming stock that eventually came south.

"I stayed on the family farm until I was about 12," she recalled. "I helped a little, but at that time I was a little too small to be important as a worker. Oh, I liked it well enough there – until I left. It's a very hard life.

"In fact, almost everybody in the family left the farm. There were 12 boys and one girl in my father's family, and every one except him left. You know, 11 boys and the girl just saying no to farming, and leaving for something better. They all came to the states. My father stayed longer than anyone – he just liked the land. But I went to school, and then convent and college, and didn't go back to farm life.

"My father went to school for about six years; my mother got about the same amount of schooling. But even though they weren't highly educated, they wanted the children to learn. They said it was important. I went to Montreal College (graduated 1938), and years later (1952) got a Master's Degree in nursing education from George Washington University. At the time I hadn't been to the South, and I liked everything except the weather in Washington. We had to wear heavy habits in those days, and it was very uncomfortable. But I did get my Master's in nursing, which has been important."

It does not appear that Sister Aldea's parents pushed her toward the religious life. She indicates she drifted toward it due to her friendships with the Gray Nuns during her teens. During her school years, she was an excellent student. Doctors who knew her at St. Mary's Hospital in Lewiston, Maine, said she was among the most gifted of nurses. Religious commitment has melded with vocational excellence in creating a most unique and accomplished individual.

Sister Aldea's professional career began in 1938, when as a young nurse she was sent to St. Mary's in Lewiston. By 1950 she was a teacher and administrator at the nursing school there, and through the 1960's served as Director of Nursing there. From 1966 to 1977 she served as general counsel to the Mother House of the order in St. Hyacinthe. In 1977 she arrived at the Hospice, late in her professional career but willing to serve where needed.

Sister Aldea administers a 245-bed facility. About two-thirds of the residents are of French-Canadian ancestry. Some pay, some receive public assistance. In many cases, elderly Franco-Americans paid their way in their early days of residence but ran out of money. The hospital costs $25 per day for private patients, and $21.12 per day for those receiving government support.

The health status of the residents varies. There are those who are in good health, and simply need a place to live. They are mobile, alert, and pleased to have such a place to stay.

Others are slowed by strokes or broken bones. Some are bedridden, attended by the facility's medical staff. Others hobble through the halls and social rooms, barely able to maintain movement. In some cases, a healthy husband will live downstairs, and his incapacitated wife will be confined to medical facilities upstairs. Or a wife, waiting for her husband's broken hip to mend, will reside elsewhere in the hospital with several women her own age.

Caring for this infirm flock appears to be a true test of the love that Sisters have for fellow man. It is trying work, yet it lacks the excitement and challenge of other areas of religious endeavor. But devotion to duty seems to come naturally for Sister Aldea. It's likely she would prefer teaching at nursing school, as she has done in the past, but administering a care center for the aged is her assignment at this point.

"They needed me, so I accepted," the 60-ish Sister explained simply.

"There's a big difference between the Hospice and St. Mary's, of course. There I was active with the students, I mixed with the many activities of the young people. Here there is not so much going on.

"The Hospice is not as challenging as St. Mary's, or the Mother House. Older people have different needs, and by the nature of things their world is much smaller. I wouldn't say the Hospice is without challenge – when I came here I had to take state examinations in order to register as an administrator of a facility receiving government money. That took much work and study, because I had been away from the field. In general, though, the pace here is slower. Not so much is going on."

Sister Aldea's presence in Mannville is another indication that the ties between Quebec and New England still exist. Born and educated in Quebec, she has split the years of her professional life between the Province and the States. Even during her years in the New England states, she managed to return to St. Hyacinthe summers. It's almost as if she followed the path set down by earlier generations. Though her knowledge of her family background is not extensive, she does know that 11 uncles left Quebec for the United States. She, too, came south.

"Speaking French and English has always helped," the soft-spoken sister commented. "In the places I was sent, like Lewiston and Mannville, we deal with so many who communicate in French.

"My life has been the Church, and the Hospice is another part of that service. There might be more exciting tasks, but this is where I'm needed.

"And as long as I'm healthy, I will serve. I could be called tomorrow to another city; I could be called back to Quebec. I go if I can.

"I've enjoyed working in the States. The people have been friendly, and I have been with my own people. But someday I will return to St. Hyacinthe. I know that. When I can't work anymore, I will retire there with the other Sisters of the order."

An imposing statue greets visitors at the Hospice de Antoine, where Sister Aldea is the head administrator. This form was created in the memory of one of the most revered of the Sisters of Charity, Marguerite D'Youville.

# 23. Brother Paul Demers: A parochial school closes in Rhode Island

The decline of the Catholic school has been one of the most visible signs of the evolution of the French-Canadian culture in New England communities. Generations of Francos were educated in neighborhood parochial schools but the number of those attending has dropped dramatically in the past three decades. One Franco-American who has witnessed this first hand is Brother Paul Demers. Brother Demers was principal of Sacred Heart Academy in Central Falls, R. I., when it closed in 1970.

Strong parochial school systems were characteristic of French neighborhoods. Franco-Americans often possessed limited resources, but they found ways to build churches, often the most striking buildings in the city. Similarly, parish members pooled their modest means to create schools to perpetuate their religion and culture.

At the turn of the century, school was taught in French. Canadian history and catechism were part of the course of study. Courses in English were offered, but certainly the grammar school or high school graduate left speaking better French than English.

Catholic schools in French neighborhoods continuing through the 40's and 50's were offering about half of their instruction in French, half in English. As the environment changed, so did the increase in the use of English. More graduates were entering fields where English was essential. When the mills were the only source of employment, a person could get by knowing only French. But later generations were finding it necessary to speak English, and thus the curriculum changed over the years. The conversion to English was required in some areas. State school authorities insisted on the use of English in states such as Maine. In Catholic schools through the 60's and 70's, therefore, English has been the primary language. State authorities put pressure on public schools, too, to produce English-speaking graduates. Some Francos remember being punished for speaking French in the school yard, even if French was their primary language at home.

As French families were assimilated into the American mainstream, the importance of the Catholic schools in Franco-American communities declined. Catholic schools of French orientation were not unique in their problems; parochial schools of Irish and Greek persuasion closed, too. The passing of the neighborhood church school was a disappointing development for many Franco-Americans nonetheless.

"Sacred Heart's school started in 1908," said Brother Demers, a member of the Sacred Heart Order. "It closed in 1970.

"It was a controversial situation. The school was having difficulty, but many parishioners did not want to see it closed. I didn't. There were always rumors that it couldn't go on, but we were there hoping that somehow it could be kept open. The students were there, but the building wasn't. It was a firetrap, so the question was whether we could build a new school.

"Well, when the decision came to close the school, I was out of town. Maybe the timing was intentional. The decision came down from on high and that was that. I had tried to fight it, or find an alternative, but there it was.

"Sacred Heart Academy was not unique in closing. A lot of schools did in the 60's and early 70's. There were a number of reasons. One factor was that the number entering the religious vocations declined sharply in the 60's. You didn't have enough teachers to staff the schools. When you brought in lay teachers, you had to pay them more. That made a big difference in the budget.

"Also, there was a refusal on the part of religious leaders to give lay people a role. The community was not involved as much as it could have been. To get the people involved is important these days.

"And the assimilation process was there. Families were relating as Americans, and they didn't put as much importance on providing a background of French culture. We weren't teaching in French, of course; it was in English. But even so, times had changed so that parents didn't see the French Catholic school as a priority.

"Schools like Sacred Heart began with a mission – to come to a community to help the French-Canadians and Franco-Americans adjust to the new country. Instruction was in French, and the schools were a buffer between the old and the new. They helped monitor the behavior of the newcomers. After families settled, they helped maintain the cultural background, they provided some of the old ways. Times changed, though, and people began leaving for the suburbs, entering new vocations. They left the churches and schools behind in the city.

"The youngsters entered public schools, where they might get French, but it would be French as a foreign language. I think that's sad. I know I studied French in parochial school and I went through those systems. I benefited."

Brother Demers grew up in an environment not unlike the surroundings of Woonsocket. He is a native of Suncook, N. H., a mill town near Manchester. His parents worked in mills, as did those in Woonsocket.

Brother Demers, 45, graduated from Sacred Heart Academy in Pomfret, Conn. After Sacred Heart he attended another Catholic institution, St. Michael's College in Winooski, Vt. He earned a masters at Providence College, also Catholic. Religious training took place at the Sacred Heart Novitiate in Pascoag, R. I. "I guess when you look back, Sacred Heart has been the big part of my life," he reflects.

After some years in the classroom, Brother Demers assumed the principalship of Sacred Heart Academy in Central Falls, just north of Providence, in 1968. Later he went to Mt. St. Charles in Woonsocket where he teaches English and Latin.

"My parents worked in the mills," said the brother. "My father, Rene Demers, was from St. Guillame, Quebec. His father was a farmer, but he worked in the mills here. My mother, Beatrice Vezina Demers, was from Penacook, N. H. There weren't very many stories in our family – my parents didn't dwell on the past, so I don't know very much about their background. Now I wish I did.

"My parents didn't urge me to go into the church. I guess I was just very close to church. I was an altar boy, I went to Catholic school, I was friendly with the brothers. I sort of drifted into it, because there was this religious orientation around me. When I went to high school, it was half French, half English. When I started teaching, though, many of the children didn't know enough French to have that kind of instruction. It was in English. The brothers had trouble getting books, too, and I remember there were better chances of obtaining books from Quebec than New York.

"But that's the way it always was with the brothers. The ties were better in Quebec. It was that way with most people in the area, too. When people would think of traveling, they'd go north to Quebec, not south. South was foreign territory.

"My life in Rhode Island reminds me of New Hampshire. The mill communities are the same; I'm with Franco-American people. It's a little slower in New Hampshire, but it's similar.

"Woonsocket has made tremendous progress since the mills shut down. And it's like Manchester in that regard. Both had to find new industries when the mills left. The mills had been everything, but all of a sudden there had to be a replacement.

"I feel at home in the Woonsocket area. I identify with the people, because it's like my background. But things are changing. Many Franco-Americans have left the city. I don't know if 50 per cent of the students at Mt. St. Charles have French surnames – less than 50 per cent of those in the city now have French names. There has been greater movement and less emphasis on Franco-American background. Other groups, like blacks, Spanish, Irish, have a sense of history. The French don't have that to the same degree. And with the passing of Catholic schools, there's even less consciousness of culture.

"There is more of an interest in genealogy today, to be sure. Everyone is interested. I should do it, too. When you're older you look back; when you're young, you're looking forward. Not many young people are looking back to their French heritage.

"I think that's sad. My life has been enriched because of it. It's helped me tremendously, and it's helped others, too.

"But many youngsters have felt that to be American, you had to go all the way. You have to deny your background to be more American. The parochial schools in many mill cities are struggling – at public schools, the inclination to assimilate is great. The school tends to have more influence than the home, and the idea is that to succeed, you have to deny your heritage. So many schools closed.

"I see a little bit of pendulum swing, though. I wouldn't say that we'll ever go back to the day when many Franco-American children went to church schools, but there seems to be more of an interest in heritage today.

"More parents, and their children, seem to be seeing that there can be an advantage to learning of one's background, and speaking the language."

Robert Fournier—A leader in New Hampshire bi-lingual education. His own need to learn English as a youngster has given him insights on the learning situation of Francos in New England.

# 24. Robert Fournier:
# The benefits of bilingualism

"When I visit schools," educator Robert Fournier says, "I tell students about a Franco-American friend of mine who represents the Cessna aircraft company in Africa. Much of Africa is French-speaking, and one reason he got that job was because of his background. He can speak two languages. He's very successful in an exciting career and his ability to speak French is the reason.

"I relate this story so young people will know of the benefits of bilingualism. Too many children learn to feel it's a liability to speak French, but that's not true. And stories like this illustrate there are definitely advantages."

Fournier, a native of Suncook, N. H., is in a pivotal position when it comes to bilingual studies. He is a state education consultant in New Hampshire in foreign languages; he also serves as state coordinator of state Title VII federal legislation aimed at French-English education programs. In addition, Fournier has been a New England representative on the National Council for Bilingual Education.

So when Fournier, who grew up speaking French, addresses the subject of bilingualism, he is drawing on ample resources and experience.

"It's well-known that far fewer young people are speaking French these days. Franco-Americans of my age, 45, spoke it as children. It was a natural thing, but the same is not true today. The parents of schoolchildren do not speak the language at home.

"These parents were hurt by their French. They did not learn English quickly, since French was their tongue. Later, they had the French accent. With me, for instance, I spent hours in front of a mirror to improve my English pronunciation. It wasn't enough to say the words over and over; you had to watch the motions of the mouth to improve. Many of today's parents worked to get rid of French for English, so they don't want to start their children in French.

"Parents see French as perpetuating the system – the system that hurt them. That might be understandable, but we are interested in pointing out the benefits of bilingualism.

"These are areas where those of French descent have been penalized. A professor at the University of New Hampshire used to ask students, 'are you French? are you Catholic? Okay, then, you start with one letter grade less.' That's hard to believe, but I know it to be true.

"Some Franco-Americans didn't test well due to their linguistic background. There are cases of youngsters' records showing them to have IQ's of 70 and 80. Well, they went on to get master's degrees and doctorates, so obviously they did not lack brains. The tests were not well-suited to their backgrounds, though.

"Many Francos entered school with poor self-image, a negative view of themselves. This is reflected in their school work. If you're ashamed of yourself, and your background, how can you excel? One reason for the bilingual program is to recognize problems in the educational system, and work to correct them. Sometimes it's difficult to convince education officials to take steps to improve conditions. You know, educators are bombarded by laws – they don't move until they're pressured to do so. They are nuts and bolts type people who are not oriented to kids. If there's a court decision, though, they take note. If it's mandated by a higher authority, they'll react. That's why work in the bilingual field is important. Someone has got to be out there to make the needs known."

Fournier runs the bilingual program in New Hampshire with consciousness of the Franco environment. He himself came from a family of mill workers in Suncook, N. H. Though the articulate educator did not work in the mills, both parents did. So did several grandparents.

"My grandparents came down from Quebec a long time ago," Fournier related. "The Fourniers arrived in New Ipswich, N. H. in about 1850 or 1860. I think my grandfather worked in the Greenville Mill, the first mill in New Hampshire.

"My mother's family, the LeBlancs, arrived about the same time, the 1855-1860 era. Apparently they didn't settle permanently at first. They would work here in the winter, and return to the farm in Quebec in summer. They kept going back and forth. Eventually the local ties became strong – they stayed, like most of the French-Canadians finally decided to stay.

"My mother worked in the mills for 45 years. My grandmother helped bring us up, because of the time my mother was away. My mother, Germaine LeBlanc Fournier, was in the weave room most of her life. In fact, when she was home her hand would involuntarily bob up and down, simulating her hand movements in the mill. It wasn't a physical condition. It was just that so many hours were spent with her hands moving over the fabric, that even in her relaxed moments her hands would be moving.

"My father, Ulric Arthur Fournier, spent most of his years in the mills, too. He was in the 'China Mills' and later Textron. He did some weaving at first, but eventually was a loom fixer. Later he was in supervisory capacities, with 300 to 350 men under him. They seemed to allow some members of the French to work out of the ghetto – if you don't have someone in mid-management, you might have difficulty controlling the group. I look back and see him as a go-between top management and the labor force.

"My father's feeling about any discrimination was that the French had to be twice as good to achieve anything. You had to put your entire heart and soul into it in order to succeed. And he did. He was taking English lessons at the same time he studied textiles — in French.

"My parents worked in the Suncook area, and I remember hearing that the region was a possible disaster target arena during World War II. They were weaving parachutes then, and federal officials had Suncook on a list of places the enemy might try to destroy. The local doctor never had to go into service, because the thinking was if there is a disastrous attack, medical professionals would be needed at once.

"It's hard to believe that a New Hampshire mill town would be the subject of such precautions, but I'm told that's what happened."

Fournier's parents and grandmother, who managed a boarding house as well as her own residence, urged young Robert Fournier on to obtain more education than they had. Fournier, therefore, was directed on a course of study designed so to avoid a career of mill work.

He attended St. John High School in nearby Concord.

"It was Irish, but most students were Italian and French from the mill ghettos."

Fournier's French accent was the source of ridicule, but practice in front of the mirror eventually minimized the problem. He graduated in 1954.

After military service and several years with Pratt and Whitney in Connecticut, Fournier took his improved English skills to the University of New Hampshire. After graduating in 1962, he taught school in West Newbury, Newmarket and Whitefield (all in New Hampshire). The genial Franco joined the state Department of Education in New Hampshire in 1967, and has since worked in a variety of programs dealing with improving linguistic skills of young Franco-Americans.

Is there an increasing Franco-American collective consciousness? he was asked.

"Yes, the consciousness is growing. There's been a whole opening of the media since World War II, and that has changed things. Television has made the world more interdependent; we've become more aware of other cultures. We're much less parochial. Now we can see more uses for language and culture than the French saw in the ghetto.

"There are individual cases of Franco-Americans standing up. A young nurse in Greenville, N. H., was unhappy about the way the schools were treating the French. She ran for school board, and she won; she ran for state legislature, and she won. She began threatening people with her ideas, and at one point a bank official ripped up her loan application because he didn't like what she stood for. But that's one example of how Francos have been identifying."

To the question of whether Franco-Americans must speak French in order to maintain their culture, Fournier replied, "Look at the Italians. They don't speak the language at all times, yet the culture in this country seems strong. I don't think it's essential, but it is a great benefit to the individuals to speak it, and good for the country, too."

Is there a Franco-American "movement" underway?

"There is a Franco-American movement underway but not at the grass roots level. There has been a lack of attention to this group. The world-wide phenomena of ethnic development is making a difference here, as TV's 'Roots' pointed out. Many Franco-Americans are what I call 'cultural amnesiacs' but that is changing.

" 'Roots' gave the impetus to Americans to search for their origin, and it permeated the Franco-American consciousness, too. In the past there was an elite among Francos, fostered by the church, that had its own cultural level but provided no conscious assistance for the lower social classes. There was a lack of goal-setting, a lack of expectation of self. That's slowly changing."

Indeed, Fournier is on the forefront of that change. His work in the New Hampshire school system is to help youngsters learn to value their origins, to form better self-images. In the lingo of educators, programs in bilingualism deal with improving self-concept, cognitive redevelopment, and multi-cultural education.

In plain talk, that means helping young Franco-Americans appreciate their heritage. And themselves.

Prof. Madeleine D. Giguere of the University of Southern Maine, one of the leading authorities on Franco-American history.

# 25. Madeleine Giguere:
# A word about strong women

As a tenured sociology professor at the University of Southern Maine in Portland, Madeleine Giguere is knowledgeable in numerous areas. One is the Franco-American studies, in which she offers a course. Of particular interest to the learned Lewiston native is the life of French-Canadian and Franco-American women. It's not unusual for her to deal with the subject of women at seminars and conferences. Scholars from other regions and disciplines will have talked for hours on economics or demographics of the French. Then Madeleine Giguere will take the podium, and, as if to say, "Well, you might have overlooked something here, "she'll deliver a revealing discourse on the valuable contributions that women have made to the Franco society over the years.

The subject of women is not her only area of expertise. She has produced several papers regarding geographical distribution of Franco residents based on the 1970 census. But she often stands alone in pursuing this area of research.

"I think if you were taking the overview of the women on the farms in Quebec, and the later Franco women who worked in the mills, you would find a consistency," said Prof. Giguere. "As the wives of habitants, they had real responsibilities. Then as the wife of a mill worker, or a wage earner herself, she was also important.

"The French women had to be competent. That was important. On the farms, she had to tend her own garden, and bring in food. She had to store certain foodstuffs, she had to plan for the months ahead. Don't forget, it wasn't a case of going into the refrigerator for more if you didn't get enough in those days. Once winter came, you relied on what you had – there was no icebox, or no supermarket down the street for most habitants. So she was responsible for this type of duty.

"And the children. There might be 12 or 14 children, and she was the director of that part of life. With so many children, she spent a good part of her young years pregnant. The French women lost many children, which was an emotional burden. The number of women lost in childbirth in those days was also high. Motherhood was not an easy role."

Giguere, whose grandparents migrated from St. Anne de Beaupre in Quebec, said that life improved for French women after they arrived in the New England states.

"For women, there was more independence in the mills," she commented. "It was work, but it gave them a little time for themselves, and a little money of their own. On the farm, it was work in the household all day long, and for what reward? In the mills, at least, they were paid for what they did. And in the early days especially, the work wasn't that bad.

"I know, I remember my great aunts saying they enjoyed it. When the looms were running, there would be time to talk, watch the children, visit in a social way. You could never do that on the farm. And there were lasting friendships made in the mills. My maternal grandmother worked in the mills when she was young. For years after she left, she met at least once a year with the girls she had known in her section of the mills. And they would talk about those old days.

"Of course, they still had their responsibilities at home. The mills operated on New Year's Day, which is a very big celebration day for the French. So there were times when women would have holiday breakfasts at 3 and 4 in the morning to mark the occasion, then go to work so they were there at 6 a.m. You can imagine what time they had to wake up to get things ready."

Professor Giguere indicated that succeeding generations of women had more choices on work, marriage and education. She herself is an example of the evolution of women in society. Just two generations removed from the farmland of Quebec, Prof. Giguere is an educated, prominent Franco-American woman making her own decisions.

She is the daughter of the late Eustache Napoleon Giguere and Dinora Cailler Giguere, themselves children of immigrants. Her grandparents on both sides came from large families, as did her parents. She was an only child, however.

Her father, raised in Lewiston, grew up to be a doctor. After attending the local parochial school, he went to St. Mary's "College" in Van Buren, Maine, then to Sherbrooke to enter the seminary. He left the religious studies, however, and enrolled in the University of Montreal, then Bowdoin Medical School. A 1921 graduate of the Brunswick, Maine College, he was believed to have been the first Lewiston native to become a doctor.

Madeleine's mother was a school teacher in the Lewiston system, certainly making that family one of the more educated in the community.

"My father didn't talk much about not going into the priesthood," she remarked. "He just told us he was glad he became a doctor.

"You know, he was one of 16 children. Yet only four survived to adulthood. Four. And he said that although losing that many children was unusual then, it wasn't unique in Lewiston . The family lived across from the canal – maybe it was the water. Or it might have been a malnutrition situation. Some families couldn't eat well, or they didn't have sound diets. But coming from a background like that, his desire to become a doctor seems natural.

"No one ever talked to me about my grandmother's feelings at losing so many children. People thought in terms of my grandfather, getting up enough money to bury one child, then having another one die, and having to pay for that one. And women then didn't attach themselves to young children as we see today.

"The society in those days had a very high infant mortality rate – parents didn't let themselves get attached to a child until maybe it was eight or 10. They couldn't, knowing they might lose a child any day. So when a youngster died, there wasn't the same grief we see today.

"Anyway, my grandmother was ambitious. She always had a rooming house, and put a lot of effort into that. Maybe it didn't bother her as much, what with the demands of her business."

Madeleine Giguere attended the same public school system in which her mother taught, graduating from Lewiston High in 1943. Not one to be tied to the community, she attended New York's College of New Rochelle (Catholic), graduating in 1947, and earned a Master's degree at Fordham (1950). Enrolled in a doctoral program at Columbia University from 1952-55, she finished her course work and passed her exams, but never completed her dissertation. The subject of her thesis involved first marriages among French-Canadian and Franco-American women in the 18th and 19th centuries.

She has taught at the college level at Boston College, St. John's University and St. Joseph's College (North Windham, Maine) before coming to the University of Maine system in the early 1970's. She strikes one as a serious, no-nonsense academic, but at the same time wouldn't think of conducting office hours without her aging dog reclining in the best chair in the room. Educated, able and respected in the academic community, Prof. Giguere is a highly successful professional woman.

"French women were often educated," she remarked to the statement that she is conspicuous as an achiever for her generation. "The Ursuline Sisters had members with doctorates; the convents were natural places for women to be educated.

"One of my courses I teach at the university is in Franco-American studies, and that's the kind of thing we bring out. I'd say about half of the students have French backgrounds. And the students differ in why they're there. Some come out of curiosity – others really want to know about their roots, and how the French settled in Maine.

"Initially, a lot of people thought it would be a gut course, that it would be an easy credit. But I've made it demanding, partly because they thought it would be easy. If they enroll in the course, they are going to learn something."

Although Prof. Giguere's academic interests are wide-ranging, some of her most interesting material does relate to women. Few scholars have directed their attention to it, and thus many of her views are fresh and original.

"The idea of French women marrying young isn't really true," she explained. "In Canada, they didn't get married at 14 or 15. If they were marrying a farmer, it was expected he would have his own land, and that didn't happen until he was a young man.

"When they came to the United States, the Franco-American girls had quite a bit of independence for that period. They were working in the mills, they were making their own money. There was no need for them to rush into marriage. They didn't have to be supported by someone else. So you had the situation of the young women waiting, maybe marrying in the early or mid-20's, or later. Or not at all.

"But generally speaking, when they began having children, they left the mills. They assumed the traditional role of staying home and taking care of the children.

"Now that changed in the 30's when the Depression came. Women would work, and make some kind of arrangements, because they had to. There weren't many jobs, and if she had one, she might keep it.

"I really don't agree with the idea that some people have that the French had a matriarchal society. The women were strong and competent; most were assuming the traditional roles of wife and mother. The men had the say.

"And they were traditional in things like childbirth. They couldn't really announce to their husbands that they thought three children was enough, and they'd stop now. No, she would be involved in the traditional role that resulted in six, eight, or 10 children. I'll say, though, that moving to the United States changed that. Studies show that Canadian women had more children than Franco-American women here at the same time. Again, there's that independence – on the farm, the family was everything, and there was no outside stimulation. In the mill communities, other things were happening. As a matter of fact, the men's French societies in the American cities were viewed as a kind of birth control device. Wives didn't mind them going off to them at night and staying late – they'd be gone for the night at least."

In addition to bringing out the presence of women in French homes, Professor Giguere's teaching also underscores the existence of subtle discrimination in New England aimed at those of French descent.

The level of education in Quebec was low, because of the early ages that children began helping with the farm work. Though the children of mill workers in New England received a greater amount of formal education, they, too, have been undereducated over the years. Now when many parents are conscious of the value of education, Prof. Giguere feels that some discrimination is involved.

"I think that many teachers have lower expectations of a child with a French name. If he or she is slow to learn, or unable to comprehend at first, they have a tendency to go on. They don't make the special effort, they assume the child is slow. It's easy for Anglo teachers to forget that these are potentially bright children, who may just be stopped for the moment.

"Even at the university level, you see an attitude. When I came here, people didn't know my background, and they told me French jokes! I told them I was French, and then I'd hear that they didn't mean it that way. Well . . .

"It's true that the French in New England did not rush toward education at first. They were mostly blue-collar workers, with those aspirations. It was felt that a high school education only was needed for a white collar job.

"And they thought that education wasn't for everyone, that some were just not destined to go to school. That was a product of their heritage of the subsistence agriculture.

"Now more families are aware of the value of education.

"I don't see school systems reacting to help Francos, though. I don't see them working to let the Francos know of opportunities, and to encourage them in the direction of more learning. And they should."

# 26. Normand Dube:
# Proud to be French . . . finally

When Normand Dube thought about choosing a major in college three decades ago, he didn't have to dwell on the decision. "I chose English," he says today. "I knew what I wanted and it was out of spite. I did not want anything to do with French, or my Franco background."

Such feelings did not originate with the 48-year-old Dube. Countless Franco-Americans have experienced the desire to separate themselves from their family roots. But they seem unusual for a man who has risen to assume one of New England's key positions in "French Fact" studies.

Dube is executive director of the Materials Center for Bi-Lingual Study of French, in Bedford, N. H. It is he who directs the creation of displays, pamphlets and (in French) books that will be used by schoolchildren in bilingual study programs. It is Dube who is at the helm of one of the few ongoing programs that work to keep French a viable medium in the increasingly Anglo world. So it appears just slightly ironic that Dube not only ignored his French roots while growing up, but was active in avoiding them.

"You could literally say I went into English out of spite," says Dube, who was born in Van Buren, Maine and grew up in Lewiston. "I majored in English in college (St. Michael's College, Winooski, Vt. – 1948) and got a Master's in English (State University of New York, Albany – 1956).

"I was turned off by being a Franco-American because I didn't understand what it was. I had supposed you had to be the perfect being, flawless, not make mistakes. You know, whenever you did something it had to be more perfect than what someone else did. But after a summer at Bowdoin College (1960) when they had a series of workshops for teachers about teaching French to Franco-Americans, I saw things differently. I started looking around, and saw that some things were good about being a Franco; others, not so good. It wasn't black and white. We were people just like anyone else, capable of making mistakes and capable of doing well.

"I wouldn't call it a conversion or anything, but I felt differently about my past. I mean, I could walk down Lisbon Street and see the beer parlors but not think that we were all bad. Growing up, we (the French) were putting ourselves on a pedestal. There were religious overtones, we were supposed to be better, to be without weaknesses. When I got over these feelings, when I viewed us as just people, I got into Franco-American studies."

Since "seeing the light" in 1960, Dube, then a teacher at Lewiston High School, switched from teaching English to French and became involved with Franco-American studies. From an instructor who had little interest in French heritage, he became one who attempted to introduce new material specifically suited for Franco-American students. Only partially successful because of administration apathy, he opted to work on his own. In 1964, he left Lewiston to seek a doctorate in foreign language study at Ohio State University.

In actuality, Dube got into the subject more deeply than even he had expected. He put eight months into his thesis ("Study of Cognitive Taxonomy Used in Language Textbooks") before department officials vetoed the idea. As the resident Franco-American, he was prevailed upon to change the thesis topic to "Guidelines to Teaching of Franco-Americans in New England."

His advanced degree (granted in 1969) made him a prime candidate for a position in bilingual education at the University of Maine, Fort Kent. Dube suggests that the university, under scrutiny by state education officials, "needed a reason to exist" and thus chose the scholarly doctor to head its program for Franco-Americans. Dube left the university shortly thereafter, to head an innovative bilingual program in the St. John Valley. After five years of what he and many others consider a successful program, Dube joined the Materials Center in 1977.

One of the most prominent, as well as the most traveled of Franco-

American academics, the soft spoken Dube is immersed in a career of bilingual education and he's a long way from turning his back on his French roots.

"I'm a fifth generation Franco-American," commented Dube in his Bedford office, located just off Route 101, west of the mill city of Manchester. "My family were farmers in Van Buren for generations. My father is Edgar Dube, my mother Antoinette Lavoie Dube. The Dube's are a very old family in the Valley. Lucien Dube, who would be my great-great-great-grandfather, was one of the first settlers of Van Buren. But they weren't Acadians from the east, they came from New Brunswick.

"There's some Indian in the family, too. My grandfather, who was 91, told us a few years ago that some of the men in the family had married Indians. Even my father hadn't known that. He was surprised. The French trappers and itinerant people often had children with Indians – at that time, and where they went, it was natural. Many families had Indian blood, though it has been considered a black mark to talk about it.

"The family moved from Van Buren to Lewiston in the 1930's. There weren't many jobs in Aroostook then. In 1934, the big wood factory closed down, and this made things even harder. So we moved to Lewiston. But we were not actually getting away from the Valley. A lot of families from the St. John area came south too, looking for work. My mother worked in the shoe works – my father was in the American Bobbin Shop, which is now closed. He was a machinist. Everyone around me worked in mills – my parents, my grandparents, two aunts who lived with us. They worked in the mills. And the family that lived next door to us were distant cousins from the Valley, they worked there too.

"I became aware of stories about the mills when I was maybe 12 or 13. They influenced me not to go into the mills. No one told me to get an education, it was just that I should avoid the mills. I did work in the mills one summer – at Bates. I was in a big room where you rolled materials from one side to another all day. Well, I never wanted to make mill work my life.

"I went to St. Dom's (St. Dominic's High School, Lewiston). I did well, I was always one of the top five in the class. But I wasn't studying because my family pushed education; I didn't read so much because I knew it would mean a better job, I just liked the knowledge. We spoke French of course. I can't remember when I started speaking English. We always spoke French in the home, regardless.

"I stayed away from being a Franco-American though. I guess it was everything, the behavior I saw, like the Saturday night brawls, the wife-beating, the foul language, the rotten kind of sex, the vulgarity, that made me feel that way. I was at the age where I made a judgment. I saw these things and said to myself, 'there's no redeeming value anywhere.'

"We were an average family – we lived in the French section where there was frustration and unhappiness, so these things happened. I avoided Lisbon Street, I stayed away from anything French.

"I was reacting to what I saw in Lewiston, but I couldn't see the other side at that time. We lived in a small area, we were a close family. I wasn't seeing the values it created. We had the two grandparents, two aunts, brothers and I, parents and next to us, cousins. I wasn't seeing the good. But there was good."

Today Dube is like many "later-day" Francos; successful and adjusted, but with clear memories of a challenging past. His position is one of the plums of Franco-American academia. The program, federally supported, with a dozen staffers, enjoys a rare combination of funds, direction and creativity.

The director, Dube, doubles as a family man, but one who has adjusted to change.

"Sure, I'd like my children to speak French, but I also recognize they have their lives to live. They'll appreciate what they have some day."

He can also point to the innovative bilingual programs throughout New England as a tangible reflection of work well done.

"Bilingual education is education in preparation for your environment, career and self-development. How much it's used depends on how much those involved think it should be developed."

Born in Van Buren, raised in Lewiston, educated throughout the East, Dube is a veteran of both Valley and Mill City mentalities. If he had to sum up how the French have been able to deal with dead-end jobs, poor living conditions and life situations with little prospect for improvement, he might respond, "born for small bread."

"The Franco-Americans had menial jobs with little hope of ever moving up, but they endured it. There's a French expression, 'born for small bread.' The way the people thought was that 'this is the way it's going to be.' There was no such thing as moving upward among the laborers. The businessmen and professionals, yes, but not the men and women who worked in the mills. They didn't expect more – they didn't get it. Mostly, the kids didn't have the training. It wasn't because the schools didn't offer it, but because there was little motivation in the children. They weren't taught to expect more, they didn't work toward achieving more.

"There were church overtones – Franco-American Catholic overtones. I remember that those in public schools were sinners. I heard that from the pulpit. The clergy believed in the way things were, too. They believed in an elite class. The elite were the laymen who were religious leaders as well as business and professional leaders. Franco-Americans weren't assimilated by reason, but by 'it was the way it was supposed to be.'

"My father, for instance, never wanted to buy a house, though at one point, he could have. He always thought that if he lost his job, he couldn't make the payment, etc. He never looked into it, how it was done, how the system could work for him. He never even bought a car until my brother made him. It was not understanding the system. We lived not to compete but to cooperate. And if you didn't understand the system, how could you dive into it and make changes?"

Yvon Labbe, director of the Franco-American resources program at the University of Maine, Orono, and editor of FAROG Forum, the bilingual newspaper that has a national circulation of close to 6,000. His is a prominent voice in new Franco-American thinking.

# 27. Yvon Labbe:
# The wave of the future?

The Franco-American presence in New England has been described as a "quiet presence." At least one voice, however, is breaking the traditional silence. It is that of ethnic organizer Yvon Labbe, and his efforts represent new directions for Franco-Americans.

Labbe is director of the Franco-American Resources Opportunity Group (F.A.R.O.G.) at the University of Maine, Orono. From that office he publishes the largest Franco-American newspaper in the country, the *FAROG Forum*. With an international circulation of 6,000 monthly copies, the *Forum* is being recognized as a leading voice of "new" Franco-American thought.

"In certain quarters I suppose I'm considered radical," says the 41-year-old editor. "People might view me that way at first, but I don't think they feel that way after we have a chance to talk, to get to know each other. We're supportive of the French fact in Maine, and New England. Our office is saying that Francos should be accepted as we are. We shouldn't feel awkward about our French language, and we should be proud of our heritage. As far as the newspaper goes, we're saying it's all right to be what we are. We are proud of being French.

"Now those aren't really radical ideas. It just takes awhile for the old line Francos to understand what we're doing."

Much of Labbe's work is couched in terms of "identity" and "self-image" and "ethnic pride." They are intangible factors which are foreign to some Franco-Americans. What the F.A.R.O.G. office has been able to accomplish in concrete terms is a clearer indication of their direction. The group has administered orientation programs for Franco-Americans entering the university. It has prevailed upon the university to offer courses in Canadian-American studies. It has helped Franco-American students arrange scholarships, and obtain tutoring. The office has provided translators for the federal judicial court in Bangor. On a more festive side, the F.A.R.O.G. sponsors soirees for students of French-Canadian ancestry. In addition, representatives of the organization have left the campus on numerous occasions to speak with business and education leaders about the needs of Franco-Americans in this region.

And there is the newspaper. More a collection of articles and opinion than a hard news publication, the *Forum* is among the best vehicles for what's going on in the world of Franco-Americans. A recent edition, for instance, gave prominent play to a decision by Maine's commissioner of education encouraging school systems to apply for bilingual education funds. It carried a United Press International story about a New Hampshire study that showed that "Franco-Americans were not receiving their due in educational and employment areas." A growing number of stories deal with matters relating to Quebec, as seen through eyes of Franco-Americans (an address by Premiere Rene Levesque was covered.)

And a particularly telling feature of the Forum are the letters written by its readers. The writers talk candidly about the Franco-American experience.

Though some personal reflections reveal one-time discomfort about being French, they bring out in glowing terms the satisfaction they have now found in their ethnic background.

About half of the articles are in French, half are in English. A key asset to the publication is that it has a clear sense of purpose: it presents positive and meaningful material relevant to Franco-Americans. It is finding an increasing degree of acceptance on all levels, though it has stirred up its share of controversy.

"We had a strong reaction from the beginning," Labbe commented. "The name, FAROG, brought to many people's minds the word frog, and there was a feeling that we shouldn't use that term because of its negative connotation. But I think that after people got used to it, they found it acceptable.

"We have a good nucleus at the university. You often hear that young Franco-Americans aren't interested in their background or culture, but we've done many things that prove otherwise. Several years ago we went to a major convention of Franco-Americans in Manchester, N. H. We weren't invited, but we knew some people inside, and they got us in. I know that some of the older people there thought we were going to do something awful, but we were happy to just talk with the leaders and let our views be known. By the end of the conference, they were willing to listen to some new voices. And they realized we cared."

Labbe, who is becoming recognized as one of the leading Franco-American strategists in the region, was born in the province of Quebec. His father spent many years as a cook in the logging camps. When Yvon was 11, the family moved to Stratton, Maine, to be closer to a new logging operation. Like many French-Canadians who came to this new country, Labbe encountered difficulty.

"I was considered bright when we moved to the states," Labbe commented, "but all of a sudden I couldn't speak the language, so I didn't do well in school. I didn't know what to expect, either, moving to the Protestant country. We were Catholics, you know, and this was a new experience. I had illusions of grandeur when we arrived but they were slowly eroded in the new country. I didn't speak the language, and not everyone was Catholic. I remember that the name Yvon was pronounced like Evonne here, and at 11 or 12 I didn't want a girl's name. So I called myself Ivan – and I still meet people who know me as Ivan Labbe.

"Because of the language problem, I didn't do well in school. My father thought I should forget about school, and work in the woods with him. Now my parents valued education, but they really thought in terms of making a living. The most important thing to them was having a job. I thought about leaving, because I didn't want to be considered one of the dummies in the class. But I stayed on."

After considerable struggling, Labbe graduated from grammar school to enter Madison High School. His school work improved, and he began making good grades. Yet his "image" seemed to work to his detriment. A group testing students' aptitudes found that he was unusually fast with working with his hands. So instead of suggesting an academic future, they urged him to enter the shoeshops where his manual skills could be best utilized.

"They were astonished at my speed, really, so they immediately suggested shoeshops. And I did some part-time work there. I decided, though, that this wasn't what I wanted to do with my life."

Labbe, instead of working with his hands, worked with his brain. By the time he graduated from Madison High, he was accomplished enough to be named as the school's representative to Boys State. As he recalls, "I didn't know what that was, but everyone told me it was an honor." With the help of benefactor Ellis Snodgrass, whom his father worked for, Labbe went off to the University of Maine, Orono.

A teaching career followed graduation. Four years at Lincoln, Maine, was followed by a year at Wellesley, Mass. Though he had a promising career at the high-paying Wellesley system as chairman of the French department, Labbe was not comfortable in that wealthy Boston suburb.

"Wellesley was a different culture for me," Labbe recalled. "There were no Franco-Americans there, and life was so different. I didn't have any access to the students. They were so programmed. They'd go to class, go to their afterschool activities, go to the guidance center – it was completely different in that community.

"That's when I decided to get back to Maine, to study and lay out a new course for myself."

Labbe returned to Orono in 1970 and in that year became part of a group that might be known as the Franco-American "Gang of Four." With Cecile Colin, Roger Pelletier and Annette Tanguay, he was able to organize a group of Francos to discuss ways to improve academic offerings to those of French-Canadian descent. The Gang of Four also was able to prevail upon the University for funds to help organize a program for Franco-Americans.

"I had an assistantship in 1970," said Labbe. "That year I met with other Francos. There were those who were full of conflict, who were involved in self-pity, things like that. But after talking and realizing how much we had in common through our heritage, we decided to do something about it. We wanted to organize a program that would make life on campus easier for Franco-Americans in this environment.

"We organized an orientation program in the summer of 1971. We wanted to go to Franco areas like Fort Kent and Caribou to talk with high school seniors who would be coming to Orono the following year. We had a problem obtaining permission to enter the schools. I guess administrators didn't want to hear there was a problem.

"It was a learning experience for us. We weren't very successful then, but that was the start of something bigger."

The following year, Labbe was able to get his program funded. The Franco-American Resources Opportunity Group captured much attention with its acronym approximating "frog." And several years later, the *FAROG Forum* emerged as tangible evidence of a vigorous Franco-American spirit. In past years, observers have seen minorities like blacks and chicanos lobby for greater opportunity, but Franco-Americans in New England were quiet. The Forum is helping to change that.

"The keystone of the entire effort here is the evolution of the people," Labbe commented. "One way in which we are trying to accomplish that is through the newspaper. I would say the whole project was an outgrowth of the late 60's and early 70's, when there was a lot of activism. Franco-Americans were not vocal. But now we are making statements that are being heard. We don't want to be ashamed of our language; we don't want to be told in class that our French is no good, and we must learn Parisian French.

"We're getting attention, too. The Quebec government is very interested in our activity, and we have contacts in France, too. They are becoming aware that there is a voice out there that speaks for Franco-Americans."

In addition to his willingness to press for the evolution of Francos, Labbe has received attention for his support of Quebec separatist Rene Levesque. Few Franco-Americans at this time appear concerned about the state of Canadian politics as it relates to Quebec. At the 1979 Franco-American convention in Providence, for instance, it was barely given passing notice. But Labbe is one Franco-American who is following developments there.

"I support the direction of Levesque's government. We support the people of Quebec. Now some people were taken back when this came out, but I don't think it's so unusual. We have a need to know

Quebec, and we have a need to be closer. If Levesque is successful in his efforts to create some kind of separate entity, he will be looking this way. They will need friends, and I think there will be a greater connection between the French-Canadians and the Franco-Americans."

Not the least of Labbe's opinions is his view on the nature of the Franco-Americans. While some see them as a passive people over the years, Labbe would dispute this.

"The public impression is that they are passive," he said. "I think they are active. They have been very active within their own society, but it has been a closed society. Much of what they've done has not been recognized by non-Francos, so you have people assuming the French are passive.

"For years living in the French context was a cultural support system. They are not as quiet as it would seem. If you sit in their kitchens and talk to them, you'll find they do know what they want."

What does Labbe see in the future?

"I definitely feel there will be a closeness among those of French descent. The Franco-Americans will have greater contact and sympathy with the French-Canadians, and vice-versa. Those of French descent in the United States and Canada will begin looking toward France for greater connections. There will be more unity on all levels in the future."

# Footnotes

1. Jacques-Donat Casanova, with the collaboration of Armour Landry, *America's French Heritage*, a joint publication of La Documentation Francaise and the Quebec Official Publisher, 1976, p. 113.
2. Mason Wade, *The French-Canadians, 1760-1967, Vol. I.*, (Toronto: MacMillan, 1968), p. 4.
3. Dr. Gerard Brault, "The French Origins of the Canadian Colonists: Toward A New Synthesis," paper delivered at the first international symposium, The Franco-American Presence in America, April 8-9, 1978, Bates College, Lewiston, Maine.
4. Wade, p. 18.
5. Casanova, p. 113.
6. French-Canadian and Acadian Genealogical Review, Vol. VI, no. 1, (Quebec; spring, 1978), p. 19.
7. Casanova, p. 86.
8. Wade, p. 3.
9. Earl of Durham, "Lord Durham's Report on the Affairs of British North America, 1839," edited by Sir Charles Lucas (New York: Augustus M. Kelley, Publishers, 1912), p. 40.
10. Ibid., p. 16.
11. The Rev. Thomas Albert, *History of Madawaska*, (Quebec: Imprimerie Franciscaine Missionnaire, 1920), p. 55.
12. Ibid.
13. Henry Wadsworth Longfellow, *Favorite Poems of Henry Wadsworth Longfellow*, "Evangeline," (Garden City, N. Y.: Doubleday and Company, Inc., 1947), pp. 316-363.
14. Albert, p. 66.
15. U. S. Bureau of the Census, Census of Population, 1970, "General Social and Economic Characteristics," interpreted by Prof. Madeleine Giguere, University of Southern Maine.
16. Research into the earliest days of the migration has been published by several writers, including Dr. Paul P. Chasse, Jacques Ducharme, and Ralph D. Vicero.
17. Steve Dunwell, *The Run of the Mill*, (Boston: David R. Godine, 1978), p. 35.
18. Benita Eisler, ed., *The Lowell Offering – Writings by New England Women (1840-45)*, (Philadelphia and New York: J. B. Lippincott Company, 1977), p. 19.
19. Dunwell, p. 97.
20. Eisler, p. 29.
21. Ralph D. Vicero, "Immigration of French-Canadians to New England, 1840-1900: A Geographical Analysis," unpublished thesis, University of Wisconsin, 1968, p. 99.
22. Luc Lacourciere, "Oral Tradition: New England and Canada."
23. Michael Guignard, "French-Canadian Migration to Biddeford," *Maine History News*, Vol. 7, No. 3, July 1972, p. 8.

222

24. Vicero, p. 289.
25. Vicero, p. 289.
26. Vicero, p. 289.
27. Robert B. Perreault, *One Piece of the Great American Mosaic – The Franco-Americans of New England*, (Manchester, N. H.: Le Canado-Americain, 1976), p. 20; utilizing material found in *Shadow of the Trees*, Jacques Ducharme (New York: Harper and Brothers, 1943).
28. Vicero, p. 275.
29. Vicero, p. 178, utilizing "Dwight Manufacturing Company papers – agent's letter book, April 12, 1859 - Feb. 1, 1860," p. 39.
30. Ibid., p. 178.
31. Dr. Paul P. Chasse, "The Church," Franco-American Ethnic Heritage Study Program, 1975, p. C-3.
32. Ibid., p. C-4.
33. Donald B. Cole, *Immigrant City: Lawrence, Massachusetts 1845-1921*, (Chapel Hill, N. C.: University of North Carolina Press, 1963), p. 65.
34. Dr. Paul P. Chasse, "Societies," Franco-American Ethnic Heritage Studies Program, 1975, p. S-2.
35. Dr. Paul P. Chasse, "Media," Franco-American Heritage Studies Program, 1975, p. M-1.
36. Chasse, "Media," pp. M-4, M-5.
37. Dr. Paul Chasse, "Labor and Economics," Franco-American Ethnic Heritage Studies Program, 1975, p. LE-4.
38. U. S. Department of Commerce, Historical Statistics of the United States, colonial times to 1970, Part 1, "Foreign-born Population, by country of birth, 1850-1970," (Washington: U. S. Government Printing Office, 1975), p. 117.
39. Ibid., p. 119.
40. Barbara Kaye Greenleaf, *America Fever – The Story of American Migration*, (New York: Four Winds Press, 1970), p. 158.
41. Vicero, p. 325.
42. Dr. Paul P. Chasse, "Education," Franco-American Ethnic Heritage Studies Program, 1975, p. E-3.
43. Dunwell, p. 144.
44. "American's Textile Industry – Bicentennial Edition," (Greenville, S. C.: Clark Publishing Co., 1976), p. 11.
45. Office of the Commissioner of Labor, Charles P. Neill, "Report on the Strike of Textile Workers in Lawrence, Mass., in 1912," (Washington: Government Printing Office, 1912), p. 19.
46. Ibid., p. 26.
47. Bill Cahn, *Mill Town*, (New York: Cameron and Kahn, 1954), p. 39.
48. "Strike of the Textile Workers in Lawrence, Mass.," p. 30.
49. Bessie Bloom Wessel, *An Ethnic Study of Woonsocket, R. I.*, (Chicago: University of Chicago Press, 1931), p. 234.
50. Dyke C. Hendrickson, "The Coming of the Franco-Americans," *The Maine Sunday Telegram*, May 8, 1977, p. D-3, col. 5.
51. President Carter's signing of Public Law 95-561 on Nov. 1, 1978, confirmed some minority status on Franco-Americans, however.
52. Dr. Paul P. Chasse, "Language and Assimilation," Franco-American Ethnic Heritage Studies Program, p. LA-4.

The Wannalancit Textile Co. in Lowell, Mass., is one of the few remaining textile factories in New England. Much has changed as it has aged. In foreground is a modern plant with landscaping, parking and modern ventilation. At right, on land once occupied by "little Canada," is federally subsidized housing. Photo was taken from a dormitory roof at the University of Lowell.

(Photo by Gordon Chibroski)

A sign of changing times—the note above the foreman's clipboard is written in English and Spanish. In past decades, the "other" language was French.

(Photo by Gordon Chibroski)

One of the last of the old mills, the Wannalancit Textile Co. in Lowell, Mass. The firm has survived in part because it has specialized—one of its major products is cloth for parachutes.

(Photo by Gordon Chibroski)

The English Conquest of North America in the mid-18th century has had repercussions on the French of this continent ever since. Here is one of the early French-Canadians to have arrived in New England—Moise Cartier of Biddeford, Maine. Cartier, widely known as Moses Quarter, is reported to have come from Quebec before 1850. This picture of Cartier, a brickmaker, was taken in 1905.

# Treaty of Paris

## Paris, February 10, 1763

**The Definitive Treaty of Peace and Friendship between his Britannick Majesty, the Most Christian King, and the King of Spain. Included here because of its tremendous impact on the lives of the French in North America.**

In the name of the Most Holy and Undivided Trinity, Father, Son, and Holy Ghost. So be it.

BE it known to all those to whom it shall, or may, in any manner, belong.

It has pleased the Most High to diffuse the spirit on union and concord among the Princes, whole divisions had spread troubles in the four parts of the world, and to inspire them with the inclination to cause the comforts of peace to succeed to the misfortunes of a long and bloody war, which having arisen between England and France, during the reign of the most serene and most potent Prince, George the Second, by the grace of God, King of Great-Britain, of glorious memory, continued under the reign of the most serene and most potent Prince, George the Third, his successor, and, in its progress, communicated itself to Spain and Portugal: Consequently, the most serene and most potent Prince, George the Third, his successor, and, in its progress, communicated itself to Spain and Portugal: Consequently, the most serene and most potent Prince, George the Third, by the grace of God, King of Great-Britain, France, and Ireland, Duke of Brunswick and Lunenbourg, Arch-Treasurer, and Elector, of the Holy Roman Empire; the most serene and most potent Prince, Lewis the Fifteenth, by the grace of God, Most Christian

King; and the most serene and most potent Prince, Charles the Third, by the Grace of God, King of Spain and of the Indies, after having laid the foundation of peace in the Preliminaries, signed at Fontain-bleau the third of November last; and the most serene and most potent Prince, Don Joseph the First, by the Grace of God, King of Portugal and of the Algarves, after having acceded thereto, determined to com-pleat, without delay, this great and important work. For this purpose, the high contracting parties have named and appointed their respec-tive Ambassadors Extraordinary and Ministers Plenipotentiary, viz. his Sacred Majesty the King of Great-Britain, the most illustrious and most excellent Lord, John Duke and Earl of Bedford, Marquess of Tavistock, $c. his Minister of State, Lieutenant General of his Armies, Keep of his Privy Seal, Knight of the most Noble Order of the Garter, and his Ambassador Extraordinary and Minister Pleni-potentiary to his most Christian Majesty; his Sacred Majesty the most Christian King, the most illustrious and most excellent Lord, Caesar Gabriel de Choiseul, Duke of Praslin, Peer of France, Knight of his Orders, Lieutenant General of his Armies and of the province of Britanny, Counsellor in all his Councils, and Ministers and Secretary of State, and of his Commands and Finances; his sacred Majesty the Catholic King, the most illustrious and most excellent Lord, Don Jerome Grimaldi, Marquis de Grimaldi, Knight of the most Christian King's Orders, Gentleman of his Catholick Majesty's Bed-Chamber in Employment; and his Ambassador Extraordinary to his most Christian Majesty; his Sacred Majesty the most Faithful King, the most illustrious and most excellent Lord, Martin de Mello and Castro, Knight Professed of the order of Christ, of his most Faithful Majesty's council, and his Ambassador; and Minister Plenipotentiary, to his most Christian Majesty.

Who, after having duly communicated to each other their full powers, in good form, copies whereof are transcribed at the end of the present treaty of peace, have agreed upon the articles, the tenor of which is as follows:

## I.

There shall be a Christian, universal, and perpetual peace, as well by sea as by land, and a sincere and constant friendship shall be re-established between their Britannick, most Christian, Catholick, and most Faithful Majesties, and between their heirs and successors, kingdoms, dominions, provinces, countries, subjects, and vassals, of what quality or condition soever they be, without exception of places or of persons; So that the high contracting parties shall give the greatest attention to maintain between themselves, and their said dominions and subjects, this reciprocal friendship and correspondence, without permitting, on either side, any kind of hostilities, by sea or by land, to be committed from henceforth, for any cause, or under any pretence whatsoever, and everything shall be carefully avoided, which might, hereafter, prejudice the union happily re-established, applying themselves, on the contrary, on every occasion, to procure for each other whatever may contribute to their mutual glory, interests, and advantages, without giving any assistance or protection, directly or indirectly, to those who would cause any prejudice to either of the high contracting parties: there shall be a general oblivion of every thing that may have been done or committed before, or since the commencement of the war, which is just ended.

## II.

The Treaties of Westphalia of 1648; those of Madrid between the crowns of Great-Britain and Spain of 1667, and 1670; the treaties of peace of Nimeguen of 1678, and 1679; of Ryswick of 1697; those of peace and of commerce of Utrecht of 1713; that of Baden of 1714; the treaty of the triple alliance of the Hague of 1717; that of the quadruple alliance of London of 1718; the treaty of peace of Vienna of 1738; the definitive treaty of Aix la Chapelle of 1748; and that of Madrid, between the crowns of Great-Britain and Spain, of 1750; as well as the treaties between the crowns of Spain and Portugal, of the 13th of February, 1668; of the 6th of February, 1715; and of the 12th of February, 1761; and that of the 11th of April, 1713, between France and Portugal, with the guaranties of Great-Britain; serve as a basis and foundation to the peace, and to the present treaty; and for this purpose, they are all renewed and confirmed in the best form, as well as all the general, which subsisted between the high contracting parties before the war, as if they were inserted here word for word, so that they are to be exactly observed, for the future, in their whole tenor, and religiously executed on all sides, in all their points, which shall not be derogated from by the present treaty, notwithstanding all that may have been stipulated to the contrary by any of the high contracting parties: and all the said parties declare, that they will not suffer any privilege, favour, or indulgence to subsist, contrary to the treaties above confirmed, except what shall have been agreed and stipulated by the present treaty.

## III.

All the prisoners made, on all sides, as well by land as by sea, and the hostages carried away, or given during the war, and to this day, shall be restored, without ransom, six weeks, at latest, to be computed from the day of the exchange of the ratification of the present treaty, each crown respectively paying the advances, which shall have been made for the subsistence and maintenance of their prisoners, by the Sovereign of the country where they shall have been detained, according to the attested receipts and estimates, and other authentic vouchers, which shall be furnished on one side and the other. And securities shall be reciprocally given for the payment of the debts which the prisoners shall have contracted in the countries, where they have been detained, until their entire liberty. And all the ships of war and merchant vessels, which shall have been taken since the expiration of the terms agreed upon for the cessation of hostilities by sea, shall likewise be restored bona fide, with all their crews and cargoes; and the execution of this article shall be proceeded upon immediately after the exchange of the ratifications of this treaty.

## IV.

His most Christian Majesty renounces all pretensions, which he has heretofore formed, or might have formed, to Nova Scotia, or Acadia, in all its parts, and guaranties the whole of it, and with all its dependencies, to the King of Great Britain: Moreover, his most Christian Majesty cedes, and guaranties to his said Britannick Majesty in full right, Canada, with all its dependencies, as well as the Island of Cape Breton, and all the other Islands and Coasts, in the gulph and river of St. Laurence, and in general, every thing that depends on the said Countries. Lands, Islands, and Coasts, with the sovereignty, property, possession, and all rights acquired by treaty, or otherwise, which the most Christian King, and the crown of France, have had, till now, over the said Countries, Islands, Lands, Places, Coasts, and their inhabitants, so that the most Christian King cedes and makes over the whole to the said King, and to the crown of Great-Britain, and that in the most ample manner and form, without restriction, and without any liberty to depart from the said cession and guaranty, under any pretence, or to distrub Great Britain in the possessions above-mentioned. His Britannick Majesty, on his side, agrees to grant the liberty of the Catholick religion to the inhabitants of Canada: He will, in consequence, give the most precise and most effectual orders, that his new Roman Catholick subjects may profess the worship of their religion, according to the rites of the Roman Church, as far as the laws of Great Britain permit. His Britannick Majesty further agrees, that the French inhabitants, or others who had been subjects of the most Christian King in Canada, may retire, with all safety and freedom, wherever they shall think proper, and may sell their estates, provided it be to the subjects of his Britannick Majesty, and bring away their effects, as well as their persons, without being restrained in their emigration, under any pretence whatsoever, except that of debts, or of criminal prosecutions: The term, limited for this emigration, shall be fixed to the space of eighteen months, to be computed from the day of the exchange of the ratification of the present treaty.

## V.

The subjects of France shall have the liberty of fishing and drying, on a part of the coasts of the island of Newfoundland, such as it is specified in the XIIIth article of the Treaty of Utrecht; which article is renewed and confirmed by the present treaty, (except what relates to the Island of Cap Breton, as well as to the other Islands and Coasts, in the mouth and in the gulph of St. Laurence): And his Britannick Majesty consents to leave to the subjects of the most Christian King, the liberty of fishing in the fulph St. Laurence, on condition that the subjects of France do not exercise the said fishery, but at the distance of three leagues from all the coasts belonging to Great Britain, as well those of the continent, as those of the Islands situated in the said gulph St. Laurence. And as to what related to the fishery on the coasts of the Island of Cape Breton, out of the said gulph, the subjects of the most Christian King shall not be permitted to exercise the said fishery, but at the distance of fifteen leagues from the coasts of the Island of Cape Breton; and the fishery on the coasts of Nova Scotia or Acadia, and every where else out of the said Gulph; shall remain on the foot of former treaties.

## VI.

The King of Great Britain cedes the islands of St. Pierre and Miquelon, in full right, to his most Christian Majesty, to serve as a shelter to the French fishermen; and his said most Christian Majesty engages not to fortify the said islands; to erect no buildings upon them, but merely for the convenience of the fishery; and to keep up them a guard of fifty men only for the police.

## VII.

In order to re-establish peace on solid and durable foundations, and to remove for ever all subject of dispute with regard to the limits of the British and Franch territories on the continent of America; it is agreed, that, for the future, the confines between the dominions of his Britannick Majesty, and those of his most Christian Majesty, in that part of the world, shall be fixed irrevocably by a line drawn along the middle of the River Mississippi, from its source, to the River Iberville, and from thence, by a line drawn along the middle of this River, and the Lakes Maurepas and Pontchartrain, to the sea: and for this purpose, the most Christian King cedes in full right, and guaranties to his Britannick Majesty, the River and Port of the Mobile, and every thing which he possesses, or ought to possess, on the left side of the River Mississippi, except the town of New Orleans, and the island in which it is situated, which shall remain to France; provided that the navigation of the River Mississippi, shall be equally free, as well to the subjects of Great Britain, as to those of France, in its whole breadth and length, from its source to the sea, and expresly that part, which is between the said island of New Orleans, and the right bank of that River, as well as the passage both in and out of its mouth: It is further stipulated, that the vessels belonging to the subjects of either nation, shall not be stopped, visited, or subjected to the payment of any duty whatsoever. The stipulations, inserted in the IVth article, in favour of the inhabitants of Canada, shall also take place, with regard to the inhabitants of the countries ceded by this article.

## VIII.

The King of Great Britain shall restore to France the islands of Guadeloupe, of Mariegalante, of D'Esirade, of Martinique, and of Bellisle; and the fortresses of these islands shall be restored in the same condition they were in, when they were conquered by the British arms; provided that his Britannick Majesty's subjects, who shall have settled in the said islands, or those who shall have any commercial affairs to settle there, or in the other places restored to France by the present treaty, shall have liberty to sell their lands and their estates, to settle their affairs, to recover their debts, and to bring away their effects, as well as their persons, on board vessels, which they shall be permitted to send to the said islands, and other places restored as above, and which shall serve for this use only, without being restrained, on account of their religion, or under any other pretence whatsoever, except that of debts, or of criminal prosecutions; and for this purpose, the term of eighteen months is allowed to his Britannick Majesty's subjects, to be computed from the day of the exchange of the ratifications of the present treaty; but, as the liberty, granted to his Britannick Majesty's subjects, to bring away their persons and their effects, in vessels of their nation, may be liable to abuses, if precautions were not taken to prevent them; it has been expresly agreed between his Britannick Majesty and his most Christian Majesty, that the number of English vessels, which shall have leave to go to the said islands and places restored to France, shall be limited, as well as the number of tons of each one; that they shall go in ballast; shall set sail at a fixed time; and shall make one voyage only, all the effects, belonging to the English, being to be embarked at the same time. It has been further agreed, that his most Christian Majesty shall cause the necessary passports to be given to the said vessels; that, for the greater security, it shall be allowed to place two French Clerks, or Guards, in each of the said vessels, which shall be visited in the landing places, and ports of the said islands, and places, restored to France, and that the merchandise which shall be found therein, shall be confiscated.

## IX.

The most Christian King cedes and guaranties to his Britannick Majesty, in full right, the islands of Grenada, and the Grenadines, with the same stipulations in favour of the inhabitants of this Colony, inserted in the IVth article for those of Canada: and the partition of the islands called neutral, is agreed and fixed, so that those of St. Vincent, Dominica, and Tobago, shall remain in full right to Great Britain, and that of St. Lucia shall be delivered to France, to enjoy the same likewise in full right: and the high contracting parties guaranty the partition so stipulated.

## X.

His Britannick Majesty shall restore to France the island of Goree in the condition it was in when conquered: and his most Christian Majesty cedes in full right, and guaranties to the King of Great Britain the River Senegal, with the forts and factories of St. Lewis, Podor, and Galam, and with all the rights and dependencies of the said River Senegal.

## XI.

In the East Indies, Great Britain shall restore to France, in the condition they are now in, the different factories, which that Crown possessed, as well as on the coast of Coromandel, and Orixa, as on that of Malabar, as also in Bengal, at the beginning of the year 1749. And his most Christian Majesty renounces all pretension to the acquisitions which he has made on the coast of Coromandel and Orixa, since the said beginning of the year 1749. His most Christian Majesty shall restore, on his side, all that he may have conquered from Great Britain, in the East Indies, during the present war; and will expresly cause Nattal and Tapanoully, in the island of Sumatra, to be restored; he engages further, not to erect fortifications, or to keep troops in any part of the dominions of the Subah of Bengal. And in order to preserve future peace on the Coast of Coromandel and Orixa, the English and French shall acknowledge Mahomet Ally Khan for lawful Nabob of the Carnatick, and Salabat Jing for lawful Subah of the Decan; and both parties shall renounce all demands and pretensions of satisfaction, with which they might charge each other, or their Indian allies, for the depredations, or pillage, committed, on the one side, or on the other, during the war.

### XII.

The Island of Minorca shall be restored to his Britannick Majesty, as well as Fort St. Philip, the same condition they were in, when conquered by the arms of the most Christian King; and with the artillery which was there, when the said Island, and the said fort were taken.

### XIII.

The town and port of Dunkirk shall be put into the state fixed by the last treaty of Aix la Chapelle, and be former treaties. The Cunette shall be destroyed immediately after the exchange of the ratifications of the present treaty, as well as the forts and batteries which defend the entrance on the side of the sea; and provision shall be made, at the same time, for the wholesomeness of the air, and for the health of the inhabitants, by some other means, to the satisfaction of the King of Great Britain.

### XIV.

France shall restore all the countries belonging to the Electorate of Hanover, to the Landgrave of Hesse, to the Duke of Brunswick, and to the Count of La Lippe Buckebourg, whichare, or shall be occupied by his most Christian Majesty's arms: the fortresses of these different countries shall be restored in the same condition they were in, when conquered by the French Arms; and the pieces of artillery, which shall have been carried elsewhere, shall be replaced by the same number, of the same bore, weight, and metal.

### XV.

In case the stipulations, contained in the XIIIth article of the preliminaries, should not be compleated at the time of the signature of the present treaty, as well with regard to the evacuations to be made by the armies of France of the fortresses of Cleves, Wezel, Guelders, and of all the countries belonging to the King of Prussia, as with regard to the evacuations to be made by the British and French armies of the countries which they occupy in Westphalia, Lower Saxony, on the Lower Rhine, the Upper Rhine, and in all the Empire; and to the retreat of the troops into the dominions of their respective Sovereigns: their Britannick, and most Christian Majesties promise to proceed, bona fide, with all the dispatch the case will permit of, to the said evacuations, the entire completion whereof they stipulate before the 15th of March next, or sooner if it can be done; and their Britannick and most Christian Majesties further engage, and promise to each other, not to furnish any succours, of any kind, to their respective allies, who shall continue engaged in the war in Germany.

## XVI.

The decision of the prizes made, in time of peace, by the subjects of Great Britain, on the Spaniards, shall be referred to the Courts of Justice of the Admiralty of Great Britain, conformably to the rules established among all nations, so that the validity of the said prizes, between the British and Spanish nations, shall be decided and judged, according to the law of nations, and according to treaties, in the courts of justice of the nation, who shall have made the capture.

## XVII.

His Britannick Majesty shall cause to be demolished all the fortifications which his subjects shall have erected in the Bay of Honduras, and other places of the territory of Spain in that part of the world, four months after the ratification of the present treaty; and his Catholick Majesty shall not permit his Britannick Majesty's subjects, or their workmen, to be disturbed, or molested, under any pretence whatsoever, in the said places, in their occupation of cutting, loading, and carrying away Logwood; and for this purpose, they may build without hindrance, and occupy, without interruption, the houses and magazines, necessary for them, for their families, and for their effects: and his Catholick Majesty assures to them, but this article, the full enjoyment of those advantages, and powers, on the Spanish coasts and territories, as above stipulated, immediately after the ratification of the present treaty.

## XVIII.

His Catholick Majesty desists, as well for himself, as for his successors, from all pretension, which he may have formed, in favour of the Guipuscoans, and other subjects, to the right of fishing in the neighborhood of the island of Newfoundland.

## XIX.

The King of Great-Britain shall restore to Spain all the territory which he has conquered in the island of Cuba, with the fortress of the Havana; and this fortress, as well as the other fortresses of the said island, shall be restored in the same condition they were in when conquered by his Britannick Majesty's arms; provided, that his Britannick Majesty's subjects, who shall have settled in the said island, restored to Spain by the present treaty, or those who shall have any commercial affairs to settle there, shall have liberty to see their lands, and their estates, to settle their affairs, to recover their debts, and to bring away their effects, as well as their persons, on board vessels which they shall be permitted to send to the said island restored as above, and which shall serve for that use only, without being restrained on account of their religion, or under any other pretence whatsoever, except that of debts, or of criminal prosecutions: And for this purpose, the term of eighteen months is allowed to his Britannick Majesty's subjects, to be computed from the day of the exchange of the ratifications of the present treaty: but as the liberty, granted to his Britannick Majesty's subjects, to bring away their persons, and their effects, in vessels of their nation, may be liable to abuses, if precautions were not taken to prevent them; it has been expresly agreed, between his Britannick Majesty and his Catholick Majesty, that the number of English vessels, which shall have leave to go to the said island restored to Spain, shall be limited, as well as the number of tons of each one; that they shall go in ballast; shall set sail at a fixed time; and shall make one voyage only; all the effects belonging to the English being to be embarked at the same time; it has been further agreed, that his Catholick Majesty shall cause the necessary passports to be given to the said vessels; that, for the greater security, it shall be allowed to place two Spanish clerks, or guards, in each of the said vessels, which shall be visited in the landing-places, and ports of the said island restored to Spain, and that the merchandize, which shall be found therein, shall be confiscated.

## XX.

In consequence of the restitution stipulated in the preceding article, his Catholick Majesty cedes and guaranties, in full right, to his Britannick Majesty, Florida, with Fort St. Augustin, and the Bay of Pensacola, as well as all that Spain possesses on the continent of North-America, to the East, or to the South-East, of the river Mississippi. And, in general, every thing that depends on the said countries and lands, with the sovereignty, property, possession, and all rights, acquired by treaties or otherwise, which the Catholick King, and the crown of Spain, have had till now, over the said countries, lands, places, and their inhabitants; so that the Catholick King cedes and makes over the whole to the said King, and to the crown of Great Britain, and that in the most ample manner and form. His Britannick Majesty agrees, on his side, to grant to the inhabitants of the countries above ceded, the liberty of the Catholic religion: he will consequently give the most express and the most effectual orders, that his new Roman Catholic subjects may profess the worship of their religion according to the rites of the Romish church, as far as the laws of Great-Britain permit. His Britannick Majesty farther agrees, that the Spanish inhabitants, or others who had been subjects of the Catholick King in the said countries, may retire, with all safety and freedom, wherever they think proper; and may sell their estates, provided it be to his Britannick Majesty's subjects, and bring away their effects, as well as their persons, without being restrained in their emigration, under any pretence whatsoever, except that of debts, or of criminal prosecutions: the term, limited for this emigration, being fixed to the space of eighteen months, to be computed from the day of the exchange of the ratifications of the present treaty. It is moreover stipulated, that his Catholick Majesty shall have power to cause all the effects, that may belong to him, to be brought away, whether it be artillery or other things.

## XXI.

The French and Spanish troops shall evacuate all the territories, lands, towns, places, and castles, of his most faithful Majesty, in Europe without any reserve, which shall have been conquered, with the same artillery, and ammunition, which were found there: And with regard to the Portuguese Colonies in America, Africa, or in the East Indies, if any change shall have happened there, all things shall be restored on the same footing they were in, and conformably to the preceding treaties which subsisted between the Courts of France, Spain, and Portugal, before the present war.

## XXII.

All the papers, letters, documents, and archives, which were found in the countries territories, towns, and places, that are restored, and those belonging to the countries ceded, shall be, respectively and bona fide, delivered, or furnished at the same time, if possible, that possession is taken, or, at least, four months after the exchange of the ratifications of the present treaty, in whatever places the said papers or documents may be found.

## XXIII.

All the countries and territories, which may have been conquered, in whatsoever part of the world, by the arms of their Britannick and most Faithful Majesties, as well as by those of their most Christian and Catholick Majesties, which are not included in the present treaty, either under the title of cessions, or under the title of restitutions, shall be restored without difficulty, and without requiring any compensations.

## XXIV.

As it is necessary to assign a fixed epoch for the restitutions, and the evacuations, to be made by each of the high contracting parties, it is agreed, that the British and French troops shall compleat, before the 15th of March next, all that shall remain to be executed of the XIIth and XIIIth articles of the preliminaries, signed the 3d day of November last, with regard to the evacuation to be made in the

Empire, or selsewhere. The island of Bell Isle shall be evacuated six weeks after the exchange of the ratifications of the present treaty, or sooner if it can be done. Guadaloupe, Desirade, Mariegalante, Martinico, and St. Lucia, three months after the exchange of the ratifications of the present treaty, or sooner if it can be done. Great-Britain shall likewise, at the end of three months after the exchange of the ratifications of the present treaty, or sooner if it can be done, enter into possession of the river and port of the Mobile,. and of all that is to form the limits of the territory of Great-Britain, on the side of the river Mississippi, as they are specified in the VIIth article. The island of Goree shall be evacuated by Great-Britain, three months after the exchange of the ratifications of the present treaty; and the island of Minorca, by France, at the same epoch, or sooner if it can be done: And according to the conditions of the VIth article, France shall likewise enter into possession of the islands of St. Peter, and of Miquelon, at the end of three months after the exchange of the ratifications of the present treaty. The Factories in the East-Indies shall be restored six months after the exchange of the ratifications of the present treaty, or sooner if it can be done. The fortress of the Havana, with all that has been conquered in the island of Cuba, shall be restored three months after the exchange of the ratifications of the present treaty, or sooner if it can be done: and, at the same time, Great-Britain shall enter into possession of the country ceded by Spain according to the XXth article. All the places and countries of his most Faithful Majesty, in Europe, shall be restored immediately after the exchange of the ratification of the present treaty: And the Portuguese colonies, which may have been conquered, shall be restored in the space of three months in the West-Indies, and of six months in the East-Indies, after the exchange of the ratifications of the present treaty, or sooner if it canbe done. All the fortresses, the restitution whereof is stipulated above, shall be restored with the artillery and ammunition, which were found there at the time of the conquest. In consequence whereof, the necessary orders shall be sent by each of the high contracting parties, with reciprocal passports for the ships shall carry them, immediately after the exchange of the ratifications of the present treaty.

## XXV.

His Britannick Majesty, as electorate of Brunswick Lunenbourg, as well for himself, as for his heirs and successors, and all the dominions and possessions of his said Majesty in Germany, are included and guarantied by the present treaty of peace.

## XXVI.

Their sacred Britannick, most Christian, Catholick, and most Faithful Majesties, promise to observe, sincerely and bona fide, all the articles contained and settled in the present treaty; and they will not suffer the same to be infringed, directly or indirectly, by their respective subjects; and the said high contracting parties, generally and reciprocally, guaranty to each other all the stipulations of the present treaty.

## XXVII.

The solemn ratification of the present treaty expedited in good and due form, shall be exchanged in this City of Paris, between the high contracting parties, in the space of a month, or sooner if possible, to be computed from the day of the signature of the present treaty.

In witness whereof, we the underwritten their Ambassadors Extraordinary, and Ministers Plenipotentiary, have signed with our hand, in their name, and in virtue of our full powers, have signed the present definitive treaty, and have caused the seal of our arms to be put thereto. Done at Paris the tenth day of February, 1763.

(L.S.) Bedford, C.P.S.

(L.S.) Choiseul, Duc de Praslin

(L.S.) El Marq. de Grimaldi

### Separate Articles

### I.

Some of the titles made use of by the contracting powers, either in the full powers, and other acts, during the course of the negotiation, or in the preamble of the present treaty, not being generally acknowledged, it has been agreed, that no prejudice shall ever result therefrom to any of the said contracting parties, and that the titles, taken or omitted, on either side, on occasion of the said negotiation, and of the present treaty, shall not be cited, or quoted as a precedent.

## II.

It has been agreed and determined; that the French language, made use of in all the copies of the present treaty, shall not become an example, which may be alledged, or made a precedent of, or prejudice, in any manner. and of the contracting powers; and that they shall conform themselves, for the future, to what has been observed, and ought to be observed, with regard to, and on the part of powers, who are used, and have a right, to give and to receive copies of like treaties in another language than French; the present treaty having still the same force and effect, as if the aforesaid custom had been therein observed.

## III.

Though the King of Portugal has not signed the present definitive treaty, their Britannick, most Christian, and Catholick Majesties, acknowledge, nevertheless; that his most Faithful Majesty is formally included therein as a contracting party, and as if he had expresly signed the said treaty: Consequently, their Britannick, most Christian, and Catholick Majesties, respectively and conjointly, promise to his most Faithful Majesty, in the most express and most binding manner, the execution of all and every the clauses, contained in the said treaty on his act of accession.

The present Separate Articles shall have the same force as if they were inserted in the treaty.

In witness hereof, We the under-written Ambassadors Extraordinary, and Ministers Plenipotentiary of their Britannick, most Christian, and Catholick Majesties, have seigned the present Separate Articles and have caused the seal of our arms to be put thereto.

Done at Paris, the 10th of February, 1763

(L.S.)  Bedford, C.P.S.

(L.S.)  Choiseul, Du de Praslin

(L.S.)  El Marq. de Grimaldi

## His Britannick Majesty's Full Power

GEORGE the third, by the grace of God, King of Great-Britain, France, and Ireland, Defender of the Faith, Duke of Brunswick and Lunenbourg, Arch-Treasurer, and Prince Elector, of the Holy Roman Empire, &c. To all and singular to whom these presents shall come, Greeting. Whereas, in order to perfect the peace, between Us and our good Brother the most Faithful King, on the one part, and our good Brothers the most Christian and Catholick Kings, on the other, which has been happily begun by the Preliminary Articles already signed at Fontainbleau the 3d of this month; and to bring the same to the desired end. We have thought proper to invest some fit person with full authority, on our part: Know ye, that We, having most entire confidence in the fidelity, judgement, skill, and ability in managing affairs of the greatest consequence, of our right trusty, and right entirely beloved cousin and Counsellor, John Duke and Earl of Bedford, Marquess of Tavistock, Baron Russel of Cheneys, Baron Russell of Thornhaugh, and Baron Howland of Streatham, Lieutenant-General of our forces, Keeper of our Privy Seal, Lieutenant and Custos Rotulorum of the countries of Bedford and Devon, Knight of our most noble order of the Garter, and our Ambassador Extraordinary and Plenipotentiary to our good Brother the most Christian King, have nominated, made, constituted, and appointed, as by these presents, we do nominate, make, constitute, and appoint Him, our true, certain, and undoubted Minister, Commissary, Deputy, Procurator, and Plenipotentiary, giving to him all and all manner of power, faculty, and authority, as well as our general and special command (yet so as that the general do not derogate from the special, or on the contrary) for Us and in our name, to meet and confer, as well singly and separately, as jointly, and in a body, with the Ambassadors, Commissaries, Deputies, and Plenipotentiaries, of the Princes, whom it may concern, vested with sufficient power and authority for that purpose, and with them to agree upon, treat, consult, and conclude, concering the re-establishing, as soon as may be, a firm and lasting peace, and sincere friendship and concord; and whatever shall be so agreed and concluded, for Us and in our name, to sign, and to make a treaty or treaties, on what shall have been so agreed and concluded, and to transact every thing else that may belong to the happy completion of the aforesaid work, in as ample a manner and form, and with the same force and effect, as We ourselves, if we were present, could do and perform; engaging and promising, on our royal word, that we will approve, ratify, and accept, in the best manner, whatever shall happen to be transacted and concluded by our said Plenipotentiary, and that We will never suffer any person to infringe or act contrary to the same, either in the whole or in part. In witness and confirmation whereof We have caused our great Seal of Great-Britain to be affixed to these presents, signed with our royal hand. Given at our Palace at St. James's, the 12th day of November., 1762, in the third year of our reign.

## His Most Christian Majesty's Full Power

LEWIS, by the grace of God, King of France and Navarre, To all who shall see these presents, Greeting. Whereas the Preliminaries, signed at Fontainebleau the 3d of November of the last year, laid the foundation of the peace re-established between us and our most dear and most beloved good Brother and Cousin the King of Spain, on the one part, and our most dear and most beloved good Brother the King of Great-Britain, and our most dear and most beloved good Brother and Cousin the King of Portugal, on the other, We have had nothing more at heart, since that happy epoch, than to consolidate and strengthen, in the most lasting manner, so salutary and so important a work, by a solemn and definitive treaty between Us and the said powers. For these causes, and other good considerations, Us thereunto moving, We trusting entirely in the capacity and experience., zeal and fidelity of our service, of our most dear and well-beloved Cousin, Caesar Gabriel de Choiseul, Duke of Praslin, Peer of France, Knight of our Orders, Lieutenant General of our Forces and of the province of Britany, Counsellor in all our Councils, Minister and Secretary of State, and of our Commands and Finances, We have named, appointed, and deputed him, and by these presents, signed with our hand, do name, appoint, and depute him, our Minister Plenipotentiary, giving him full and absolute power to act in that quality, and to confer, negotiate, treat, and agree, jointly with the Minister Plenipotentiary of our most dear and most beloved good Brother the King of Great-Britain, the Minister Plenipotentiary of our most dear and most beloved good Brother and Cousin the King of Spaine, and the Minister Plenipotentiary of our most dear and most beloved good Brother and Cousin the King of Portugal, vested with full powers, in good form, to agree, conclude, and sign, such articles, conditions, conventions, declarations, definitive treaty, accessions, and other acts whatsoever, that he shall judge proper for securing and strengthening the great work of peace, the whole with the same latitude and authority, that We ourselves might do, if We were there in person, even though there should be something which might require a more Special order than what is contained in these present's, promising on the faith and word of a King, to approve, keep firm and stable forever. to fulfill and execute punctually, all that our said Cousin, the Duke of Praslin, shall have stipulated, promised, and signed, in virtue of the present full power, without ever acting contrary thereto, or permitting any thing contrary thereto, for any cause, or under any pretence whatsoever, as also to cause our letters of ratification to be expedited in good form, and to cause them to be delivered, in order to be exchanged within the time that shall be agreed upon. For such is our pleasure. In witness whereof, we have caused our Seal to be put to these presents. Given at Versailles the 7th day of the month of February, in the year of Grace 1763, and of our reign the forty-eighth. Signed Lewis, and on the fold, by the King, the Duke of Choiseul. Sealed with the great Seal of yellow Wax.

### His Catholick Majesty's full Power

DON CARLOS, by the grace of God, King of Castille, of Leon, of Arragon, of the two Sicilies, of Jerusalem, of Navarre, of Granada, of Toledo, of Valencia. of Galicia. of Majorca, of Seville, of Sardinia, of Cordova, of Corsica, of Murcia, of Jaen, of the Algarves, of Algecira, of Gibraltar, of the Canary Islands, of the East and West-Indies, Islands and Continent, of the Ocean, Arch-Duke of Austria, Duke of Burgundy, of Brabant and Milan, Count of Hapsburg, of Flanders, of Tirol and Barcelona: Lord of Biscay and of Molino &c Whereas preliminaries of a solid and lasting peace between this Crown, and that of France as the one part, and that of England and Portugal on the other, were concluded and signed in the Royal Residence of Fontainebleau, the 3d of November of the present year, and the respective ratifications thereof exchange on the 22d of the same month, by Ministers authorized for that purpose, wherein it is promised, that a definitive treaty should be forthwith entered upon, having established and regulated the chief points upon which it is to turn: and whereas in the same manner as I granted to you, Don Jerome Grimaldi, Marquis deGrimaldi, Knight of the Order of the Holy Ghost, Gentleman of my Bed-Chamber with employment, and my Ambassador Extraordinary to the most Christian King, my full power to treat, adjust, and sign the before-mentioned preliminaries, it is necessary to grant the same to you, or to some other, to treat, adjust, and sign the promised definitive treaty of peace as aforesaid: therefore, as you the said Don Jerome Grimaldi, Marquis de Grimaldi, are at the convenient place, and as I have every day fresh motives, from your approved fidelity and zeal, capacity and prudence, to entrust to you this, and other like concerns of my Crown, I have appointed you my Minister Plenipotentiary, and granted to you my full power, to the end, that, in my name, and representing my person, you may treat, regulate, settle and sign the said definitive treaty of peace between my Crown, and that of France on the one part, that of England, and that of Portugal on the other, with the Ministers who shall be equally and specially authorized by their respective Sovereigns for the same purpose; acknowledging, as I do from this time acknowledge, as accepted and ratified, whatever you shall so treat, conclude and sign; promising on my Royal Word, that I will observe and fulfill the same, will cause it to be observed and fulfilled, as if it had been treated, concluded and signed by myself. In witness whereof, I have caused these presents to be dispatched, signed by my hand, sealed with my privy seal, and countersigned by my underwritten Counsellor of State, and first Secretary for the department of State and of War. Buen Retiro, the tenth of December, 1762.

(Signed)  I The King

(Lower)  Richard Wall

**Declaration of his most Christian Majesty's Plenipotentiary, with regard to the Debts due to the Canadians.**

THE KING of Great Britain having desired, that the payment of the letters of exchange and bills, which had been delivered to the Canadians for the necessaries furnished to the French troops, should be secured, his most Christian Majesty, entirely disposed to render to every one that justice which is legally due to them, has declared, and does declare, that the said bills, and letters of exchange, shall be punctually paid, agreeably to a liquidation made in a convenient time, according to the distance of the places, and to what shall be possible, taking care, however, that, the bills and letters of exchange, which the French subjects may have at the time of this declaration, but not confounded with the bills and letters of exchange, which are in the possession of the new subjects of the King of Great Britain.

In witness whereof, we the underwritten Minister of his most Christian Majesty, duly authorized for this purpose, have signed the present declaration, and caused the Seal of our Arms to be put thereto.

Done at Paris the 10th of February, 1763.

(L.S.) Choiseul Duc de Praslin

**Declaration of His Britannick Majesty's Ambassador Extra-ordinary and Plenipotentiary, with regard to the limits of Bengal in the East Indies.**

WE the underwritten Ambassador Extraordinary and Plenipotentiary of the King of Great Britain, in order to prevent all subject of dispute on account of the limits of the Dominions of the Subah of Bengal, as well as of the Coast of Coromandel and Orixa, declare, in the Name and by order of his said Britannick Majesty, that the said Dominions of the Subah of Bengal shall be reputed not to extend farther than Yanaon exclusively, and that Yanaon shall be considered as included in the north part of the Coast of Coromandel or Orixa.

In witness whereof, we the underwritten Minister Plenipotentiary of his Majesty the King of Great Britain, have signed the present declaration, and have caused the Seal of our Arms to be put thereto.

Done at Paris the 10th of February, 1763.

(L.S.) Bedford, C.P.S.

### Accession of his most Faithful Majesty.

In the Name of the Most Holy and Undivided Trinity, Father, Son, and Holy Ghost. So be it.

BE it known to all those to whom it shall, or may, belong; the Ambassadors and Plenipotentiaries of his Britannick Majesty, of his most Christian Majesty, and of his Catholick Majesty, having concluded and signed at Paris, the 10th of February of this year, a definitive treaty of peace, and separate articles, the tenor of which is as follows.

### Fiat Intertio

And the said Ambassadors and Plenipotentiaries having in a friendly manner invited the Ambassador and Minister Plenipotentiary of his most Faithful Majesty to accede thereto in the Name of his said Majesty; the underwritten Ministers Plenipotentiary, viz. On the part of the most serene and most potent Prince, George the Third, by the grace of God, King of Great-Britain, France, and Ireland, Duke of Brunswick, and Lunenbourg, Arch-Treasurer, and Elector of the Holy Roman Empire, the most illustrious and most Excellent Lord, John Duke and Earl of Bedford, Marquess of Tavistock, &c. Minister of State to the King of Great Britain, Lieutenant-General of his forces, Keeper of his Privy Seal, Knight of the most noble order of the Garter, and his Ambassador Extraordinary and Plenipotentiary to his most Christian Majesty; and on the part of the most Serene and most Potent Prince, Don Joseph the first, by the Grace of God, King of Portugal ad of the Algarves, the most illustrious and most Excellent Lord, Martin de Mello and Castro, Knight professed of the Order of Christ, of his most Faithful Majesty's Council, and his Ambassador and Minister Plenipotentiary to his most Christian Majesty, in virtue of their full powers, which they have communicated to each other, and of which copies shall be added at the end of the present act, having agreed upon what follows; viz. His most Faithful Majesty desiring most sincerely to in the speedy re-establishment of peace, accedes, in virtue of the present act, to the said definitive treaty and separate articles, as they are above transcribed, without any reserve or exception, in the firm confidence that every thing that is promised to his said Majesty, will be bona fide fulfilled, declaring at the same time, and promising to fulfill, with equal fidelity, all the articles, clauses, and conditions, which concern him. On his side, his Britannick Majesty accepts the present accession of his most Faithful Majesty, and promises likewise to fulfill, without any reserve or exception, all the articles, clauses, and conditions contained in the said definitive treaty and separate articles above inserted. The ratifications of the present treaty shall be exchanged in the space of one month, to be computed from this day, or sooner if it can be done.

In witness whereof, we, Ambassadors and Ministers Plenipotentiary of his Britannick Majesty, and of his most Faithful Majesty, have signed the present act, and have caused the seal of our arms to be put thereto.

Done at Paris, the 10th of February 1763.

> (L.S.)  Bedford, C.P.A.
>
> (L.S.)  De Mello et Castro

## His most faithful Majesty's full Power

DON JOSEPH, by the grace of God, King of Portugal, and of the Algarves, on this side the Sea, and on that side in Africa. Lord of Guinea, and of the conquest, navigation, commerce of Ethiopa, Arabia, Persia, and India, &c. I make known to those who shall see these my letters Patent, that desiring nothing more than to see the flame of war, which has raged so many years in all Europe, extinguished, and to co-operate (as far as depends upon me) towards its being succeeded by a just peace, established upon solid principles; and being informed, that great part of the belligerant powers entertain the same pacifick dispositions, I am to nominate a person, to assist, in my name, at the assemblies and conferences to be held upon this important business, who, by his nobility, prudence and dexterity, is worthy of my confidence; whereas these several qualities concur in Martin de Mello de Castro, of my council, and my Envoy Extraordinary and Plenipotentiary to the Court of London; and as from the experience I have, that he has always served me to my satisfaction, in everything I have charged him with, relying, that I shall, from henceforward, have fresh cause for the confidence I have placed in him, I nominate and constitute him my Ambassador and Plenipotentiary, in order that he may, as such, assist, in my name, at any congresses, assemblies, or conferences, as well publick, as private, in which the business of pacification may be treated; negotiating and agreeing with the Ambassadors, and Plenipotentiaries of the said belligerant powers, whatever may relate to the said peace; and concluding what he shall negociate between me and my belligerent Kings and Princes, under the conditions he shall stipulate in my Royal Name: therefore, for the above purposes, I grant him all the full powers and authority, general and special, which may be necessary; and I promise, upon the faith and word of a King, that I will acknowledge to be firm and valid, and will ratify within the time agreed upon, whatever shall be contracted and stipulated by my said Ambassador and Plenipotentiary, with the aforesaid Ambassadors and Ministers of the belligerant Kings and Princes, who shall be furnished by them with equal powers: In witness whereof, I have ordered these presents to be made out, signed by myself, sealed with the Seal of my Arms thereunto affixed, and countersigned by my Secretary and Minister of State for foreign affairs and war. Given at the Palace of our Lady of Ajuda, the eighteenth day of September, of the year from the Birth of our Lord Jesus Christ, 1762.

The King.

Locus Sigrilli Pendentis.

Don Lewis Da Cunha

Letters Patent whereby your Majesty is pleased to nominate Martin de Mello de Castro to be your Ambassador and Plenipotentiary for the negotiation and conclusion of peace, in the form above set forth.

For your Majesty's Inspection.

**Declaration of his most Faithful Majesty's Ambassador and Minister Plenipotentiary, with regard to alternating with Great Britain and France.**

WHEREAS on the conclusion of the negotiation of the definitive treaty, signed at Paris this 10th day of February, a difficulty arose as to the order of signing, which might have retarded the conclusion of the said treaty. We the underwritten, Ambassador and Minister Plenipotentiary of his most Faithful Majesty, declare, that the alternative observed, on the part of the King of Great Britain, and the most Christian King, with the most Faithful King, in the act of accession of the court of Portugal, was granted by their Britannick and Most Christian Majesties, solely with a view to accelerate the conclusion of the definitive treaty, and by that means, the more speedily to consolidate so important and so salutary a work; and that this complaisance of their Britannick and most Christian Majesties shall not be made any precedent for the future; the court of Portugal shall not alledge it as an example in their favor; shall derive therefrom no right, title, or pretention, for any cause, or under any pretence whatsoever.

In witness whereof, We, Ambassador and Minister Plenipotentiary of his most Faithful Majesty, duly authorized for this purpose, have signed the present declaration, and have caused the seal of our arms to be put thereto.

Done at Paris, the 10th of February, 1763.

(L.S.)  Martin De Mello Et Castro

---

Source: National Material Development Center, Bedford, N. H.

# A Guide to the

# Residences of Franco-Americans

# in New England

# Appendix A

**Percent French Mother Tongue Population for Selected States**

| Area | Total Population | Fr. Mo. Tongue | % Fr. Mo. Tongue |
|---|---|---|---|
| Maine | 993,663 | 141,489 | 14.2 |
| New Hampshire | 737,681 | 112,278 | 15.2 |
| Vermont | 444,330 | 42,193 | 9.5 |
| Massachusetts | 5,688,903 | 367,194 | 6.4 |
| Rhode Island | 948,844 | 101,270 | 10.7 |
| Connecticut | 3,031,705 | 142,118 | 4.7 |
| Louisiana | 3,640,442 | 572,262 | 15.4 |
| New York | 18,236,882 | 208,801 | 1.4 |
| New Jersey | 7,168,143 | 44,445 | .6 |
| Pennsylvania | 11,793,864 | 33,723 | .3 |
| Ohio | 10,650,903 | 32,014 | .3 |
| Illinois | 11,109,450 | 51,942 | .5 |
| Indiana | 5,193,665 | 14,777 | .3 |
| Michigan | 8,875,068 | 81,684 | .9 |
| Wisconsin | 4,417,731 | 24,317 | .6 |
| Minnesota | 3,304,971 | 28,413 | .7 |
| Missouri | 4,676,495 | 13,980 | .3 |
| Maryland | 3,922,391 | 22,072 | .6 |
| Virginia | 4,648,478 | 22,693 | .5 |
| Florida | 6,789,383 | 64,378 | .9 |
| Texas | 11,195,416 | 90,902 | .8 |
| Washington | 3,405,161 | 24,540 | .7 |
| California | 19,957,304 | 200,784 | 1.0 |
| United States | 203,210,158 | 2,598,400 | 1.3 |

The following question was asked to determine mother tongue: "What language other than English was usually spoken in this person's home when he was a child?"

Source: U. S. Bureau of the Census, Census of Population, 1970, *General Social and Economic Characteristics*, Selected States, Table 49.
Percentages computed by Franco-American Files, University of Maine at Portland-Gorham.

# *Appendix B*

**Percent Distribution of French Mother Tongue Population
by Selected States**

| Area | Fr. Mo. Tongue | % Fr. Mo. Tongue |
|------|------|------|
| Maine | 141,489 | 5.4 |
| New Hampshire | 112,278 | 4.3 |
| Vermont | 42,193 | 1.6 |
| Massachusetts | 367,194 | 14.1 |
| Rhode Island | 101,270 | 3.9 |
| Connecticut | 142,118 | 5.5 |
| Louisiana | 572,262 | 22.0 |
| New York | 208,801 | 8.0 |
| New Jersey | 44,445 | 1.7 |
| Illinois | 51,942 | 2.0 |
| Michigan | 81,684 | 3.1 |
| Florida | 64,378 | 2.5 |
| Texas | 90,902 | 3.5 |
| California | 200,784 | 7.7 |
| Other States | 376,668 | 14.7 |
| | | |
| United States | 2,598,408 | 100.0 |

Source: U. S. Bureau of the Census, Census of Population, 1970,
*General Social and Economic Characteristics*, United States
Summary, Tables 146, 147.
Percentages computed by Franco-American Files, University of Maine
at Portland-Gorham.

# Appendix C

### Number and Percent of Selected Foreign
### Mother Tongue Populations in the United States, 1970

|  | Native Population | Foreign Born | Total Population | % Total Population |
|---|---|---|---|---|
| United States | 193,590,856 | 9,619,302 | 203,210,158 | 100.0% |
| French | 2,187,828 | 410,580 | 2,598,408 | 1.3 |
| German | 4,891,519 | 1,201,535 | 6,093,054 | 3.0 |
| Polish | 2,018,026 | 414,912 | 2,437,938 | 1.2 |
| Yiddish | 1,155,877 | 438,116 | 1,593,993 | 0.8 |
| Italian | 3,118,321 | 1,025,994 | 4,144,315 | 2.0 |
| Spanish | 6,127,343 | 1,696,240 | 7,823,583 | 3.8 |

Source: U. S. Bureau of the Census, Census of Population, 1970,
*General Social and Economic Characteristics*,
United States Summary, Tables 146, 147.

# Appendix D

### Percent French Mother Tongue for Towns
### and Places of 10,000 - 50,000: New Hampshire, 1970

|  | Total Population | Fr. Mo. Tongue | % Fr. Mo. Tongue |
|---|---|---|---|
| Berlin | 15,256 | 9,224 | 60.5 |
| Claremount | 14,221 | 2,465 | 17.3 |
| Concord | 30,022 | 2,740 | 9.1 |
| Derry Town | 11,712 | 1,045 | 8.9 |
| Dover | 21,002 | 2,937 | 14.0 |
| Hudson Town | 10,873 | 1,990 | 18.3 |
| Keene | 20,467 | 1,199 | 5.9 |
| Laconia | 14,888 | 3,173 | 21.3 |
| Portsmouth | 26,059 | 1,158 | 4.4 |
| Rochester | 17,938 | 3,810 | 21.2 |
| Salem Town | 20,142 | 2,087 | 10.4 |

Percentages computed by Franco-American Files, University of Maine
at Portland-Gorham.

# Appendix E

### Percent French Mother Tongue for Towns and Places of 50,000 or more: New Hampshire

|  | Total Population | Fr. Mo. Tongue | % Fr. Mo. Tongue |
|---|---|---|---|
| Manchester | 87,754 | 27,777 | 31.7 |
| Nashua | 55,820 | 15,289 | 27.4 |

Percentages computed by Franco-American Files, University of Maine at Portland-Gorham.

# Appendix F

### Percent French Mother Tongue for Towns and Places of 10,000 - 50,000: Maine, 1970*

|  | Total Population | Fr. Mo. Tongue | % Fr. Mo. Tongue |
|---|---|---|---|
| Auburn | 24,151 | 6,938 | 28.7 |
| Augusta | 21,945 | 6,419 | 29.3 |
| Bangor | 33,168 | 1,861 | 5.6 |
| Biddeford | 19,983 | 12,268 | 61.4 |
| Brunswick Center | 10,867 | 2,156 | 19.8 |
| Brunswick Town | 16,195 | 2,488 | 15.4 |
| Caribou | 10,419 | 2,470 | 23.7 |
| Kittery | 11,028 | 474 | 4.3 |
| Lewiston | 41,779 | 25,037 | 59.9 |
| Portland | 65,116 | 2,747 | 4.2 |
| Presque Isle | 11,452 | 1,576 | 13.8 |
| Saco | 11,678 | 3,331 | 28.5 |
| Sanford Center | 10,457 | 4,333 | 41.4 |
| Sanford Town | 15,722 | 5,997 | 38.1 |
| South Portland | 23,312 | 906 | 3.9 |
| Waterville | 18,192 | 5,456 | 30.0 |
| Westbrook | 14,444 | 2,487 | 17.2 |

*Source: U. S. Department of Commerce, Bureau of the Census, Census of Population, 1970, *General Social and Economic Characteristics*, Maine, Tables 102 and 81.

# *Appendix G*

**Percent French Mother Tongue:**
**Maine Towns of Under 10,000 and**
**with 400 or more French Language Persons***

|                         | Total Population | Fr. Mo. Tongue | % Fr. Mo. Tongue |
|-------------------------|------------------|----------------|------------------|
| Ashland Town            | 1,809            | 604            | 33.4             |
| Berwick Town            | 3,136            | 469            | 15.0             |
| Brewer                  | 9,300            | 499            | 5.4              |
| Eagle Lake              | 979              | 933            | 95.3             |
| Fairfield Town          | 5,684            | 799            | 14.1             |
| Fort Fairfield Town     | 4,837            | 628            | 12.9             |
| Fort Kent Town          | 4,587            | 3,929          | 85.9             |
| Frenchville             | 1,487            | 1,441          | 96.9             |
| Gorham                  | 7,839            | 444            | 5.7              |
| Grand Isle              | 755              | 736            | 97.5             |
| Jackman Town            | 869              | 413            | 47.5             |
| Jay Town                | 3,951            | 728            | 18.5             |
| Kennebunk Town          | 5,578            | 445            | 8.0              |
| Kittery Town            | 11,028           | 474            | 4.3              |
| Limestone Town          | 10,360           | 645            | 7.4              |
| Lisbon                  | 6,649            | 1,135          | 17.3             |
| Livermore Falls Town    | 3,450            | 777            | 22.5             |
| Madawaska Town          | 5,622            | 4,977          | 89.1             |
| Madison Town            | 4,482            | 628            | 14.7             |
| Mexico Town             | 4,309            | 672            | 15.6             |
| Millinocket Town        | 7,544            | 993            | 12.8             |
| Old Orchard Beach Town  | 5,404            | 977            | 18.1             |
| Old Town City           | 9,057            | 1,763          | 19.5             |
| Orono Town              | 9,967            | 768            | 7.7              |
| Rumford Town            | 9,363            | 1,993          | 21.3             |
| Skowhegan Town          | 7,607            | 925            | 12.2             |
| South Berwick Town      | 3,488            | 484            | 13.9             |
| St. Agatha              | 883              | 850            | 96.5             |
| St. Francis Plantation  | 1,110            | 876            | 78.9             |
| Topsham Town            | 5,133            | 674            | 13.1             |
| Van Buren Town          | 4,102            | 3,844          | 93.9             |
| Wallagrass Plantation   | 534              | 512            | 95.9             |
| Webster                 | 1,623            | 491            | 31.6             |
| Winslow                 | 7,299            | 2,882          | 39.5             |

*Source: U. S. Department of Commerce, Bureau of the Census,
Census of Population, 1970, Fourth Count, (Population)
Summary Tape.

258

# Appendix H

**Percent French Mother Tongue for Towns
and Places of 10,000 - 50,000: Rhode Island, 1970**

| | Total Population | Fr. Mo. Tongue | % Fr. Mo. Tongue |
|---|---|---|---|
| Barrington | 17,572 | 497 | 2.8 |
| Bristol | 17,845 | 718 | 4.0 |
| Burrillville | 10,087 | 2,307 | 22.9 |
| Central Falls | 18,716 | 6,793 | 36.3 |
| Coventry | 22,938 | 3,805 | 16.6 |
| Cumberland | 26,617 | 5,184 | 19.5 |
| East Providence | 48,123 | 1,700 | 3.5 |
| Johnston | 22,036 | 957 | 4.3 |
| Lincoln | 16,177 | 4,561 | 28.2 |
| Middletown | 29,800 | 635 | 2.1 |
| Newport | 34,562 | 1,058 | 3.1 |
| Newport East | 10,285 | 227 | 2.2 |
| North Kingstown | 29,781 | 990 | 3.3 |
| North Providence | 24,352 | 1,252 | 5.1 |
| Portsmouth | 12,521 | 585 | 4.7 |
| Smithfield | 13,453 | 1,291 | 9.6 |
| South Kingstown | 16,913 | 541 | 3.2 |
| Tiverton | 12,559 | 1,766 | 14.1 |
| Warren | 10,520 | 1,187 | 11.3 |
| Westerly Center | 13,588 | 377 | 2.8 |
| Westerly | 17,322 | 546 | 3.2 |
| West Warwick | 24,352 | 5,947 | 24.4 |
| Woonsocket | 46,820 | 26,579 | 56.8 |

Source: U. S. Bureau of Census, *1970 Census of Population, General Social and Economic Characteristics, Rhode Island.*
Percentages computed by Franco-American Files, University of Maine at Portland-Gorham.

# Appendix I

**Percent French Mother Tongue for Towns
and Places 50,000 or more: Rhode Island, 1970**

|            | Total Population | Fr. Mo. Tongue | % Fr. Mo. Tongue |
|------------|-----------------|----------------|-------------------|
| Cranston   | 73,032          | 2,513          | 3.4               |
| Pawtucket  | 76,992          | 13,409         | 17.4              |
| Providence | 179,231         | 6,663          | 3.7               |
| Warwick    | 83,650          | 4,191          | 5.0               |

Source: U. S. Bureau of Census, *1970 Census of Population, General
Social and Economic Characteristics, Rhode Island.*
Percentages computed by Franco-American Files, University of Maine
at Portland-Gorham.

# Appendix J

**Percent French Mother Tongue for Towns
and Places of 10,000 - 50,000: Vermont, 1970**

|                  | Total Population | Fr. Mo. Tongue | % Fr. Mo. Tongue |
|------------------|-----------------|----------------|-------------------|
| Barre            | 10,209          | 1,608          | 15.8              |
| Bennington       | 14,586          | 825            | 5.7               |
| Brattleboro      | 12,494          | 690            | 5.5               |
| Burlington       | 38,635          | 4,622          | 12.0              |
| Essex            | 10,951          | 1,140          | 10.4              |
| Rutland          | 19,293          | 1,025          | 5.3               |
| South Burlington | 10,032          | 1,136          | 11.3              |
| Springfield      | 10,063          | 460            | 4.6               |

Percentages computed by Franco-American Files, University of Maine
at Portland-Gorham.

# *Appendix K*

### Percent French Mother Tongue for Towns
### and Places of 10,000 - 50,000: Massachusetts, 1970

| | Total Population | Fr. Mo. Tongue | % Fr. Mo. Tongue |
|---|---|---|---|
| Abington | 12,369 | 281 | 2.3 |
| Acton | 14,770 | 345 | 2.3 |
| Adams Center | 11,239 | 1,791 | 15.9 |
| Adams Town | 11,772 | 1,800 | 15.3 |
| Agawam Town | 21,669 | 1,822 | 8.4 |
| Amesbury Center | 10,093 | 2,020 | 20.0 |
| Amesbury Town | 11,610 | 2,278 | 19.6 |
| Amherst Center | 17,926 | 375 | 2.1 |
| Amherst Town | 25,976 | 481 | 1.9 |
| Andover Town | 23,695 | 903 | 3.8 |
| Athol Town | 11,298 | 1,317 | 11.7 |
| Attleboro | 32,907 | 4,147 | 12.6 |
| Auburn Town | 15,310 | 1,241 | 8.1 |
| Barnstable Town | 19,842 | 477 | 2.4 |
| Bedford Town | 13,513 | 481 | 3.6 |
| Bellingham Town | 13,967 | 3,531 | 25.3 |
| Belmont Town | 28,342 | 561 | 2.0 |
| Beverly | 38,326 | 2,230 | 5.8 |
| Billerica Town | 31,648 | 1,252 | 4.0 |
| Bourne Town | 12,636 | 452 | 3.6 |
| Braintree | 35,040 | 464 | 1.3 |
| Bridgewater Town | 11,829 | 333 | 2.8 |
| Burlington Town | 21,980 | 489· | 2.2 |
| Canton Town | 17,100 | 226 | 1.3 |
| Chelmsford | 31,391 | 1,791 | 5.7 |
| Chelsea | 30,639 | 856 | 2.8 |
| Clinton Town | 13,383 | 441 | 3.3 |
| Concord Town | 16,148 | 387 | 2.4 |
| Danvers | 26,231 | 1,689 | 6.4 |
| Dartmouth | 18,788 | 1,398 | 7.4 |
| Dedham Town | 26,955 | 360 | 1.3 |
| Dracut Town | 18,214 | 5,280 | 29.0 |
| Easthampton | 13,046 | 2,052 | 15.7 |
| East Longmeadow | 12,989 | 799 | 6.2 |
| Easton | 12,157 | 155 | 1.3 |
| Everett | 42,500 | 683 | 1.6 |
| Fairhaven | 16,332 | 1,447 | 8.9 |
| Falmouth | 16,133 | 324 | 2.0 |
| Fitchburg | 43,343 | 10,195 | 23.5 |
| Fort Devens | 13,053 | 211 | 1.6 |
| Foxborough | 14,218 | 386 | 2.7 |
| Gardner | 19,748 | 6,023 | 30.5 |

(continued next page)

## APPENDIX K
(continued)

|  | Total Population | Fr. Mo. Tongue | % Fr. Mo. Tongue |
|---|---|---|---|
| Gloucester | 27,938 | 562 | 2.0 |
| Clifton | 11,627 | 1,598 | 13.7 |
| Greenfield Center | 14,642 | 830 | 5.7 |
| Greenfield Town | 18,082 | 1,011 | 5.6 |
| Hanover Town | 10,107 | 151 | 1.5 |
| Harvard Town | 13,426 | 230 | 1.7 |
| Haverhill | 46,144 | 4,473 | 9.7 |
| Hingham | 18,803 | 296 | 1.6 |
| Holbrook | 11,775 | 285 | 2.4 |
| Holden | 12,559 | 489 | 3.9 |
| Holliston | 12,069 | 329 | 2.7 |
| Hudson Center | 14,138 | 965 | 6.8 |
| Hudson Town | 16,084 | 1,068 | 6.6 |
| Ipswich Town | 10,750 | 702 | 6.5 |
| Leominster | 32,939 | 7,281 | 22.1 |
| Lexington | 31,890 | 517 | 1.6 |
| Longmeadow Town | 15,630 | 406 | 2.6 |
| Ludlow | 17,461 | 2,090 | 12.0 |
| Lynnfield | 10,861 | 165 | 1.5 |
| Marblehead Town | 21,295 | 326 | 1.5 |
| Marlborough | 27,936 | 3,029 | 10.8 |
| Marshfield | 15,223 | 311 | 2.0 |
| Melrose | 33,222 | 739 | 2.2 |
| Methuen | 35,456 | 4,406 | 12.4 |
| Middleborough | 13,607 | 613 | 4.5 |
| Milfred Center | 13,740 | 379 | 2.8 |
| Milfred Town | 19,352 | 562 | 2.9 |
| Millbury Town | 12,149 | 2,136 | 17.6 |
| Milton | 27,190 | 207 | 0.8 |
| Natick | 31,095 | 873 | 2.8 |
| Needham | 29,676 | 416 | 1.4 |
| Newburyport | 15,807 | 867 | 5.5 |
| North Adams | 19,195 | 2,628 | 13.7 |
| Northampton | 29,643 | 2,037 | 6.9 |
| North Andover | 16,247 | 882 | 5.4 |
| North Attleborough | 18,618 | 2,462 | 13.2 |
| Northbridge | 11,795 | 2,550 | 21.6 |
| North Reading | 11,264 | 348 | 3.1 |
| Norwood | 30,867 | 439 | 1.4 |
| Oxford | 10,345 | 1,359 | 13.1 |
| Palmer | 11,682 | 1,536 | 13.1 |
| Peabody | 48,080 | 1,779 | 3.7 |
| Pembroke | 11,193 | 168 | 1.5 |
| Plymouth | 18,375 | 532 | 2.9 |
| Randolph | 27,035 | 345 | 1.3 |

(continued next page)

## APPENDIX K
### (continued)

| | Total Population | Fr. Mo. Tongue | % Fr. Mo. Tongue |
|---|---|---|---|
| Reading | 22,539 | 576 | 2.6 |
| Revere | 43,159 | 541 | 1.3 |
| Rockland Town | 15,751 | 347 | 2.2 |
| Salem | 40,543 | 7,414 | 18.3 |
| Saugus | 25,123 | 920 | 3.7 |
| Scituate | 16,973 | 235 | 1.4 |
| Seekonk | 11,162 | 905 | 8.1 |
| Sharon | 12,367 | 111 | 0.9 |
| Shrewsbury | 19,294 | 1,013 | 5.3 |
| Somerset | 17,647 | 2,888 | 1.6 |
| Southbridge Center | 14,261 | 5,350 | 37.5 |
| Southbridge Town | 17,057 | 6,078 | 35.6 |
| South Hadley | 17,104 | 2,503 | 14.6 |
| Stoneham Town | 20,713 | 407 | 2.0 |
| Stoughton | 23,429 | 266 | 1.1 |
| Sudbury | 13,506 | 361 | 2.7 |
| Swampscott | 13,583 | 210 | 1.5 |
| Swansea | 12,594 | 2,239 | 17.8 |
| Taunton | 43,756 | 2,813 | 6.4 |
| Tewksbury | 22,753 | 1,183 | 5.2 |
| Wakefield | 25,402 | 905 | 3.6 |
| Walpole | 18,149 | 302 | 1.7 |
| Wareham | 11,492 | 386 | 3.4 |
| Watertown | 39,295 | 1,009 | 2.6 |
| Wayland | 13,456 | 333 | 2.5 |
| Webster Center | 12,435 | 1,891 | 15.2 |
| Webster Town | 14,917 | 2,371 | 15.9 |
| Wellesley | 28,073 | 565 | 2.0 |
| Westborough | 12,594 | 507 | 4.0 |
| Westfield | 31,433 | 1,453 | 4.6 |
| Westford | 10,365 | 993 | 9.6 |
| Weston | 10,886 | 182 | 1.7 |
| West Springfield | 28,542 | 2,055 | 7.2 |
| Westwood | 12,746 | 235 | 1.8 |
| Whitman | 12,982 | 301 | 2.3 |
| Wilbraham | 12,112 | 641 | 5.3 |
| Wilmington | 17,107 | 449 | 2.6 |
| Winchester | 22,136 | 358 | 1.6 |
| Winthrop | 20,335 | 395 | 1.9 |
| Woburn | 37,406 | 602 | 1.6 |
| Yarmouth | 12,033 | 336 | 2.8 |

Source: U. S. Bureau of the Census, *Census of Population, 1970,*
*General Social and Economic Characteristics, Massachusetts,*
Table 102.
Percentages computed by Franco-American Files, University of Maine
at Portland-Gorham.

# Appendix L

**Percent French Mother Tongue for Towns and
Places of 50,000 or more: Massachusetts, 1970**

|  | Total Population | Fr. Mo. Tongue | % Fr. Mo. Tongue |
|---|---|---|---|
| Arlington | 53,576 | 1,160 | 4.3 |
| Boston | 641,056 | 10,452 | 1.6 |
| Brockton | 89,040 | 3,011 | 3.4 |
| Brookline | 58,886 | 940 | 1.6 |
| Cambridge | 100,417 | 3,513 | 3.5 |
| Chicopee | 66,676 | 13,589 | 20.4 |
| Fall River | 96,976 | 17,115 | 17.6 |
| Framingham | 64,048 | 1,631 | 2.5 |
| Holyoke | 50,051 | 8,169 | 16.3 |
| Lawrence | 66,915 | 11,695 | 17.5 |
| Lowell | 94,280 | 19,187 | 20.4 |
| Lynn | 90,289 | 5,850 | 6.5 |
| Malden | 56,127 | 1,629 | 2.9 |
| Medford | 64,389 | 994 | 1.5 |
| New Bedford | 101,527 | 14,260 | 14.0 |
| Newton | 91,051 | 2,041 | 2.2 |
| Pittsfield | 57,115 | 2,840 | 5.0 |
| Quincy | 87,966 | 1,500 | 1.4 |
| Somerville | 88,732 | 2,137 | 1.8 |
| Springfield | 163,916 | 15,330 | 7.8 |
| Waltham | 61,582 | 7,611 | 5.4 |
| Weymouth | 54,575 | 1,036 | 1.5 |
| Worcester | 176,617 | 14,008 | 7.0 |

Source:  U. S. Bureau of the Census, *Census of Population, 1970,
General Social and Economic Characteristics, Massachusetts,*
Table 81.

Percentages computed by Franco-American Files, University of Maine
at Portland-Gorham.

# *Appendix M*

**Percent French Mother Tongue for Towns
and Places of 50,000 or more: Connecticut, 1970**

|  | Total Population | Fr. Mo. Tongue | % Fr. Mo. Tongue |
|---|---|---|---|
| Bridgeport | 156,542 | 2,784 | 3.6 |
| Bristol | 55,487 | 8,747 | 15.8 |
| Danbury | 50,781 | 1,174 | 2.3 |
| East Hartford | 57,583 | 5,562 | 9.7 |
| Fairfield | 56,252 | 1,063 | 1.9 |
| Greenwich | 59,395 | 1,156 | 2.0 |
| Hartford | 158,017 | 12,073 | 7.6 |
| Meridan | 55,959 | 3,806 | 6.8 |
| Milford | 50,858 | 1,191 | 2.1 |
| New Britain | 83,441 | 6,515 | 6.3 |
| New Haven | 137,721 | 7,829 | 0.7 |
| Norwalk | 79,192 | 1,792 | 1.5 |
| Stamford | 108,848 | 1,170 | 0.7 |
| Waterbury | 108,032 | 6,984 | 5.0 |
| West Hartford | 68,031 | 2,512 | 2.9 |
| West Haven | 52,851 | 765 | 1.2 |

Percentages computed by Franco-American Files, University of Maine at Portland-Gorham.

# *Appendix N*

**Percent French Mother Tongue for Towns
and Places of 10,000 - 50,000: Connecticut, 1970**

| | Total Population | Fr. Mo. Tongue | % Fr. Mo. Tongue |
|---|---|---|---|
| Enfieldtown | 46,214 | 3,760 | 8.1 |
| Farmington Town | 14.390 | 660 | 4.6 |
| Glastonbury Town | 20,651 | 737 | 3.6 |
| Groton Town | 38,685 | 1,217 | 3.1 |
| Guilford Town | 12,033 | 190 | 1.6 |
| Hamden Town | 49,357 | 602 | 1.2 |
| Killingly Town | 13,809 | 3,276 | 23.7 |
| Ledyard Town | 14,431 | 339 | 2.3 |
| Manchester Town | 47,994 | 1,883 | 6.0 |
| Mansfield Town | 19,994 | 732 | 3.7 |
| Middletown | 36,946 | 939 | 2.5 |
| Monroe Town | 12,197 | 175 | 1.4 |
| Montville Town | 15,662 | 695 | 4.4 |
| Naugatuck | 22,965 | 755 | 3.3 |
| New Canaan | 17,816 | 258 | 1.4 |
| Newington | 26,037 | 1,363 | 5.2 |
| New London | 31,589 | 814 | 2.6 |
| New Milford | 14,601 | 333 | 2.3 |
| Newtown | 16,942 | 384 | 2.3 |
| North Branford | 10,778 | 155 | 1.4 |
| North Haven | 22,120 | 369 | 1.7 |
| Norwich | 41,433 | 4,067 | 9.8 |
| Orangetown | 13,524 | 179 | 1.3 |
| Plainfield | 11,957 | 3,100 | 25.9 |
| Plainville Town | 16,733 | 1,975 | 11.8 |
| Plymouth Town | 10,321 | 876 | 8.5 |
| Ridgefield Town | 17,256 | 272 | 1.6 |
| Rocky Hill Town | 11,103 | 573 | 5.2 |
| Seymour Town | 12,776 | 185 | 1.4 |
| Shelton | 27,294 | 584 | 2.1 |
| Sinsburytown | 17,475 | 473 | 2.7 |
| Southington Town | 30,946 | 2,739 | 8.9 |
| South Windsor | 15,553 | 1,408 | 9.1 |
| Stonington Town | 15,946 | 531 | 3.3 |
| Storrs | 10,691 | 236 | 2.2 |
| Stratford Town | 49,699 | 1,147 | 2.3 |
| Torrington | 31,952 | 1,400 | 4.4 |
| Trumbulltown | 32,388 | 537 | 1.7 |

(continued next page)

| | Total Population | Fr. Mo. Tongue | % Fr. Mo. Tongue |
|---|---|---|---|
| Vernontown | 27,237 | 1,807 | 6.6 |
| Wallingford Town | 35,714 | 1,484 | 4.2 |
| Waterford Town | 17,227 | 424 | 2.5 |
| Watertown Town | 18,610 | 1,434 | 7.7 |
| Westport Town | 27,403 | 505 | 1.8 |
| Wethersfield Town | 26,662 | 895 | 3.4 |
| Willimantic | 14,402 | 2,652 | 18.4 |
| Wilton Town | 13,572 | 361 | 2.7 |
| Winchester Town | 11,173 | 722 | 6.5 |
| Windham Town | 19,626 | 3,598 | 18.3 |
| Windsor Locks Town | 15,055 | 1,074 | 7.1 |
| Windsor Town | 22,502 | 1,124 | 5.0 |
| Walcott Town | 12,428 | 1,472 | 11.8 |

Percentages computed by Franco-American Files, University of Maine
at Portland-Gorham.

# *Appendix O*

**Percent French Mother Tongue for
Standard Metropolitan Statistical Areas
of 250,000 or more: Connecticut, 1970**

| | Total Population | Fr. Mo. Tongue | % Fr. Mo. Tongue |
|---|---|---|---|
| Bridgeport | 390,022 | 7,543 | 1.9 |
| Hartford | 663,845 | 40,988 | 6.2 |
| New Haven | 355,621 | 4,476 | 1.3 |
| Springfield, Chicopee, Holyoke, Mass.-Conn. | 529,890 | 57,533 | 10.9 |

Percentages computed by Franco-American Files, University of Maine
at Portland-Gorham.

Source: Research of Professor Madeleine Giguere, University of Maine,
Portland-Gorham.

(Source: Research of Professor Madeleine Giguere, University of Maine,
Portland-Gorham.)